THE
ENGLISH
LIBRARY

General Editor JAMES SUTHERLAND

Emeritus Professor of Modern Literature
University College, London

ENGLISH SATIRIC POETRY

POETRY

Dryden to Byron

Edited by

James Kinsley

Professor of English Studies, University of Nottingham

and

James T. Boulton

Professor of English Literature, University of Nottingham

UNIVERSITY OF SOUTH CAROLINA PRESS

Columbia, S.C.

Published 1966 in Great Britain by
EDWARD ARNOLD (PUBLISHERS) LTD.
41 Maddox Street, London W.1

Published 1970 in the United States of America by the
UNIVERSITY OF SOUTH CAROLINA PRESS
Columbia, S.C. 29208

Standard Book Number: 87249-155-2
Library of Congress Catalog Card Number: 74-116470

Manufactured in Great Britain

General Preface

THE design of this series is to present fully annotated selections from English literature which will, it is hoped, prove satisfactory both in their breadth and their depth. To achieve this, some of the volumes have been planned so as to provide a varied selection from the poetry or prose of a limited period, which is both long enough to have developed a literary movement, and short enough to allow for adequate representation of the chief writers and of the various cross-currents within the movement. Examples of such periods are the late seventeenth century and the early eighteenth century. In other volumes the principle of selection is to present a literary kind (e.g. satirical poetry, the literary ballad). Here it is possible to cover a longer period without sacrificing the unified and comprehensive treatment which is the governing idea for the whole series. Other volumes, again, are designed to present a group of writers who form some kind of "school" (e.g. the Elizabethan sonneteers, the followers of Ben Jonson), or who were closely enough linked for their work to be brought together (e.g. the poetry of Johnson and Goldsmith).

Each volume has a full critical introduction. Headnotes, a special feature of this series, provide relevant background and critical comment for the individual poems and prose pieces. The footnotes are for the most part explanatory, giving as briefly as possible information about persons, places, allusions of one kind or another, the meaning of words, etc., which the twentieth-century reader is likely to require. Each selection aims at providing examples of the best work of the authors represented, but it is hoped that the inclusion of some less familiar pieces not available in any other collection will widen the reader's experience and enjoyment of the literature under review. The series is intended for use in universities and the upper forms of schools.

Much of the best poetry written between 1660 and the time of the English romantic poets was satirical, and in this volume Professor James Kinsley and Professor James T. Boulton have made a selection of satirical poems ranging from Dryden's *Mac Flecknoe* to

Byron's *The Vision of Judgment*. Among the other well-known poets represented are Rochester, Swift, Pope, Johnson, Churchill, Goldsmith and Burns; but, in keeping with the expressed aim of this series, the student will also find some less familiar names, such as Soame Jenyns, "Peter Pindar" and William Gifford, whose best work invites comparison with that of their more famous contemporaries. In making their selection the editors have given thought to illustrating the various modes of satire during this period, ranging as they say, from comedy to diatribe. In their Introduction they question whether the primary function of satire is corrective, and are inclined to find the basis of its appeal in "a delight in the observation of folly, . . . intensified and refined by literary art". Today, when the satirist is once again in fashion, this volume, which presents some of the finest and liveliest work of the great age of English verse satire, should prove a welcome addition to the series of Arnold's English Texts.

Contents

Introduction

SATIRE is "the fine art of calling names". The disposition of some men makes them consistently satiric in their writing; that of most men provokes them to satire in some moods and circumstances. The satiric temper is kaleidoscopic, volatile. It expresses itself in modes ranging from comedy to diatribe; it pervades many literary kinds—drama, the novel, the essay, and even the lyric. The poems in this book, however, illustrate satire in its restricted but primary form, from a period when it not only vitalised many literary genres but became in itself a major kind of poetry.

English poets contributed to the medieval tradition of "complaint", and the Elizabethans and Jacobeans attempted (with fitful success) to naturalise Roman formal satire, especially that of Persius and Martial.[1] But the main neo-classical tradition begins, in England, with Dryden and the Restoration. There are many reasons for this. Religious and political feeling ran high. Despite the autocratic gestures of Charles II and James II, the atmosphere of court and parliament made the free expression of opinion comparatively safe. The times may have been less spacious than those of Queen Elizabeth, but they were much easier for independent spirits to survive in. This was, too, the first age of the professional writer, who has a special concern with political affairs and social criticism. In the sphere of poetry, Renaissance enthusiasm for the classics had widened to accommodate not only the matter and style of Roman literature, but its forms; and the native tradition in satire, from the Elizabethans to Marvell, awaited enrichment from a fuller critical understanding of the achievement of Juvenal and Horace. The "character", imitated from classical literature by the Elizabethans, had been established as a minor prose form by Earle, Overbury, and the Stuart historians; and Butler and Marvell had transplanted it in verse satire.[2] Finally, the art of the heroic couplet, a uniquely appropriate medium for satiric writing, had been brought to a high finish both in England and in France. In satire as in other kinds, Dryden poured new wine into an old bottle. He innovated little; but he brought his distinctive poetic character, with all his qualities of mind and style, to satire; raising it to the level of his Latin models both in intrinsic excellence and in reputation as a genre worth the attention of the best poets.

[1] See John Peter, *Complaint and Satire in Early English Literature*, 1956, chs. 1-5.
[2] See D. Nichol Smith, *Characters from . . . the Seventeenth Century*, 1918.

Dryden's *Discourse concerning the Original and Progress of Satire*, published in 1693 as an introduction to his translations of Juvenal and Persius, is important as a historical survey of Latin satire. It provides a fine critical comparison of Juvenal, Persius and Horace, and a statement of Dryden's own views—developed in his long study of the classical poets and his own practice—on the theory and craft of satire. What he has to say is crucial to an understanding of the whole English Augustan tradition. The basis of Roman satire, in its mature forms, is a moral concern; it is "of the nature of Moral Philosophy; as being instructive" and not (as it is commonly regarded in England and France) merely invective. What Persius teaches "might be taught from Pulpits, with more profit to the Audience, than all the nice Speculations of Divinity"; Horace is praised for "Copious, and Profitable . . . Instructions of Humane Life". But Dryden is in no danger of preferring moral instruction to aesthetic pleasure: "I wou'd willingly divide the Palm betwixt [*Juvenal* and *Horace*;] upon the two Heads of Profit and Delight, which are the two Ends of Poetry in general. . . . Juvenal is the more delightful Author." In the end, his delight in reading Horace is "but languishing":

> *Juvenal* is of a more vigorous and Masculine Wit, he gives me as much Pleasure as I can bear: He fully satisfies my Expectation, he Treats his Subject home: His Spleen is rais'd, and he raises mine: I have the Pleasure of Concernment in all he says; He drives his Reader along with him. . . . When he gives over, 'tis a sign the Subject is exhausted; and the Wit of Man can carry it no farther.[1]

This emphasis on the delightfulness of satire—not narrowly aesthetic, but judiciously appreciating the art with which the poet handles his *matter*—was new in English criticism. Traditionally the satirist claims a moral justification. But although the didactic element in any literary form is difficult to define, and in none more difficult than in satire, a study of the best classical satire does not substantiate the view that its primary function is corrective. There is in human nature a vein of malice—a delight in the observation of folly, an inclination to laugh uncharitably at others. This pleasure, intensified and refined by literary art, is the basis of satire's appeal. But we prefer such an appeal to have a veneer of morality and justice: our appetite for abuse, for the expression of motiveless malignity or sheer misanthropy, is primitive, embarrassing, and spasmodic. Any critic of men and manners has to adopt a posture of moral superiority, and the social satirist who takes upon himself the ridicule of folly and vice—whether in personal or in general terms—is free to do so only as long as he does not display folly and vice himself: his assumed superiority to his victims gives

[1] *The Poems of John Dryden*, ed. James Kinsley, 1958, ii. 637, 643, 647, 649.

his criticism a moral sanction. The moralist proper is above all constructive —he reproves in order to correct; and although he may use satiric devices to give sparkle or force to his writing, the more he employs what are essentially destructive devices the less likely he is to achieve a moral end. It has seldom mattered to the satirist, on the other hand, "to what lies he has stooped so long as he moralised his song". He may not feel strongly on what he writes about; he must feel what he writes.[1] Beneath the appearance or the reality of passion, the justification of satire is its art. A man, the Earl of Rochester told Bishop Burnet,

> could not write with life, unless he were heated with Revenge, for to make a Satire without Resentments, upon the cold Notions of Philosophy, was as if a man would in cold blood cut men's throats, who had never offended him. And he said, the lyes in these Libels came often in as ornaments that could not be spared without spoiling the beauty of the Poem.[2]

Dryden himself, in the prefaces to his satires, wears the mask of the moralist and reformer; but the gravity with which he wears it is ironic. "The true end of *Satyre*", he tells the reader of *Absalom and Achitophel*, "is the amendment of Vices by correction"; he treats Absalom (less his victim than Achitophel's) with compassion, and hopes for his "Reconcilement . . . to David". But he begins to smile as he extends the same charity to Achitophel, whom he believed to be incorrigible: "I have not, so much as an uncharitable Wish against [him]; but, am content to be Accus'd of a good natur'd Errour; and, to hope with *Origen*, that the Devil himself may, at last, be sav'd." There is nothing of the moralist in his retrospective comment on *Absalom and Achitophel*, twelve years later, in the *Discourse . . . of Satire*:

> The Character of *Zimri* [Buckingham] . . . is, in my Opinion, worth the whole Poem: 'Tis not bloody, but 'tis ridiculous enough. And he for whom it was intended, was too witty to resent it as an injury. . . . I avoided the mention of great Crimes, and apply'd my self to the representing of Blind-sides, and little Extravagancies: To which, the wittier a Man is, he is generally the more obnoxious [exposed, liable]. It

[1] A. M. Clark, "The Art of Satire", in *Studies in Literary Modes*, 1946, p. 42. Cf. p. 41: "The satirist . . . is under no obligation to his subject except to render it with the fullest art at his command, and satire can be as free from a real indignation or contempt as any other poetry can be free from any precipitating cause but the author's imagination and a desire to exercise it and his art."

[2] *Cambridge History of English Literature*, 1912, viii. 214.

succeeded as I wish'd; the Jest went round, and he was laught at in his turn who began the Frolick.[1]

The poem had been written for Charles II in the crisis of his political fortunes, and it helped to ensure as well as to adorn his triumph over the Whigs; but to Dryden, its permanent achievement lay in its art.

The study of Roman satire—especially Juvenal's—persuaded Dryden that this kind of poetry was, at its highest, a species of epic.[2] He had, moreover, an ambivalent attitude to heroic poetry itself: such a poetry represents past or ideal human achievement and carries implicit criticism of present social realities; and the heroic mode could therefore, with some alloy of parody or irony, perform a high satiric function in an unheroic society.[3]

It is this general attitude, as much as Boileau's specific success with the "poëme héroï-comique" (see infra, p. 23), that underlies Dryden's first venture in satire, Mac Flecknoe; his second "witty heroic poem", Absalom and Achitophel;[4] and the mock-heroic poetry of Pope, The Rape of the Lock and The Dunciad. But satire of this kind could not be evolved in mere imitation of Juvenal—for all Dryden's admiration for his saeva indignatio and declamatory grandeur; much less could it take the "crabbed" Persius or the familiar Horace as models. A refined, oblique, subtle ironic style had to be worked out anew. Dryden's final statement on the matter (again emphasising the principle of pleasure rather than reformation) illuminates his own work, and establishes the way of proceeding in high formal satire for the next generation of English poets:

> ... the nicest and most delicate touches of Satire consist in fine Raillery. ... 'Tis not Reading, 'tis not imitation of an Author, which can produce this fineness: It must be inborn, it must proceed from a Genius, and particular way of thinking, which is not to be taught; and therefore not to be imitated by him who has it not from Nature: How easie it is to call

[1] Poems, ed. cit., ii. 655.

[2] Cf. Milton's earlier reiteration, at a time when the level of English satire was low, of the Aristotelian view: "For a Satyr as it was borne out of a Tragedy, so ought to resemble his parentage, to strike high, and adventure dangerously at the most eminent vices among the greatest persons, and not to creepe into every blinde Taphouse that fears a Constable more than a Satyr" (Apology [for] Smectymnuus, 1642, in Works, Columbia edn., 1931, iii. 329; Aristotle, Poetics, i. 7).

[3] Cf. W. Frost, Dryden and the Art of Translation, 1955, ch. iv; E. M. W. Tillyard, The English Epic and its Background, 1954, ch. vii, "...this addition of the burlesque to the serious, potentially Dryden's original contribution to the course of the English epic, was something true ... to his age."

[4] See Ian Jack, Augustan Satire 1660–1750, 1952, ch. iv.

Rogue and Villain, and that wittily! But how hard to make a Man appear a Fool, a Blockhead, or a Knave, without using any of those opprobrious terms! To spare the grossness of the Names, and to do the thing yet more severely. . . . This is the Mystery of that Noble Trade. . . . Neither is it true, that this fineness of Raillery is offensive. A witty Man is tickl'd while he is hurt in this manner; a Fool feels it not. The occasion of an Offence may possibly be given, but he cannot take it . . . there is still a vast difference betwixt the slovenly Butchering of a Man, and the fineness of a stroak that separates the Head from the Body, and leaves it standing in its place. . . .[1]

The source of the primary heroic strain in Augustan satire, exemplified by Dryden and Pope, is the Roman epic. But the Roman satirists made their own direct contribution. A second neo-classical satiric mode, less exalted but more pervasive, and again exemplified by Pope, is epistolary. "I have not the courage", Pope wrote to Swift,

> to be such a satyrist as you, but I would be as much, or more, a philosopher. You call your satires, Libels; I would rather call my satires, Epistles: They will consist more of morality than wit, and grow graver, which you will call duller. I shall leave it to my Antagonists to be witty (if they can) and content myself to be useful, and in the right.[2]

The model here is Horace: cultured, ironic, unromantic, *parcus deorum cultor et infrequens*, an appropriate teacher and *elegentiae arbiter* for the eighteenth century. Dryden thought that Horace's fault in satire was "too much lowness"; a style "according to his Subject; that is generally groveling".[3] But to the next generation, less ready to take the strain of the heroic in art or in life, the civilised, relaxed Horatian *causerie* made an immediate appeal. A poet wishing to write "Epistles after the Model given us by *Horace*", says the *Spectator*, must have

> a thorough Knowledge of Mankind . . . and the prevailing Humours of the Age . . . must have his Mind well seasoned with the finest Precepts of Morality. . . . He must be a Master of refined Raillery, and understand the Delicacies, as well as the Absurdities of Conversation. He must have a lively Turn of Wit, with an easie and concise manner of Expression; Every thing he says, must be in a free and disengaged Manner. He must . . . appear a Man of the World throughout.[4]

[1] *Poems, ed. cit.*, ii. 655.
[2] *The Correspondence of Alexander Pope*, ed. G. Sherburn, 1956, iii. 366. Cf. Dryden on Roman satire, *supra*, p. 10.
[3] *Poems, ed. cit.*, ii. 645, 649-50.   [4] No. 618.

The Horatian epistle—free and familiar in style, flexible in structure—is the pattern not only of Pope's *Imitations of Horace* but also of the *Moral Essays* and the *Epistle to Arbuthnot* (p. 50). But Pope's stylistic range is much wider than that prescribed by the *Spectator;* there are many passages of eulogy, autobiography, self-justification, many satiric "characters" and assaults of great rhetorical intensity, which fall below or rise above the "middle" style that is the Horation norm.[1]

Horace, says the critic Dennis, typifies the "Comick Satirist . . . more agreeable to the discerning Part of a Court, and a great Capital" because of his familiarity with men and affairs. But there is another kind of satirist, represented by Juvenal, who shows

> almost every where . . . Anger, Indignation, Rage, Disdain, and the violent Emotions and vehement Style of Tragedy. . . . Will not the Tragick Satire, which like Tragedy fetches its Notions from Philosophy and from common Sense, be in all probability more acceptable to Universities and Cloisters, and all those Recluse and Contemplative Men . . . suppos'd to have Philosophy from Study, and common Sense from Nature?[2]

Juvenal, who had maintained his place in poetic tradition through the great translation by Dryden and others (1693), but without exercising much influence on modern satire, made his direct contribution in Johnson's *Vanity of Human Wishes* (p. 75). The gravity and force of Juvenal's rhetoric, the philosophical generality of his thought, and his stoic dignity, appealed to Johnson as Horace could not have done. The *saeva indignatio* of Juvenal is replaced by an eighteenth-century melancholy,[3] and the stoicism by Christian faith; but the *Vanity* is an imitation in the highest sense—an ambitious departing, as Edward Young called it, from "great predecessors" (*Conjectures on Original Composition*, 1759):

> the farther from them in similitude, the nearer you are to them in excellence: you rise by it into an original: become a noble collateral, not a humble descendant from them.

[1] It may be noted here that in Scotland the Horatian epistle was given a distinctive familiar humour by Allan Ramsay, Fergusson, and Burns. The stanza they chose and perfected—"Standart *Habby*", traditionally comic-elegiac—is that used by Burns in *Holy Willie's Prayer* (p. 125), a poem with medieval antecedents and otherwise quite unrelated to the Augustan satiric tradition.

[2] *To Matthew Prior, Esq.; upon the Roman Satirists* (1721); *Critical Works*, ed. E. N. Hooker, ii (1943), 219.

[3] Cf. Scott, *Life of Johnson:* "The deep and pathetic morality of the *Vanity of Human Wishes* has often extracted tears from those whose eyes wander dry over pages professedly sentimental."

Joseph Warton, indeed, thought that "the imitations of Horace by Pope, and of Juvenal by Johnson, are preferable to their originals in the appositeness of their examples, and in the poignancy of their ridicule".[1]

The practice of imitation (in Young's sense) continued through the century: Cowper imitated Horace; Gifford's *Baviad* (1794) was a "paraphrastic imitation" of Persius's Satire I; and even Wordsworth, in 1795, attempted an imitation of Juvenal, Satire VIII. But in Young's *Conjectures* itself there were signs that this tradition was failing to satisfy current taste. "New thought", "rare imagination and singular design", were preferred to imitation, and Young contrasted "the well-accomplished scholar" with "the divinely-inspired enthusiast".[2] The scholar was "up to the knees in antiquity . . . treading the sacred footsteps of great examples with the blind veneration of a bigot saluting the papal toe". Richard Hurd rejected classical models even more firmly: "we read *Imitation* with somewhat of his languor who listens to a twice-told tale". The study of great models was harmful; for "they *prejudice* our judgment in favour of their abilities, and so lessen the sense of our own; and they intimidate us with this splendour of their renown'.[3]

Though later eighteenth-century satirists went on following the established *genre*, almost out of habit, we can now recognise the changes of attitude, values, and practice which led to the ultimate rejection of the Augustan tradition. Charles Churchill, the most vigorous satirist between Johnson and Byron, detected symptoms of decline in the mellifluous emptiness of much contemporary poetry:

> Verses must run, to charm a modern ear,
> From all harsh, rugged interruptions clear:
> Soft let them breathe, as Zephyr's balmy breeze;
> Smooth let their current flow as summer seas;
> Perfect then only deem'd when they dispense
> A happy tuneful vacancy of sense.[4]

Paradoxically, he held Pope's example responsible: because of the harmonious flow of each line with "equal beauty", Pope's "excellence, unvaried, tedious grows". In the debate (to which Johnson contributed in his *Lives*) on the respective merits of Dryden and Pope, Churchill cast his vote for

[1] *The Adventurer*, No. 133, 12 February 1754.

[2] "Enthusiast", which gave Joseph Warton the title for a poem on the love of nature in 1744, had been a pejorative term for Swift and still was for Johnson. With Young's contrast, cf. Churchill, *The Author*, ll. 13 ff. (*infra*, p. 105).

[3] *Letters on Chivalry and Romance* (1762), ed. E. Morley, 1911, pp. 7, 9.

[4] *The Apology*, 1761, ll. 340-5.

Dryden. But in his own use of satire's "mighty Flail" he often turned back
to pre-Restoration techniques. Churchill, said Horace Walpole in a letter to
Sir Horace Mann (15 November 1764), "had great powers; but besides the
facility of outrageous satire, almost all his compositions were wild and
extravagant, executed on no plan, and void of the least correction". Churchill himself confirms this in *Gotham* (1764; ii. 165-78):

> Had I the pow'r, I could not have the time,
> Whilst spirits flow, and Life is in her prime,
> Without a sin 'gainst Pleasure, to design
> A plan, to methodize each thought, each line
> Highly to finish, and make ev'ry grace,
> In itself charming, take new charms from place.
> Nothing of Books, and little known of men,
> When the mad fit comes on, I seize the pen,
> Rough as they run, the rapid thoughts set down,
> Rough as they run, discharge them on the Town.
> Hence rude, unfinish'd brats, before their time,
> Are born into this idle world of rime,
> And the poor *slattern* MUSE is brought to bed
> With all her imperfections on her head.

The classical ideal of polished, disciplined writing—"pruned by length of
time and many an erasure", as Horace said—could scarcely be rejected more
decisively. Gone, too, are the concern for stylistic propriety and the notion
of satire as a "sacred Weapon, left for Truth's defence":

> But now, *Decorum* lost, I stand
> *Bemus'd*, a Pencil in my hand,
> And, dead to ev'ry sense of shame,
> Careless of Safety and of Fame,
> The names of Scoundrels minute down,
> And Libel more than half the Town.[1]

Some way below the surface the ideals which are explicit in Pope's *Epilogue
to the Satires* still linger; but they do not now determine Churchill's attitude
or manner. The transition to Gifford's swingeing invective in the *Epistle to
Peter Pindar* (p. 160) was not difficult to make.

A significant shift in critical—as well as moral and social—values is shown
in the fate of the concept of "wit", which was central to Augustan satire.
This term implies—with much else that cannot be taken account of here[2]—

[1] *The Ghost*, iv (1763), 727-32.

[2] See, for instance, W. Empson, *The Structure of Complex Words*, 1951; *The
Poems of John Dryden*, ed. James Kinsley, 1958, iv. 1829, 1956-7; C. S. Lewis,
Studies in Words, 1960, ch. 4.

an incisive, evaluating intelligence which operates through verbal dexterity and achieves (says Corbyn Morris) "the Lustre *resulting from the* quick Elucidation *of one Subject, by a just and unexpected* Arrangement *of it* with another".[1] Aesthetic pleasure is derived from the juxtaposition of two apparently disparate objects or ideas in order to illuminate the nature of one of them—Shadwell and John the Baptist, Addison and Cato, Hervey and "a well-bred spaniel"; surprise is justified by the resultant insight. This "lustre" of wit had been recognised from the time of Dryden, as we have seen, as a main element in satire. But the climate of opinion had changed. Corbyn Morris, though he does not deny wit a place (as Blackmore had done) "in Works where severe Knowledge and Judgment are chiefly exercis'd",[2] agrees with Locke that "Wit consists in something that is not perfectly conformable to Truth, and good Reason".[3] By captivating the reader through subtlety and the force of surprise, wit leads him away from truth. Such a faculty was unlikely to commend itself to an age which responded to the novels of Defoe and Richardson, the *Serious Call* (1728) of William Law "to live by reason, and glorify God", and the equally influential preaching of Wesley. Wit in its more general and social sense, especially as displayed in repartee, was out of fashion. In Blackmore's view a "mere Wit" was likely to be "more inclin'd than others to Levity and dissolute Manners"; he threatened public morality as well as literary values. By 1732 the *Gentleman's Magazine* could report that "few People of Distinction trouble themselves about the Name of Wit, fewer understand it, and hardly any have honoured it with their Example".[4] In literature, wit came to be associated with trivia, permissible in light verse and letters.[5] "Men of wit, or elegant taste", said Joseph Warton in 1756, are incapable of "the higher scenes of poetry".[6]

"Wit" gradually gave place in esteem to "humour": a quality which, says Corbyn Morris,

in the Representation of the *Foibles* of *Persons* in *real Life*, frequently exhibits very *generous benevolent* Sentiments of Heart; And these, tho' exerted in a particular odd Manner, justly command Fondness and Love.—Whereas in the allusions of Wit, *Severity, Bitterness,* and *Satire,*

[1] *An Essay towards fixing the True Standards of Wit, Humour, Raillery, Satire, and Ridicule,* 1744, p. 1; probably the best discussion of the subject in the first half of the century.

[2] "Essays upon Wit", in *Essays,* 1716, p. 199.   [3] *Essay,* 1744, p. xv.

[4] Blackmore, *op. cit.; Gentleman's Magazine,* July 1732, p. 861.

[5] *Essay on Wit* (anon.), 1748, p. 15.

[6] *Essay on Pope,* 1806 edn., I. vii.

are frequently exhibited.—And where these are avoided, not worthy amiable Sentiments of the *Heart*, but quick unexpected Efforts of the *Fancy*, are presented.[1]

These views, published in the same decade as Fielding's two major novels, remind us that Morris's contemporaries preferred Parson Adams and Tom Jones to the heroes—Horner, Dorimant, and the like—of Restoration comedy. Morris himself preferred Falstaff to Jonson's wit-characters; and later, the tone of Goldsmith's comedies had a close affinity with the good nature displayed in his satire, *Retaliation* (p. 100). In the later part of the century men looked more kindly on "raillery"—what Morris calls pleasing the reader "by some little *Embarrassment* of a *Person*"—than on satire, the aim of which was "to scourge *Vice*, and to deliver it up to your just *Detestation*".[2] When Wordsworth referred to the "spice of malignity" which he thought essential in satire, he was right to find it in Pope but wrong to attribute it to "the more redoubted Peter [Pindar]".[3] Pindar's forte was comedy rather than malignity. Indeed, he contrasted his own "humour" with the "satire" of Churchill and Junius:

> Compar'd to them, whose pleasure was to stab,
> Lord! I'm a melting medlar to a crab!
>   My humour of a very diff'rent sort is:
> Their satire's horrid hair-cloth; mine is silk:
> I am a pretty nipperkin of milk;
>   They, two enormous jugs of *aqua-fortis*.

> Compar'd to their high floods of foaming satire,
> My rhyme's a rill—a thread of murmuring water:
> A whirlwind they, that oaks like stubble heaves;
> I, zephyr whisp'ring, sporting through the leaves.[4]

He says he is "playful as the sportive kitten"—and we recall Pope's comparison of the satirist with a falcon stooping to truth; he says his satire "tickles", but his "only instrument's a *feather*"—and we remember that Dryden's "tickling" satire separated the head from the body in one fine stroke. "Pray let me laugh, my Lords . . . my laughing muscles can't lie still." This was the dominant mood of Pindar's satire; the laughter was different in kind from that in *Mac Flecknoe*, for example, or in *New Morality*, the only complete poem written in the Augustan manner at the end of the century.

---

[1] *Op. cit.*, pp. 24-5.   [2] *Ibid.*, p. 37.
[3] *Early Letters*, ed. E. de Selincourt, 1935, p. 155.
[4] "Expostulatory Odes", IX, in *Works*, ii (1797), 107.

There are further reasons for the decline of the Augustan satiric mode. Critics began to admit the emptiness of the traditional claim, seldom held with complete conviction (cf. *supra*, pp. 10-11), that satire is corrective. "Could Boileau to reform a nation hope?" asked Thomas Warton; "A Sodom can't be mended by a Pope." The same view informed his brother Joseph's *Essay on Pope*.[1] It was also recognised that Augustan satire had been the product of a social situation, and could not outlive radical social change. The *Gentleman's Magazine* (July 1732) related the rise of satire to the aristocratic fashion of "wit" at the Restoration and in the early eighteenth century; its decline was related to the social inferiority of would-be wits in the 1730's, whose "Stations in Life are not eminent enough to dazzle us into Imitation". The "superiority of the moderns in all the species of ridicule" had been due, says Joseph Warton, to the "improved state of conversation"; the "*artificial* and *polished*" manners of a wealthy and elegant aristocracy had inspired the best of Pope's satires.[2] But by the middle of the century the court and aristocracy no longer provided a cultural centre. (The point is vividly made in the first plate of Hogarth's *Marriage à la Mode*, depicting the union of decayed aristocratic fortunes with the wealth of the merchant middle class.)

Finally, the English Augustans had written "for the first time in a tone that was peculiar to the upper ranks of society, and upon subjects that were almost exclusively interesting to them";[3] and their satiric tradition declined before the evolution of a society dominated by the bourgeoisie and finding satisfaction in a non-urban poetry that was simple, sensuous, and passionate. When there was excitement in the idea that "our very peasants show that the seeds of poetry exist in the rude soil of their minds"; when Wordsworth could regard a grocer's opinion of his poetry as significant; or when he could dismiss Dryden's language as "necessarily" not imaginative because "there is not a single image from Nature in the whole body of his works"[4]— then Augustan satire had become an alien *genre*. Dryden, Pope, and Johnson did not respond to an "impulse from a vernal wood"; nor were their successors likely to find satiric stimulus there.

The poets who appealed to the new sensibility were not the Augustans but Spenser, Shakespeare in his romantic comedies, and the Milton of *L'Allegro* and *Il Penseroso*:

[1] T. Warton, *A Fragment of Satire*; J. Warton, *Essay*, 1806 edn., ii. 364.
[2] *The Adventurer*, No. 133, 12 February 1754; *Essay on Pope*, 1806 edn., ii. 402.
[3] Francis Jeffrey, *Literary Criticism*, ed. D. Nichol Smith, 1910, p. 27 (1816).
[4] *Letters of Anna Seward*, 1811, iii. 320; *Letters of Wordsworth: Middle Years*, ed. E. de Selincourt, 1937, i. 187; *Early Letters*, 1935, p. 541.

What are the lays of artful Addison,
Coldly correct, to Shakespear's warblings wild?[1]

It was expected that Pope would be remembered for his *Elegy to the Memory of an Unfortunate Lady* and *Eloisa to Abelard* rather than for his satires. Apart from these Ovidian poems, Joseph Warton asked, "what is there transcendently sublime or pathetic in Pope?" In Pope's famous couplet, "That not in Fancy's maze he wander'd long . . .", is "our author's own declaration . . . that he early left the *more poetical* provinces of his art, to become a moral, didactic, and satiric poet". And Warton adds a memorable statement of the new creed: "Wit and Satire are transitory and perishable, but Nature and Passion are eternal."[2] So, when Byron tried to defend Pope as "the great moral poet of all times", he was fighting a battle lost half a century before. Warton had willingly recognised in Pope "the *First* of all *Ethical* authors in verse"; but it was "the sublime and the pathetic", not moral wisdom, which were "the two chief nerves of all genuine poetry". Here was the beginning of the critical attitude to the Augustans, especially to Dryden and Pope, which was exemplified by Jeffrey, Wordsworth, Hazlitt, and most fully by Arnold.

The Augustan satiric tradition did not die at Warton's behest. Its form, the heroic couplet, had first to be superseded; and that proved slow and difficult. Despite the popularity of blank verse from quite early in the eighteenth century, the disciplined compactness of the couplet went on proclaiming the Augustan belief in logic and judgment: it was as appropriate a form for poets like the authors of *New Morality* (see p. 154) as it had been for satirists a century before. Courtenay's tone is closer to Byron's than to Pope's (see p. 143), and he is noticeably less at ease in the couplet than Jenyns half a century earlier (see p. 69), but he accepts the traditional form. But the new sensibility required other vehicles of expression, for the lyric, the ode, and the long descriptive or reflective poem. Negatively, the couplet had been too closely associated with satire and depreciated with it. Hugh Blair's view, set out in lectures at Edinburgh from 1759 onwards, is representative:

> The principal defect in rhyme, is the full close which it forces upon the ear, at the end of every couplet. Blank Verse is freed from this. . . . Hence it is particularly suited to subjects of dignity and force, which demand

[1] Joseph Warton, *The Enthusiast*, 1744. Cf. Thomas Warton's preference for "Spenser's wildly-warbled song" over even the "happiest art" of Pope's "Attic page"; *The Pleasures of Melancholy*, 1747.

[2] *Essay on Pope*, i. 313; ii. 255, 330. (The second volume did not appear until 1782, but most of it was written soon after the publication of the first volume in 1756.)

more free and manly numbers than rhyme. The constraint and strict regularity of rhyme are unfavourable to the sublime, or to the highly pathetic strain. . . . It is best adapted to compositions of a temperate strain, where no particular vehemence is required in the sentiments, nor great sublimity in the Style; such as Pastorals, Elegies, Epistles, Satyres, &c. To these, it communicates that degree of elevation which is proper for them, and without any other assistance sufficiently distinguishes the Style from Prose.[1]

Other critics—like Warton—found the antithetical mode wearisome; some, like Keats, thought it contemptible—"musty laws lined out with wretched rule"; and for Wordsworth it revealed a moral defect in the poet who relied exclusively on it.[2]

When Byron continued the couplet tradition in *English Bards and Scotch Reviewers* (1809) he was responding to its resurgence in the glut of political satire—mostly of a minor kind—during and after the French Revolution, and in the poems of Gifford (see p. 160) for whom, together with Pope, he had a high regard. But he did not thoroughly know himself. His performance shows only that the social, moral, and literary situation in which Augustan satire flourished was past:

He imitates the surface, the idiom, the rhetorical devices of Augustan satire, but fails to experience or reproduce its essence; and so one finds in *English Bards* a coarsening of the traditional techniques—clumsy attempts at bathos, for example, commonplace antitheses, crude ridicule, lame epigrams, and heavy-handed irony.[3]

Byron was not, like the Augustans, defending the standards of a cultivated audience with whom he felt himself identified; he was totally at odds with the accepted values of his time, a rebel, a contemptuous alien in society. So, despite his intellectual sympathies with the earlier satirists, he needed a different form to express his flamboyant, irreverent, and reckless genius. In making the superb choice of *ottava rima*, he turned his back on the Augustan tradition. That was now dead. It is ironic, however, that the decisive rejection of the neo-classical form should have been made by the one Romantic poet who believed Pope to be "the moral poet of all civilisation", and who hoped that "as such . . . he will one day be the national poet of all mankind".[4]

[1] *Lectures on Rhetoric and Belles Lettres*, 1783, ii. 331-2.
[2] Warton, *Essay on Pope*, ii. 146; Keats, "Sleep and Poetry", l. 195; Wordsworth, "Upon Epitaphs", *Prose Works*, ed. A. B. Grosart, 1876, ii. 60-1.
[3] Andrew Rutherford, *Byron*, 1961, pp. 21-2.
[4] *Letters and Journals*, 1922, v. 560.

John Dryden

MAC FLECKNOE

THE occasion of Dryden's satire on the poet Thomas Shadwell is unknown. *Mac Flecknoe* was published by Dryden in 1684; but a pirated edition appeared in 1682, and there is good evidence that the poem was circulating in manuscript some years earlier. Since 1670 Dryden and Shadwell had been conducting, in their prefaces and dedications, an irregular debate on wit, humour, rhyme, and other matters. This controversy is the basis of *Mac Flecknoe*: Shadwell is represented as a literary dunce, unable to write with true wit or to appreciate it in others. But the poem was probably provoked by some personal quarrel: for Dryden, as he claimed towards the end of his life, seldom resorted to lampoon but "suffer'd in silence; and possess'd my Soul in quiet"; and he had been carrying on a critical argument with Shadwell for nearly ten years without displaying any personal animosity.

Mac Flecknoe is essentially lampoon—a severe personal attack on Shadwell; but the abuse is elevated and refined by the language and rhetorical devices of epic. This is the first substantial mock-heroic poem in English, and Dryden's earliest illustration of his belief that satire is a species of heroic poetry. Its immediate model was Boileau's recent "poëme héroï-comique", *Le Lutrin* (1674), which Dryden later described as "the most Beautiful, and most Noble kind of Satire. Here is the Majesty of the Heroique, finely mix'd with the Venom of the other; and raising the Delight which otherwise wou'd be flat and vulgar, by the Sublimity of the Expression."

> All humane things are subject to decay,
> And when Fate summons, Monarchs must obey:
> This *Fleckno* found, who, like *Augustus*, young
> Was call'd to Empire, and had govern'd long:
> 5   In Prose and Verse, was own'd, without dispute
> Through all the Realms of *Non-sense*, absolute.
> This aged Prince now flourishing in Peace,
> And blest with issue of a large increase,
> Worn out with business, did at length debate
> 10 To settle the succession of the State:

3 *Fleckno*: Richard Flecknoe (d. 1678?), dramatist and poetaster. "How natural the connection of thought is betwixt a bad Poet and *Fleckno*" (Dryden, 1680). (Mac Flecknoe: his "son".)

And pond'ring which of all his Sons was fit
To Reign, and wage immortal War with Wit;
Cry'd, 'tis resol_vd; for Nature pleads that He
Should onely rule, who most resembles me:
15   *Sh——* alone my perfect image bears,
Mature in dullness from his tender years.
Sh—— alone, of all my Sons, is he
Who stands confirm'd in full stupidity.
The rest to some faint meaning make pretence,
20   But *Sh——* never deviates into sense.
Some Beams of Wit on other souls may fall,
Strike through and make a lucid intervall;
But *Sh——*'s genuine night admits no ray,
His rising Fogs prevail upon the Day:
25   Besides his goodly Fabrick fills the eye,
And seems design'd for thoughtless Majesty:
Thoughtless as Monarch Oakes, that shade the plain,
And, spread in solemn state, supinely reign.
Heywood and *Shirley* were but Types of thee,
30   Thou last great Prophet of Tautology:
Even I, a dunce of more renown than they,
Was sent before but to prepare thy way;
And coursly clad in *Norwich* Drugget came
To teach the Nations in thy greater name.
35   My warbling Lute, the Lute I whilom strung

15-24 The repetition of the hero's name is imitated from Cowley's
Biblical epic, *Davideis*, iv. Lines 21-4 parody a passage in *Davideis*, i.
29 *Heywood and Shirley:* Thomas Heywood (*c.* 1574–1641) and James
Shirley (1596–1666), dramatists. Cf. ll. 100-3.
32-4 *sent . . . greater name:* Cf. Matt. iii. 3-4. Flecknoe and Shadwell are
prophets, priests, and kings of Dullness; cf. ll. 118-19, 214-17.
33 *Norwich Drugget:* a coarse woollen fabric. Shadwell was born at
Weeting, Norfolk.
35 *My warbling Lute:* Cf. Marvell, "Fleckno, an English Priest at Rome".
Dryden was not the only satirist to make fun of Shadwell's claim (in
Psyche, 1675) to have "some little knowledge" of music, "having been bred,
for many years of my Youth, to some performance in it".

When to King *John* of *Portugal* I sung,
Was but the prelude to that glorious day,
When thou on silver *Thames* did'st cut thy way,
With well tim'd Oars before the Royal Barge,
40 Swell'd with the Pride of thy Celestial charge;
And big with Hymn, Commander of an Host,
The like was ne'er in *Epsom* Blankets tost.
Methinks I see the new *Arion* Sail,
The Lute still trembling underneath thy nail.
45 At thy well sharpned thumb from Shore to Shore
The Treble squeaks for fear, the Bases roar:
Echoes from *Pissing-Ally*, *Sh*—— call,
And *Sh*—— they resound from *A*—— *Hall*.
About thy boat the little Fishes throng,
50 As at the Morning Toast, that Floats along.
Sometimes as Prince of thy Harmonious band
Thou weild'st thy Papers in thy threshing hand.
St. *Andre*'s feet ne'er kept more equal time,
Not ev'n the feet of thy own *Psyche*'s rhime:
55 Though they in number as in sense excell;
So just, so like tautology they fell,
That, pale with envy, *Singleton* forswore   ⎫
The Lute and Sword which he in Triumph bore,   ⎬
And vow'd he ne'er would act *Villerius* more.   ⎭

37-50 A parody of Waller's court poem *Of the Danger His Majesty . . .
Escaped . . . at Saint Andrews.*

42 *in Epsom Blankets tost:* the punishment of Sir Samuel Hearty, an ass
who "takes himself to be a Wit", in Shadwell's *The Virtuoso* (1676).

43 *Arion:* mythical poet and musician.

47-8 *Pissing-Ally:* probably the passage which ran from the Strand to
Holywell Street. *A[ston] Hall:* not identified.

53 *St Andre:* a French dancing-master whose company was brought over
by the Duke of Monmouth to take part in Shadwell's opera, *Psyche*, at
Dorset Garden in February 1675.

57-9 *Singleton:* one of Charles II's musicians, who were often employed
in the theatre. *Villerius:* a character in Davenant's operatic *Siege of Rhodes*
(1656), ridiculed with his armour and lute in *The Rehearsal* (1672), Act V.

60   Here stopt the good old *Syre*; and wept for joy
     In silent raptures of the hopefull boy.
     All arguments, but most his Plays, perswade,
     That for anointed dullness he was made.
         Close to the Walls which fair *Augusta* bind,
65   (The fair *Augusta* much to fears inclin'd)
     An ancient fabrick, rais'd t'inform the sight,
     There stood of yore, and *Barbican* it hight:
     A watch Tower once; but now, so Fate ordains,
     Of all the Pile an empty name remains.
70   From its old Ruins Brothel-houses rise,
     Scenes of lewd loves, and of polluted joys.
     Where their vast Courts the Mother-Strumpets keep,
     And, undisturb'd by Watch, in silence sleep.
     Near these a Nursery erects its head,
75   Where Queens are form'd, and future Hero's bred; ⎫
     Where unfledg'd Actors learn to laugh and cry, ⎪
     Where infant Punks their tender Voices try,   ⎬
     And little *Maximins* the Gods defy.   ⎭
     Great *Fletcher* never treads in Buskins here,
80   Nor greater *Johnson* dares in Socks appear.

61 *the hopefull boy*: Shadwell, obese and 36 years old. A satiric application of Cowley's pedantic note (*Davideis*, ii, n. 28) on "the *Hebrew* use of the word *Boy*" for the 36-year-old David.

64-5 *Augusta*: the ancient name for London, "to fears inclin'd" during the crisis of the Popish Plot (1678-81).

72-3 *Where . . . silence sleep*: Parodying Cowley, *Davideis*, i:
            Where their vast *Court* the *Mother-Waters* keep,
            And undisturb'd by *Moons* in silence sleep.
Watch: i.e. watchmen.

74 *a Nursery*: erected by Lady Davenant in 1661; one of several schools for actors formed after the Restoration.

76-7 *Where . . . Voices try*: Parodying Cowley, *Davideis*, i:
            Beneath the Dens where *unfletcht Tempests* lye,
            And infant *Winds* their tender *Voices* try.
Punks: whores.

78 *Maximins*: ranting stage heroes. Maximin is the Roman tyrant in Dryden's *Tyrannick Love* (1670).

80 *greater Johnson*: Cf. ll. 172-86.

But gentle *Simkin* just reception finds
Amidst this Monument of vanisht minds:
Pure Clinches, the suburbian Muse affords;
And *Panton* waging harmless War with words.

85 Here *Fleckno*, as a place to Fame well known,
Ambitiously design'd his *Sh*——'s Throne.
For ancient *Decker* prophesi'd long since,
That in this Pile should Reign a mighty Prince,
Born for a scourge of Wit, and flayle of Sense:

90 To whom true dulness should some *Psyches* owe,
But Worlds of *Misers* from his pen should flow;
Humorists and *Hypocrites* it should produce,
Whole *Raymond* families, and Tribes of *Bruce*.
Now Empress *Fame* had publisht the Renown

95 Of *Sh*——'s Coronation through the Town.
Rows'd by report of Fame, the Nations meet,
From near *Bun-Hill*, and distant *Watling-street*.
No *Persian* Carpets spread th' Imperial way,
But scatter'd Limbs of mangled Poets lay:

100 From dusty shops neglected Authors come,
Martyrs of Pies, and Reliques of the Bum.

81 *Simkin:* a simpleton; a character in crude dramatic "drolls". *Panton* (l. 84) was probably another.

82 *this Monument of vanisht minds:* Davenant's description of a library, "Th' assembled souls of all that Men held wise" (*Gondibert*, II. v. 36), assimilated to satire by a quibble on *vanisht*.

83 *Clinches:* quibbles, plays on words; which Dryden regarded as "false Wit", a "clownish kind of Raillery". Cf. ll. 204-8, note.

87 *ancient Decker:* Thomas Dekker (1572–1632), playwright and pamphleteer; apparently a jocular reference only.

90-3 *some Psyches . . . Bruce:* Shadwell's early plays, *Psyche* (1675), *The Miser* (1672), *The Humorists* (1671) and *The Hypocrite* (now lost). Raymond is a wit in *The Humorists*, Bruce another in *The Virtuoso* (1676).

94 *Empress Fame:* Cf. Virgil, *Aeneid*, iv. 173 ff.

101 *Martyrs of Pies:* cf. Dryden, *Of Dramatic Poesie, An Essay* (1668): ". . . he is the very *Withers* of the City: they have bought more Editions of his Works then would serve to lay under all their Pies at the Lord Mayor's Christmass".

Much *Heywood*, *Shirly*, *Ogleby* there lay,
But loads of *Sh*—— almost choakt the way.
Bilk't *Stationers* for Yeomen stood prepar'd,
105   And *H*—— was Captain of the Guard.
The hoary Prince in Majesty appear'd,
High on a Throne of his own Labours rear'd.
At his right hand our young *Ascanius* sat[e]
Rome's other hope, and pillar of the State.
110   His Brows thick fogs, instead of glories, grace,
And lambent dullness plaid arround his face.
As *Hannibal* did to the Altars come,
Sworn by his *Syre* a mortal Foe to *Rome*;
So *Sh*—— swore, nor should his Vow bee vain,
115   That he till Death true dullness would maintain;
And in his father's Right, and Realms defence,
Ne'er to have peace with Wit, nor truce with Sense.
The King himself the sacred Unction made,
As King by Office, and as Priest by Trade:
120   In his sinister hand, instead of Ball,
He plac'd a mighty Mug of potent Ale;
Love's Kingdom to his right he did convey,
At once his Sceptre and his rule of Sway;
Whose righteous Lore the Prince had practis'd young,
125   And from whose Loyns recorded *Psyche* sprung.

---

102 *Heywood, Shirly, Ogleby:* cf. ll. 29–30. John Ogilby (1600–76) was a Scottish dancing-master turned poet, printer, translator, and cartographer. Dryden derided (and made use of) his versions of Virgil and Homer.

105 *H*——: Henry Herringman, Dryden's publisher until 1678, and publisher of Shadwell's plays, 1673–8.

108–11 *Ascanius:* Virgil's "magnae spes altera Romae" (*Aen.* xii. 168). Dryden parodies Virgil's "ecce levis", &c. (*ibid.*, ii. 682–4).

112 *Hannibal did . . . come:* Livy, *Hist.* xxi. 1.

120–1 *In his sinister hand . . . Ale:* After coronation the sovereign leaves Westminster Abbey with the orb in the left hand and the sceptre (l. 123) in the right.

122 *Love's Kingdom:* Flecknoe's "Pastoral Trage-Comedy" (1664).

His Temples last with Poppies were o'erspread,
That nodding seem'd to consecrate his head:
Just at that point of time, if Fame not lye,
On his left hand twelve reverend *Owls* did fly.
130   So *Romulus*, 'tis sung, by *Tyber's Brook*,
Presage of Sway from twice six Vultures took.
Th' admiring throng loud acclamations make,
And Omens of his future Empire take.
The *Syre* then shook the honours of his head,
135   And from his brows damps of oblivion shed
Full on the filial dullness: long he stood,   )
Repelling from his Breast the raging God;   }
At length burst out in this prophetick mood:)
    Heavens bless my Son, from *Ireland* let him reign
140   To farr *Barbadoes* on the Western main;
Of his Dominion may no end be known,
And greater than his Father's be his Throne.
Beyond loves Kingdom let him stretch his Pen;
He paus'd, and all the people cry'd *Amen*.
145   Then thus, continu'd he, my Son advance
Still in new Impudence, new Ignorance.

126 *Poppies:* emblems of sterility and sleep (Virgil, *Georgics*, i. 78, and *Aen.* iv. 486).

129-32 *Owls:* emblems of apparent sagacity and real stupidity. For the omen of the vultures see Plutarch's Life of Romulus.

134 *shook the honours . . . head:* parodying classical descriptions of Jupiter (cf. Virgil, *Aen.* x. 113–15).

135-6 *from his brows . . . dullness:* parodying Cowley's account of the anointing of Saul in *Davideis*, iv: Samuel

> with great rules fill'd his *capacious mind*.
> Then takes the sacred *Vial*, and does shed
> A *Crown* of mystique drops around his head.

137-8 *Repelling . . . prophetick mood:* parodying Virgil's account of the Sibyl (*Aen.* vi. 46–51 and 77–82).

139 *from Ireland:* cf. l. 202. Ireland was traditionally associated with dullness. Cf. *Dunciad*, I. i. 25.

144 *all the people cry'd Amen:* Nehemiah viii. 6.

Success let others teach, learn thou from me
Pangs without birth, and fruitless Industry.
Let *Virtuoso's* in five years be Writ;
150   Yet not one thought accuse thy toyl of wit.
Let gentle *George* in triumph tread the Stage,
Make *Dorimant* betray, and *Loveit* rage;
Let *Cully, Cockwood, Fopling,* charm the Pit,
And in their folly shew the Writers wit.
155   Yet still they fools shall stand in they defence,
And justifie their Author's want of sense.
Let 'em be all by thy own model made
Of dullness, and desire no foreign aid:
That they to future ages may be known,
160   Not Copies drawn, but Issue of thy own.
Nay let thy men of wit too be the same,
All full of thee, and differing but in name;
But let no alien *S—dl—y* interpose
To lard with wit thy hungry *Epsom* prose.
165   And when false flowers of *Rhetorick* thou would'st cull.
Trust Nature, do not labour to be dull;
But write thy best, and top; and in each line,
Sir *Formal's* oratory will be thine.

147–8 *Success let others teach:* Cf. Virgil, *Aen.* xii. 435–6, "disce puer . . .
fortunam ex aliis".

149 *Virtuoso's in five years:* A deliberate misreading of Shadwell's reference,
in the Dedication of *The Virtuoso,* to "the *Humorists,* written five years
since". In the Prologue to *The Virtuoso,* Shadwell sneers at "Drudges of the
Stage" who, like Dryden, are "bound to scribble twice a year". Cf. Pope,
Epistle to Dr. Arbuthnot, l. 40.

151 *gentle George:* the nickname of the dramatist Sir George Etherege.
Lines 152–3 refer to characters in Etherege's comedies: Dorimant, Mrs.
Loveit and Fopling in *The Man of Mode,* Cully in *The Comical Revenge,* and
Cockwood in *She wou'd if she cou'd.*

163–4 *let . . . Epsom prose:* Sir Charles Sedley wrote a prologue for
Shadwell's *Epsom-Wells* (1673), and was reputed (Shadwell says, by "some
industrious Enemies of mine") to have contributed to the play itself.

168 *Sir Formal:* "The most *Ciceronian* Coxcomb: the noblest Orator
breathing" in *The Virtuoso.*

Sir *Formal*, though unsought, attends thy quill,
170 And does thy *Northern Dedications* fill.
Nor let false friends seduce thy mind to fame,
By arrogating *Johnson's* Hostile name.
Let Father *Fleckno* fire thy mind with praise,
And Uncle *Ogleby* thy envy raise.
175 Thou art my blood, where *Johnson* has no part;
What share have we in Nature or in Art?
Where did his wit on learning fix a brand,
And rail at Arts he did not understand?
Where made he love in Prince *Nicander's* vein,
180 Or swept the dust in *Psyche's* humble strain?
Where sold he Bargains, Whip-stitch, kiss my Arse,
Promis'd a Play and dwindled to a Farce?
When did his Muse from *Fletcher* scenes purloin,
As thou whole *Eth'ridg* dost transfuse to thine?
185 But so transfus'd as Oyl on Waters flow,
His always floats above, thine sinks below.

170 *thy Northern Dedications:* By 1678 Shadwell had dedicated five plays
to the Duke or the Duchess of Newcastle.

173-4 *Let Father . . . raise:* cf. Virgil, *Aen*. iii. 342-3, ". . . et pater Aeneas
et avunculus . . . Hector".

175 *where Johnson has no part:* Dryden's main charge against Shadwell had
been that, despite his devotion to Ben Jonson's comedy, he did not understand Jonson's wit.

179-80 *Prince Nicander* pursues Psyche, in Shadwell's opera, with "Industrious Love" and exalted rhetoric. The Prologue to *Psyche* says that the
author's "Subject's humble, and his Verse is so".

181 *sold . . . Bargains:* wrote prurient dialogue, *double entendre*. *Whip-
stitch . . . Arse:* vulgar ejaculations made by Sir Samuel Hearty in *The
Virtuoso*.

182 *Promis'd a Play . . . Farce:* Shadwell presented *The Virtuoso* as an essay
in "Humour, Wit, and Satyr", and hit at "impossible, unnatural Farce
Fools, which some intend for Comical, who think it the easiest thing in the
World to write a Comedy".

184 *whole Eth'ridg dost transfuse:* an exaggeration. There are similar
situations in *Epsom-Wells* and Etherege's *She wou'd if she cou'd*.

185-6 *so transfus'd . . . sinks below:* "That *Oyl* mixt with any other liquor,
still gets uppermost, is perhaps one of the chiefest *Significancies* in the
Ceremony of *Anointing Kings* and *Priests*" (Cowley, *Davideis*, iv, note 28).

This is thy Province, this thy wondrous way,
New Humours to invent for each new Play:
This is that boasted Byas of thy mind,

190 By which one way, to dullness, 'tis inclin'd.
Which makes thy writings lean on one side still,
And in all changes that way bends thy will.
Nor let thy mountain belly make pretence
Of likeness; thine 's a tympany of sense.

195 A Tun of Man in thy Large bulk is writ,
But sure thou 'rt but a Kilderkin of wit.
Like mine thy gentle numbers feebly creep,
Thy Tragick Muse gives smiles, thy Comick sleep.
With whate'er gall thou sett'st thy self to write,

200 Thy inoffensive Satyrs never bite.
In thy fellonious heart, though Venom lies,
It does but touch thy *Irish* pen, and dyes.
Thy Genius calls thee not to purchase fame
In keen Iambicks, but mild Anagram:

205 Leave writing Plays, and chuse for thy command
Some peacefull Province in Acrostick Land.
There thou maist wings display and Altars raise,
And torture one poor word Ten thousand ways.
Or if thou would'st thy diff'rent talents suit,

210 Set thy own Songs, and sing them to thy lute.

189-90 *This ... inclin'd:* A parody of Shadwell's definition (based on Jonson) in the Epilogue to *The Humorists*:

> A Humor is the Byas of the Mind,
> By which with violence 'tis one way inclin'd:
> It makes our Actions lean to one side still,
> And in all Changes that way bends the will.

194 *likeness:* i.e. to Jonson. *tympany:* morbid swelling.

195 *A Tun of Man:* a Falstaff (Shakespeare, 1 *Henry IV*, II. iv. 440).

196 *Kilderkin:* the fourth part of a tun.

202 *but touch ... and dyes:* i.e. overcome by a greater poison. Shadwell complained that Dryden gave him "the *Irish* name of *Mack*, when he knows I never saw Ireland till I was three and twenty years old, and was there but four Months" (Dedication of Juvenal, *Sat.* x, 1687).

204-6 *mild Anagram ... Acrostick:* devices of "false" wit. Cf. ll. 83-4; the *Spectator*, nos. 61-3.

He said, but his last words were scarcely heard,
For *Bruce* and *Longvil* had a *Trap* prepar'd,
And down they sent the yet declaiming Bard.
Sinking he left his Drugget robe behind,
215   Born upwards by a subterranean wind.
The Mantle fell to the young Prophet's part,
With double portion of his Father's Art.

212–13 *Bruce . . . declaiming Bard:* In *The Virtuoso*, III, Bruce and Longvil drop Sir Formal, "yet declaiming", through a trap-door.

215–17 *Born upwards . . . Art:* A parody of 2 Kings ii. 9–13. Elijah's mantle fell as he ascended to heaven; Flecknoe's is delivered from below.

Charles Sackville

TO MR. EDWARD HOWARD, ON HIS PLAYS

THIS simple piece of scurrility, typical of Restoration lampoon, was addressed (*c.* 1680) by Sackville (1638–1706), Earl of Dorset and Dryden's patron and friend, to the Honourable Edward Howard. "Foolish Ned" was a son of the Earl of Berkshire (cf. ll. 31-2), and Dryden's brother-in-law. Between 1663 and 1678 he had published half a dozen bad plays. Dorset wrote a companion piece to Howard, "On his Incomparable Incomprehensible Poem . . . *The British Princess*" (1669) *Works*, 1749.

Thou damn'd antipodes to common sense,
Thou foil to Flecknoe, pr'ythee tell from whence
Does all this mighty stock of dullness spring?
Is it thy own, or hast it from Snow-hill,
5   Assisted by some ballad-making quill?
No, they fly higher yet, thy plays are such
I'd swear they were translated out of Dutch.

2 *Flecknoe:* see *Mac Flecknoe*, l. 3, note.
4 *Snow-hill:* in the Liberties, beyond Newgate.
7 *Dutch:* at this time the type of heavy witlessness.

B

Fain wou'd I know what diet thou dost keep,
If thou dost always, or dost never sleep?
10 Sure hasty-pudding is thy chiefest dish,
With bullock's liver, or some stinking fish:
Garbage, ox-cheeks, and tripes, do feast thy brain,
Which nobly pays this tribute back again.
With daizy roots thy dwarfish muse is fed,
15 A giant's body with a pigmy's head.
Can'st thou not find among thy num'rous race ⎤
Of kindred, one to tell thee, that thy plays }
Are laught at by the pit, box, galleries, nay, stage? ⎦
Think on 't a while, and thou wilt quickly find
20 Thy body made for labour, not thy mind.
No other use of paper thou should'st make,
Than carrying loads and reams upon thy back.
Carry vast burthens 'till thy shoulders shrink,
But curst be he that gives thee pen and ink:
25 Such dangerous weapons shou'd be kept from fools,
As nurses from their children keep edg'd-tools:
For thy dull fancy a muckinder is fit
To wipe the slabberings of thy snotty wit:
And though 'tis late, if justice could be found,
30 Thy plays like blind-born puppies shou'd be drown'd.
For were it not that we respect afford
Unto the son of a heroic lord,
Thine in the ducking-stool shou'd take her seat,
Drest like her self in a great chair of state;
35 Where, like a muse of quality she 'd die, ⎤
And thou thy self shalt make her elegy, }
In the same strain thou writ'st thy comedy. ⎦

9 *always, or . . . never sleep:* being both soporific and prolific.
10 *hasty-pudding:* "instant" porridge, pap.
18 *nay, stage:* i.e. even those who act them.
27 *muckinder:* bib.
33 *ducking-stool:* a chair on the end of a plank, used to duck disorderly women.

John Wilmot

A LETTER FROM ARTEMISA IN THE TOWN
TO CLOE IN THE COUNTRY

By the Earl of Rochester (1647–1680), one of the most brilliant, and notorious, of the Restoration court wits; first published as a broadside in 1679, and here reprinted from Rochester's *Poems . . . on Several Occasions*, 1691. The poem is an early example of the epistolary satire which became a common Augustan mode in both verse and prose. Its style is appropriately colloquial —in a fluid, chattering, feminine way. But it rises to the generalised rhetoric that modern satire inherited from the medieval "complaint" (cf. ll. 36-72), and to broad social commentary, part cynical (cf. ll. 101-35, 171-88) and part serious. Rochester's theme is illustrated in two female "characters": one encountered by the narrator (ll. 73 ff.)—as Donne, following Horace's example, meets his "motley humorist" (*Satyre* I)—and presented to Cloe in a long, semi-dramatic monologue (ll. 95-145, 169-255) with commentary by Artemisa; the other, Corinna (ll. 189-255), presented *within* that monologue in the kind of biographical set piece—a "Whore's Progress"—that became a major device in English Augustan satire.

> *Cloe*, by your command, in Verse I write:
> Shortly you'l bid me ride astride, and fight:
> Such Talents better with our Sex agree,
> Than lofty flights of dangerous Poetry.
> 5   Among the men, I mean the men of Wit,
> (At least they pass'd for such before they writ)
> How many bold Advent'rers for the Bays,
> Proudly designing large returns of praise;
> Who durst that stormy, pathless World explore;
> 10 Were soon dasht back, and wreckt on the dull shore,
> Broke of that little stock they had before.
> How wou'd a Womans tott'ring Barque be tost,
> Where stoutest Ships (the Men of Wit) are lost?
> When I reflect on this, I straight grow wise:
> 15 And my own self I gravely thus advise:

7 *the Bays:* the garland worn by a champion in a poetic contest.
10 *dull:* sad, melancholy.

Dear *Artemisa*! Poetry 's a Snare:
Bedlam has many Mansions: have a care:
Your Muse diverts you, makes the Reader sad:
You think your self inspir'd; He thinks you mad.
20 Consider too, 'twill be discreetly done,
To make your self the Fiddle of the Town.
To find th' ill-humour'd pleasure at their need:
Curst when you fail, and scorn'd when you succeed.
Thus, like an arrant Woman, as I am,
25 No sooner well convinc'd writing 's a shame;
That *Whore* is scarce a more reproachful Name
Than Poetess——
Like Men that marry, or like Maids that woo,
Because 'tis the very worst thing they can do:
30 Pleas'd with the contradiction, and the sin,
Methinks I stand on Thorns till I begin.
    Y' expect to hear, at least, what Love has past
In this lewd Town, since you and I saw last;
What Change has happen'd of intrigues, and whether
35 The old ones last, and who and who 's together.
But how, my dearest *Cloe*, shou'd I set
My Pen to Write, what I wou'd fain forget?
Or name that lost thing *Love*, without a Tear,
Since so debauch'd by ill-bred-Customs here?
40 *Love*, the most gen'rous Passion of the Mind;
The softest Refuge Innocence can find:
The safe Director of unguided Youth:
Fraught with kind Wishes, and secur'd by Truth:
That Cordial drop Heav'n in our Cup has thrown,
45 To make the nauseous draught of life go down:
On which one onely blessing God might raise,
In Lands of Atheists, Subsidies of Praise:

17 *Bedlam:* the asylum of St Mary of Bethlehem, near London Wall
(1676); the madhouse. *many Mansions:* John xiv. 2.
21 *Fiddle:* mirthmaker, joke. Cf. Pope, *Dunciad*, i. 224; "At once the Bear
and Fiddle of the town".
35 *'s together:* i.e. in a love affair.
44 *Cordial:* (a) belonging to the heart; (b) warm, sweetening.

For none did e're so dull, and stupid, prove,
But felt a God, and blest his Pow'r in Love:
50 This only Joy, for which poor we were made,
Is grown, like Play, to be an arrant Trade:
The Rooks creep in, and it has got, of late,
As many little Cheats, and Tricks, as that.
But, what yet more a Woman's Heart wou'd vex,
55 'Tis chiefly carry'd on by our own Sex:
Our silly Sex, who, born like Monarchs, free,   ⎫
Turn Gipsies for a meaner Liberty;   ⎬
And hate Restraint, tho' but from Infamy: ⎭
That call whatever is not common nice,   ⎫
60 And, deaf to Nature's Rule, or Love's advice, ⎬
Forsake the Pleasure to pursue the Vice.   ⎭
To an exact Perfection they have brought
The action Love; the passion is forgot.
'Tis below Wit, they tell you, to admire;
65 And ev'n without approving they desire.
Their private Wish obeys the publick Voice,
'Twixt good and bad whimsey decides, not choice.
Fashions grow up for tast, at Forms they strike;
They know what they wou'd have, not what they like.
70 *Bovy* 's a Beauty, if some few agree   ⎫
To call him so, the rest to that degree   ⎬
Affected are, that with their Ears they see. ⎭

Where I was visiting the other Night,
Comes a fine Lady, with her humble Knight,

49 *felt:* became conscious of; but echoing Acts xvii. 27: "feel after [God], and find him, though he be not far".

51 *Play:* gambling.   *arrant:* notorious.

52 *Rooks:* cheats.

58 *Infamy:* the loss, through criminal offence, of a citizen's rights.

59 *nice:* fastidious, over-strict.

61 *the Pleasure:* i.e. of natural and faithful love.

64 *below Wit:* unsophisticated, unfashionable.

68 *Forms:* accepted, conventional standards.

70 *Bovy:* James Bovey (b. 1622), a lawyer, notoriously ugly, and by this time retired, ailing, and a widower.

75   Who had prevail'd with her, through her own Skill,
     At his Request, though much against his Will,
     To come to *London*——
     As the Coach stopt, I heard her Voice, more loud
     Than a great-bellied Woman's in a Croud;
80   Telling the Knight that her Affairs require
     He, for some hours, obsequiously, retire.
     I think she was asham'd he shou'd be seen:
     Hard Fate of Husbands! the Gallant had been,
     Though a diseas'd, ill-favour'd Fool, brought in.
85   Dispatch, says she, the business you pretend,
     Your beastly visit to your drunken Friend.
     A Bottle ever makes you look so fine;
     Methinks I long to smell you stink of Wine.
     Your Country drinking Breath 's enough to kill:
90   Sour Ale corrected with a Lemmon Pill.
     Prithee, farewell; we'll meet again anon.
     The necessary Thing bows, and is gone.
     She flies up stairs, and all the haste does show
     That fifty Antick Postures will allow,
95   And then burst out—Dear Madam, am not I
     The strangest, alter'd, Creature: let me dye
     I find my self ridiculously grown,
     Embarrast with my being out of Town:
     Rude and untaught, like any Indian Queen;
100 My Country Nakedness is strangely seen.
     How is Love govern'd? Love that rules the state;
     And pray who are the men most worn of late?
     When I was marri'd, Fools were all-a-mode;

83 *Gallant:* gentleman of fashion, suitor.

90 *Lemmon Pill:* lemon-peel, to sweeten the breath.

94 *Antick:* grotesque, affected.

96 *let me dye:* exclamatory; "let me die if I do not . . .".

99 *Indian Queen:* a primitive. The title of a notably successful heroic play by Dryden and Sir Robert Howard (1663-4).

102 *worn:* cultivated, enjoyed; a *double-entendre.*

103 *all-a-mode:* in the fashion. The erroneous anglicisation is common.

The men of Wit were held then incommode:
105 Slow of Belief, and fickle in Desire,
Who, e're they'll be perswaded, must enquire;
As if they came to spie, and not to admire.
With searching-wisdom, fatal to their ease,
They still find out why, what may, shou'd not please:
110 Nay, take themselves for injur'd, when we dare
Make 'em think better of us than we are:
And, if we hide our Frailties from their sights,
Call us deceitful Jilts, and Hypocrites:
They little guess, who at our Arts are griev'd,
115 The perfect joy of being well deceiv'd.
Inquisitive, as jealous Cuckolds, grow;
Rather than not be knowing, they will know,
What being known, creates their certain woe.
Women should these, of all Mankind, avoid;
120 For wonder by clear Knowledge, is destroy'd.
Woman, who is an arrant Bird of night,
Bold in the dusk, before a Fools dull Sight
Must flie, when Reason brings the glaring light.
But the kind easie Fool, apt to admire
125 Himself, trusts us, his Follies all conspire
To flatter his, and favour our desire.
Vain of his proper Merit, He, with ease,
Believes we love him best, who best can please:
On him our gross, dull, common Flatt'ries pass;
130 Ever most happy when most made an Ass:
Heavy to apprehend; though all Mankind
Perceive us false, the Fop, himself, is blind.
Who, doating on himself,—
Thinks every one that sees him of his mind.
135 These are true Womens Men—here, forc'd to cease
Through want of Breath, not Will, to hold her peace;
She to the Window runs, where she had spi'd
Her much esteem'd, dear, Friend, the Monkey ty'd:

104 *incommode:* inconvenient, troublesome.
127 *proper:* own, personal, peculiar.
132 *Fop:* foolish dandy, coxcomb.

With forty Smiles, as many antick bows,
140   As if 't had been the Lady of the House:
The dirty, chatt'ring Monster she embrac'd;
And made it this fine tender Speech at last.

Kiss me, thou curious Minature of Man;
How odd thou art, how pretty, how japan:
145   Oh! I could live and dye with thee: then on,
For half an Hour, in Complements she ran.
I took this time to think what Nature meant,
When this mixt thing into the world she sent,
So very wise, yet so impertinent.
150   One that knows ev'ry thing, that God thought fit
Shou'd be an Ass through choice, not want of Wit.
Whose Foppery, without the help of sense,
Cou'd ne're have rose to such an excellence.
Nature 's as lame in making a true Fop
155   As a Philosopher; the very Top,
And Dignity of Folly, we attain
By studious search, and labour of the Brain:
By Observation, Counsel, and deep Thought:
God never made a Coxcomb worth a Groat.
160   We owe that Name to Industry and Arts;
An Eminent Fool must be a Fool of parts.
And such a one was she; who had turn'd o're
As many Books as Men; lov'd much, read more:
Had discerning Wit; to her was known
165   Ev'ry one's Fault, or Merit, but her own.
All the good Qualities that ever blest
A Woman so distinguish'd from the rest,
Except Discretion only, she possest.
And now *Mon Cher* Dear Pug, she cries, adieu;
170   And the Discourse, broke off, does thus renew.

139 *antick:* exaggerated, grotesque.

144 *japan:* "japanned", glossy black.

149 *impertinent:* absurd, silly. Cf. ll. 256-7.

154 *lame:* infirm, incompetent.

169 *Pug:* a term of endearment. Cf. the *Spectator*, no. 499; "I heard her call him dear Pugg, and found him to be her favourite monkey".

You smile to see me, who the World perchance
Mistakes to have some wit, so far advance
The interest of Fools, that I approve
Their Merit more, than Men of Wit, in love.
175 But, in our Sex, too many Proofs there are
Of such, whom Wits undo, and Fools repair.
This, in my Time, was so observ'd a Rule,
Hardly a Wench in Town but had her Fool.
The meanest, common Slut, who long was grown
180 The jeast, and scorn, of ev'ry Pit-Buffoon;
Had yet left Charms enough to have subdu'd
Some Fop or other; fond to be thought lewd.
Foster could make an *Irish* Lord a *Nokes*;
And *Betty Morris* had her City Cokes.
185 A Woman's ne're so ruin'd, but she can
Be still reveng'd on her undoer, Man:
How lost soe'ere, She'l find some Lover more,
A more abandon'd Fool than she a Whore.

That wretched thing *Corinna*, who has run
190 Through all the sev'ral ways of being undone:
Cozen'd at first by Love, and living then
By turning the too-dear-bought-cheat of Men:
Gay were the hours, and wing'd with joy they flew,
When first the Town her early Beauties knew:
195 Courted, admired, and lov'd, with Presents fed;
Youth in her Looks, and Pleasure in her Bed:
'Till Fate, or her ill Angel, thought it fit
To make her doat upon a man of Wit:
Who found 'twas dull to love above a day,
200 Made his ill-natur'd jeast, and went away.
Now scorn'd of all, forsaken and opprest,
She's a *Memento Mori* to the rest;

182 *fond:* pleased.
183-4 *Foster . . . Morris:* probably whores. *Nokes . . . Cokes:* slang for
"simpleton". James Nokes the comedian was famous for his "simpleton"
parts.   **200** *jeast:* jeer.
202 *Memento Mori:* "remember that you have to die"; a warning of death.

Diseas'd, decay'd, to take up half a Crown
Must Mortgage her Long Scarf, and Manto Gown;
205 Poor Creature, who unheard of, as a Flie,
In some dark hole must all the Winter lye;
And want, and dirt, endure a whole half year,
That, for one month, she Tawdry may appear.
In *Easter* Term she gets her a new Gown;
210 When my young Master's Worship comes to Town;
From Pedagogue, and Mother, just set free;
The Heir and Hopes of a great Family:
Who with strong Beer, and Beef, the Country rules;
And ever since the Conquest, have been Fools;
215 And now, with careful prospect to maintain
This Character, lest crossing of the Strain
Should mend the Booby-breed; his Friends provide
A Cousin of his own to be his Bride;
And thus set out,—
220 With an Estate, no Wit, and a young Wife:
The solid Comforts of a Coxcomb's Life;
Dunghil and Pease forsook, he comes to Town,
Turns Spark, learns to be lewd, and is undone;
Nothing suits worse with Vice than want of sense;
225 Fools are still wicked at their own expence.
This o're-grown School-Boy lost-*Corinna* wins;
At the first dash to make an Ass begins;
Pretends to like a man that has not known
The Vanities or Vices of the Town:
230 Fresh is the youth, and faithful in his love,
Eager of joys which he does seldom prove:

204 *Long Scarf:* carried decoratively, and often adorned with lace. *Manto:* manteau, a loose gown; misspelt through association with "Mantua".

208 *Tawdry:* cheaply decked out.

209-10 *In Easter . . . Town:* Cf. Dryden, *Sir Martin Mar-all* (1667), I: "I came up, Madam, as we Country-Gentlewomen use, at an *Easter*-Term . . . to see a New Play, buy a new Gown . . . and so down again to sleep with my Fore-fathers."

222 *Pease:* pease-meal, country fare.

231 *prove:* try, experience.

Healthful and strong, he does no pains endure,
But what the Fair One he adores, can cure.
Grateful for favours, does the Sex esteem,
235 And libels none for being kind to him.
Then of the lewdness of the Town complains,
Rails at the Wits, and Atheists, and maintains
'Tis better than good sense, than Pow'r, or Wealth
To have a Blood untainted, youth, and health.
240 The unbred Puppy, who had never seen
A Creature look so gay, or talk so fine,
Believes, then falls in love, and then in debt;
Mortgages all, ev'n to the ancient Seat,
To buy his Mistress a new House for Life;
245 To give her Plate, and Jewels, robs his Wife.
And when to th' height of fondness he is grown,
'Tis time to poyson him, and all 's her own.
Thus, meeting in her common Arms his Fate,
He leaves her Bastard Heir to his Estate:
250 And, as the Race of such an Owl deserves,
His own dull, lawful Progeny he starves.
Nature (that never made a thing in vain,
But does each Insect to some end ordain)
Wisely provokes kind-keeping Fools, no doubt,
255 To patch up Vices, Men of Wit wear out.

      Thus she ran on two hours, some grains of sense
Still mixt with vollies of impertinence,
But now 'tis time I shou'd some pity show
To *Cloe*, since I cannot chuse but know,
260 Readers must reap what dullest Writers sow.

---

246 *fondness*: infatuation.

248 *common*: promiscuous, open to all.

250 *Owl*: Cf. *Mac Flecknoe*, ll. 129-32, note.

254 *kind-keeping*: keeping a mistress. Cf. Dryden, *The Kind Keeper* (1678), a dramatic "*Satyr* against our crying sin".

257 *impertinence*: silliness. Cf. l. 149.

By the next Post I will such stories tell,
As, joyn'd to these, shall to a Volume swell;
As true as Heav'n, more infamous than Hell.
But you are tir'd, and so am I.

                                        Farewel.

Jonathan Swift

A SATIRICAL ELEGY ON THE DEATH OF
A LATE FAMOUS GENERAL

THE DAY OF JUDGEMENT

"THE choice of his numbers [the octosyllabic couplet] is suitable enough to
his design as he has managed it; but, in any other hand, the shortness of his
verse, and the quick returns of rhyme, had debased the dignity of style."
The words are Dryden's in *The Original and Progress of Satire;* he was speaking of Butler but might well have said the same of Swift. Two reservations,
however, would have to be made: first that Swift can achieve a distinctive,
if mordant, "dignity"—notice the way he moves from savage bitterness at
the opening of the *Satirical Elegy* to a memorable expression, at the close, of
a traditional theme akin to Johnson's in *The Vanity of Human Wishes;* and
second, that in any case he did not aim at stylistic elevation. Swift's primary
object was complete intelligibility of statement. In his view the poet—like
"the Young Gentleman lately enter'd into Holy Orders"—must make
himself unequivocally understood, must honestly communicate his view of
things as they are. Hence Swift's own rejection of whatever is superfluous;
the absence from his verse of the allusive richness of language used by Pope
or Johnson; and his avoidance of literary ornaments or commonplaces.

> Nor let my Votaries show their Skill
> In apeing lines from *Cooper's Hill;*
> For know I cannot bear to hear,
> The Mimicry of *deep, yet clear.*

This is one of his instructions to the poet in *Apollo's Edict;* he heeds his own
advice, Soame Jenyns does not (see below p. 70).

Marlborough—the "late General" who died on 16 June 1722—had
previously excited Swift's animus. In the *Examiner* paper No. 28 (1711), in
the pamphlet *The Conduct of the Allies* (1711), and in the poem *The Fable of
Midas* (1712), Swift had denounced his avarice, his love of prominence, and
his concern for family rather than national interests. A similar revulsion

informs the *Satirical Elegy* (1722), but the final lines of the poem involve all creatures of kings and concisely state a central theme of the First Book of *Gulliver's Travels*. The final line is a check to human pride in general like that administered by Hamlet's remark: "Why may not imagination trace the noble dust of Alexander, till a' find it stopping a bung-hole?"

The generality of this vision occupies the whole of *The Day of Judgement* (1731?). The savage indignation of the Fourth Book of *Gulliver's Travels* is missing, but the tone of the King of Brobdingnag's withering repudiation of human pretensions is strongly recalled. Life had become for Swift (as he wrote to Pope on 20 April 1731) "a ridiculous tragedy"; the poem gives trenchant expression to this view. The end of *The Dunciad*, and Hogarth's print, *The Bathos or Finis*—with their vision of the overthrow of "the World's mad Business"—show that it was shared by others among Swift's contemporaries.

The text of the *Satirical Elegy* follows that given in Swift's *Works*, edited by Deane Swift, 1765; the text of *The Day of Judgement* is that in *St. James's Chronicle*, 9-12 April 1774, where it was first published.

A SATIRICAL ELEGY

His Grace! impossible! what dead!
Of old age too, and in his bed!
And could that Mighty Warrior fall?
And so inglorious, after all!
5   Well, since he's gone, no matter how,
The last loud trump must wake him now:
And trust me, as the noise grows stronger,
He'd wish to sleep a little longer.
And could he be indeed so old
10   As by the news-papers we're told?
Threescore, I think, is pretty high;
'Twas time in conscience he should die.
This world he cumber'd long enough;
He burnt his candle to the snuff;
15   And that's the reason, some folks think,
He left behind *so great a s——k*.
Behold his funeral appears,
Nor widow's sighs, nor orphan's tears,
Wont at such times each heart to pierce,
20   Attend the progress of his herse.

9-10 *And could . . . told:* Marlborough died at the age of 72.

But what of that, his friends may say,
He had those honours in his day.
True to his profit and his pride,
He made them weep before he dy'd.
25   Come hither, all ye empty things,
Ye bubbles rais'd by breath of Kings;
Who float upon the tide of state,
Come hither, and behold your fate.
Let pride be taught by this rebuke,
30 How very mean a thing's a Duke;
From all his ill-got honours flung,
Turn'd to that dirt from whence he sprung.

THE DAY OF JUDGEMENT

With a Whirl of Thought oppress'd,
I sink from Reverie to Rest.
An horrid Vision seiz'd my Head,
I saw the Graves give up their Dead.
5 Jove, arm'd with Terrors, burst the Skies,
And Thunder roars, and Light'ning flies!
Amaz'd, confus'd, its Fate unknown,
The World stands trembling at his Throne.
While each pale Sinner hangs his Head,
10 Jove, nodding, shook the Heav'ns, and said,
"Offending Race of Human Kind,
By Nature, Reason, Learning, blind;
You who thro' Frailty step'd aside,
And you who never fell—*thro' Pride*;
15 You who in different Sects have shamm'd,
And come to see each other damn'd;
(So some Folks told you, but they knew
No more of Jove's Designs than you)
The World's mad Business now is o'er,
20 And I resent these Pranks no more.
I to such Blockheads set my Wit!
I damn such Fools!—Go, go, you're bit."

22 *bit:* i.e. deceived.

Anon

THE VICAR OF BRAY

THIS poem (set to the air *The Country Garden*), spoken by the time-serving parson who has accommodated himself to the changing religious climate of five reigns, is conjecturally dated *c.* 1720. However, the prototype of the speaker was probably Symon Aleyn (1540–88), himself the Vicar of Bray, Berkshire, who was twice Papist and twice Protestant between the time of Henry VIII and Elizabeth. When charged with being a time-server he is said to have answered: "Not so, for I always kept my principle, which is this, to live and die the vicar of Bray" (Thomas Fuller, *The History of the Worthies of England*, ed. P. A. Nuttall, 1840, i. 113). The Vicar was already proverbial in Berkshire when Fuller published his *Worthies* in 1662; by 1715 (in the *Appeal to Honour and Justice*) Defoe felt able to use his name as a synonym for "turncoat", on the assumption that the allusion would be generally understood.

Despite its apparent simplicity the poem is an accomplished satire. The consistent viewpoint of the speaker—that religion is concerned solely with material advantage—provides a strictly logical framework; the cumulative evidence of his successful accommodation gives an ironic momentum to the poem; and the humorous tone, which stems from the speaker's permissive morality, conveys the writer's contempt while maintaining a tacit admiration for the vicar's adroit behaviour. As a piece of self-exposure—though in a different satiric mood—it is worthy of comparison with Burns's (admittedly more subtle) *Holy Willie's Prayer*. It is set to music in *Calliope, or the Musical Miscellany. A select Collection* (1788).

> In CHARLES the Second's Golden Days
>   When Loyalty no Harm meant,
> A furious High Churchman I was,
>   And so I got Preferment;
> 5 Unto my Flock I daily preach'd
>   Kings were by God appointed,
> And damn'd was he, that durst resist,
>   Or touch the Lord's Anointed.
>
>   Chor. *That this is Law, I will maintain*
> 10   *Unto my dying Day, Sir,*

That whatsoever King shall reign,
   I will be Vicar of Bray, Sir.

When Royal JAMES possess'd the Crown,
   And Pop'ry grew in Fashion,
15 The penal Laws I hooted down,
   And read the Declaration;
The Church of *Rome* I found would fit,
   Full well my Constitution,
And had become a Jesuit,
20   But for the Revolution.

That this is Law, I will maintain, &c.

When WILLIAM our Deliverer came,
   To heal the Nations Grievance,
I turn'd the Cat in Pan again,
25   And swore to him Allegiance;
Old Principles I did revoke,
   Set Conscience at a distance;
Passive Obedience was a Joke,
   A Jest was Non-resistance.

30 *That this is Law, I will maintain,* &c.

15 *penal Laws:* James II, himself a Roman Catholic, gradually reduced the pressure of these anti-Roman Catholic measures and finally made them inoperative. (They had prohibited Roman Catholic rites, made it a felony to harbour a priest, and high treason to convert any subject to Catholicism.)

16 *Declaration:* James insisted that the second Declaration of Indulgence (April 1688) should be read in Anglican Churches. Many Anglican priests strongly resisted its concessions to dissenters (including Roman Catholics); seven bishops were prosecuted for their resistance.

20 *Revolution:* the "Glorious Revolution" on the deposition of James II and accession of William III.

24 *turn'd the . . . Pan:* i.e. changed his position from motives of self-interest.

28-9 *Passive Obedience . . . resistance:* The non-juring clergy who refused, in 1689, to take the oath of allegiance to William because he was not the hereditary monarch showed their disapproval through (in modern terms) passive resistance.

When Gracious ANN became our Queen,
   The Church of *Englands* Glory,
Another Face of Things were seen,
   And I became a Tory;
35 Occasional Conformest base
   I damn'd, and such Evasion,
And swore the Church wou'd ruin'd be
   From such Prevarication.

That this is Law, I will maintain, &c.

40 When GEORGE in Pudding-time came o'er,
   And moderate Men look'd big, Sir.
My principles I chang'd once more,
   And so became a Whig, Sir;
And thus Preferment I procur'd
45   From our great Faith's Defender,
And every now and then abjur'd
   The Pope and the Pretender.

That this is Law, I will maintain, &c.

Th' Illustrious House of *Hanover*,
50   And Protestant Succession,
To these I lustily will swear
   While they can keep Possession,

32 *The Church . . . Glory:* In her first speech from the Throne, in May 1702, Anne declared: "My own principles must always keep me entirely firm to the interests and religion of the Church of England, and will incline me to countenance those who have the truest zeal to support it."

34 *Tory:* During Anne's reign the Tory party was in the ascendant, led, first, by Godolphin and Harley; then, after the dismissal of Godolphin in 1710, by Harley and St. John.

35 *Occasional Conformest:* True to his new-found High Anglicanism, the Vicar of Bray despises the practice of those non-conformists who, in order to qualify for public office, "occasionally conformed" by taking communion in an Anglican Church. High Anglicans (notably Dr. Henry Sacheverell) virulently attacked the practice.

40 *Pudding-time:* i.e. a favourable moment.

43 *Whig:* George I regarded the Tories as his enemies; the Whigs were in power throughout his reign.

And in my Faith and Loyalty
  I never once will falter,
55 And GEORGE my lawful King shall be,
  Unless the Times shall alter.

That this is Law, I will maintain
  Unto my dying Day, Sir.
That whatsoever King shall reign,
60 *I will be Vicar of Bray, Sir.*

Alexander Pope

AN EPISTLE

from Mr. Pope, to Dr. Arbuthnot

Neque sermonibus Vulgi dederis te, nec in Praemiis *humanis spem posueris rerum tuarum: suis te oportet illecebris ipsa* Virtus *trahat ad verum decus. Quid de te alii loquantur, ipsi videant, sed loquentur tamen.*

TULLY

THIS is the most intensely personal of Pope's satiric poems. Its occasion, as the Advertisement makes clear, was an attack on him in two verse epistles by Lady Mary Wortley Montague and Lord Hervey in 1733; and one of the three substantial portraits in the poem is of Hervey (ll. 305–33). It is, Pope wrote just before the *Epistle* was published on 2 January 1735, "a just vindication from slanders of all sorts, and slanderers of what rank or quality soever". This broader theme is described in a letter of 25 August 1734 to his old friend Arbuthnot, who had been urging him to keep clear of the dangerous traffic in personal satire: "I determine to address to you one of my Epistles, written by piecemeal many years [the main early sections are ll. 193–214, 289–304, 406–19], & wch I have now made haste to put together; wherein the Question is stated, what were, & are my Motives of writing, the objections to them, & my answers . . . [and I] take this occasion of testifying . . . my Obligation & Friendship for, & from, you, for so many years." Pope indeed sets out his "Motives of writing" (see ll. 125–46, 173–90, 334–59) and his "answers" (e.g. ll. 75–108), and he pays closing tribute to Arbuthnot (see also ll. 27–8, 133–4). But the scope of the *Epistle* is much wider than his letters, or his description of it in the Advertisement as "a Sort of Bill of Complaint", suggest. It is a comprehensive vindication of his motives and practice as a satirist—and indeed of the art of satire itself; for the *persona* of the poet is, for all the autobiographical detail, more general and timeless than "Mr. Pope", and his interlocutor is more of an articulate social conscience than "Dr. Arbuthnot". Pope follows the informal epistolary model of Horace; but beneath the casual, discursive movement of his talk there is a firm logical structure. The *Epistle* is no mere satiric miscellany. Pope's stylistic range is wide: from colloquial intimacy to exalted rhetoric, from the commonplace to the fantastic or from the trivial to the cosmic in a few lines (cf. ll. 1–10; 86–8, note); in his "characters", from the Theophrastan generality of ll. 287–302 to the pointed gravity—appropriately senatorial—of the "Atticus" portrait (ll. 193–214) and the nightmare violence of "Sporus" (ll. 305–33). (See B. Boyce, *The Character Sketches in Pope's Poems*, 1962, pp. 59–62, 81 ff.). But these styles are patterned within the framework of the *Epistle*. Pope's half-comic distress in the midst of swarming poetasters sharpens (l. 69) into criticism of dunces and libellers; his first self-portrait—a figure of honest charity, suffering long, not easily provoked, thinking as little evil as he can (ll. 125–192)—is offset, in the first climax of the poem, by the portrait of "Atticus", the oblique, ungenerous, dishonest literary arbiter (ll. 193–214). The image of this Cato in his senate makes a transition to Pope's next defensive line—"I sought no homage from the Race that write"—which is again illustrated by a contrasting "character": that of the corrupt patron, Bufo, and his worthless flatterers (ll. 231–44). The portrait of patronage negligent of merit makes a transition to Pope's third representation of himself as an independent artist (ll. 261 ff.); his initial theme—the importunate, offensive, and corrupt—is resumed in a fuller, oratorical style (ll. 283–304); and a third climax is reached in the illustrative "character" of "Sporus". On the level of intensity set by this picture, Pope moves on into his final self-portrait (ll. 334 ff.) in what is almost incantation. The *Epistle*, then, is a kind of poetic suite in five movements, each with its own style and tempo, and the second, third and fourth composed on the same broad pattern of "vindication" and "character".

Pope's epigraph is from Cicero, *De Republica*, vi. 23: "You will not surrender to the talk of the crowd, or put your faith in human rewards for what you do. Virtue should attract you to true glory for her own sake. Let what others say of you be their own affair; they will say it anyhow." The text is that of the first edition, corrected from that of 1739.

ADVERTISEMENT

This Paper is a Sort of Bill of Complaint, begun many years since, and drawn up by snatches, as the several Occasions offer'd. I had no thoughts of publishing it, till it pleas'd some Persons of Rank and Fortune [the Authors of *Verses to the Imitator of Horace*, and of

4 *the Authors:* Lady Mary Wortley Montagu and Lord Hervey (see the *Epistle*, ll. 101, 305).

5 an *Epistle to a Doctor of Divinity from a Nobleman at Hampton Court,*]
to attack in a very extraordinary manner, not only my Writings
(of which being publick the Publick judge) but my *Person, Morals,*
and *Family,* whereof to those who know me not, a truer Information
may be requisite. Being divided between the Necessity to say
10 something of *Myself,* and my own Laziness to undertake so awk-
ward a Task, I thought it the shortest way to put the last hand to
this Epistle. If it have anything pleasing, it will be That by which
I am most desirous to please, the *Truth* and the *Sentiment*; and if
any thing offensive, it will be only to those I am least sorry to offend,
15 the *Vicious* or the *Ungenerous.*

Many will know their own Pictures in it, there being not a
Circumstance but what is true; but I have, for the most part spar'd
their *Names,* and they may escape being laugh'd at, if they please.

I would have some of them know, it was owing to the Request
20 of the learned and candid Friend to whom it is inscribed, that I
make not as free use of theirs as they have done of mine. However
I shall have this Advantage, and Honour, on my side, that whereas
by their proceeding, any Abuse may be directed at any man, no
Injury can possibly be done by mine, since a Nameless Character
25 can never be found out, but by its *Truth* and *Likeness.*

> Shut, shut the door, good *John*! fatigu'd I said,
> Tye up the knocker, say I'm sick, I'm dead,
> The Dog-star rages! nay 'tis past a doubt,
> All *Bedlam,* or *Parnassus,* is let out:
> 5 Fire in each eye, and Papers in each hand,
> They rave, recite, and madden round the land.
>   What Walls can guard me, or what Shades can hide?
> They pierce my Thickets, thro' my Grot they glide,
> By land, by water, they renew the charge,
> 10 They stop the Chariot, and they board the Barge.

1 *John:* Pope's servant and gardener, John Serle.

3 *The Dog-star:* Sirius, associated with distracting heat and with the
Roman practice of poetic recitation in August (Horace, *Odes,* III. xiii. 9;
Juvenal, *Sat.* iii. 8-9). With ll. 5-6 cf. Horace's *recitator acerbus* (*De Arte
Poetica,* ll. 474-6).

8 *my Grot:* the celebrated grotto at Pope's house at Twickenham.

10 *the Barge:* taking him down the Thames to London.

No place is sacred, not the Church is free,
Ev'n *Sunday* shines no *Sabbath-day* to me:
Then from the *Mint* walks forth the Man of Ryme,
Happy! to catch me, just at Dinner-time.
15   Is there a Parson, much be-mus'd in Beer,
A maudlin Poetess, a ryming Peer,
A Clerk, foredoom'd his Father's soul to cross,
Who pens a Stanza when he should *engross*?
Is there, who lock'd from Ink and Paper, scrawls
20 With desp'rate Charcoal round his darken'd walls?
All fly to *Twit'nam*, and in humble strain
Apply to me, to keep them mad or vain.
Arthur, whose giddy Son neglects the Laws,
Imputes to me and my damn'd works the cause:
25 Poor *Cornus* sees his frantic Wife elope,
And curses Wit, and Poetry, and *Pope*.
    Friend to my Life, (which did not you prolong,
The World had wanted many an idle Song)
What *Drop* or *Nostrum* can this Plague remove?
30 Or which must end me, a Fool's Wrath or Love?

13 *the Mint:* a sanctuary for debtors at Southwark, where Henry VIII had a mint.

15 *a Parson . . . be-mus'd:* the participle suggests the name of the Rev. Lawrence Eusden (1688–1730), lately poet laureate.

17 *cross:* thwart.

18 *engross:* transcribe (lit. write large) a legal document.

19-20 *scrawls . . . walls:* Cf. Boileau, *L'Art Poétique*, i. 22; "Charbonner de ses vers les murs d'un cabaret".

23 *Arthur . . . Son:* Arthur Moore (d. 1730) and his son James (1702–34). The father was a business man and politician; the son, a man of some wealth and a minor poet who offended and then attacked Pope.

25 *Cornus:* a cuckold (Lat. *cornu*, a horn).

27 *Friend:* John Arbuthnot (1667–1735), Scottish physician and man of letters; with Pope and Swift, a founder of the satiric Scriblerus Club (1713–14); at this time dying.

28 *The World . . . Song:* echoing Dryden, *Absalom and Achitophel*, l. 197.

29 *Drop . . . Nostrum:* medicine taken in drops . . . quick remedy.

A dire Dilemma! either way I'm sped,
If Foes, they write, if Friends, they read me dead.
Seiz'd and ty'd down to judge, how wretched I!
Who can't be silent, and who will not lye;
35   To laugh, were want of Goodness and of Grace,
And to be grave, exceeds all Pow'r of Face.
I sit with sad Civility, I read
With honest anguish, and an aking head;
And drop at last, but in unwilling ears,
40   This saving counsel, "Keep your Piece nine years."
    Nine years! cries he, who high in *Drury-lane*
Lull'd by soft Zephyrs thro' the broken Pane,
Rymes e're he wakes, and prints before *Term* ends,
Oblig'd by hunger and Request of friends:
45   "The Piece you think is incorrect: why take it,
I'm all submission, what you'd have it, make it."
Three things another's modest wishes bound,
My Friendship, and a Prologue, and ten Pound.
Pitholeon sends to me: "You know his Grace,
50   I want a Patron; ask him for a Place."
Pitholeon libell'd me—"but here's a Letter
Informs you Sir, 'twas when he knew no better.

32 *read me dead:* cf. Horace, *De Arte Poetica*, l. 475, "quem vero arripuit, tenet occiditque legendo".

33 *ty'd down to judge:* like the poetaster's victim in Wycherley, *The Plain Dealer*, v. 3.

40 *Keep . . . nine years:* Cf. Horace, *De Arte Poetica*, ll. 386-9; Dryden, *Mac Flecknoe*, l. 149, note.

41 *high:* i.e. in a garret.

43 *Term:* the legal term and publishers' season.

44 *Request of friends:* a common pretext to disguise poverty.

48 *a Prologue:* to help launch his new play.

49 *Pitholeon:* "The name taken from a foolish Poet at *Rhodes*, who pretended much to *Greek*" (Pope; see Horace, *Sat.* I. x. 22); representing Leonard Welsted (1688–1747), translator of Longinus, and perhaps also Thomas Cooke (1703–56), translator of Hesiod and libeller of Pope in the *London Journal* (cf. l. 54). On Welsted, see also p. 70, note.

50 *Place:* post, employment.

Dare you refuse him? *Curl* invites to dine,
He'll write a *Journal*, or he'll turn *Divine*."
55   Bless me! a Packet.—"'Tis a stranger sues,
A Virgin Tragedy, an Orphan Muse."
If I dislike it, "Furies, death and rage!"
If I approve, "Commend it to the Stage."
There (thank my Stars) my whole Commission ends,
60   The Play'rs and I are, luckily, no friends.
Fir'd that the House reject him, "'Sdeath I'll print it
And shame the Fools—your int'rest, Sir, with *Lintot*."
Lintot, dull rogue! will think your price too much.
"Not Sir, if you revise it, and retouch."
65   All my demurrs but double his attacks,
At last he whispers "Do, and we go snacks."
Glad of a quarrel, strait I clap the door,
Sir, let me see your works and you no more.
    'Tis sung, when *Midas'* Ears began to spring,
70   (*Midas*, a sacred Person and a King)
His very Minister who spy'd them first,
(Some say his Queen) was forc'd to speak, or burst.
And is not mine, my Friend, a sorer case,
When ev'ry Coxcomb perks them in my face?
75   "Good friend forbear! you deal in dang'rous things,
I'd never name Queens, Ministers, or Kings;
Keep close to Ears, and those let Asses prick,
'Tis nothing"—Nothing? if they bite and kick?
Out with it, *Dunciad*! let the secret pass,
80   That Secret to each Fool, that he's an Ass:

53 *Curl:* Edmund Curll (1675–1747), a disreputable bookseller and an enemy of Pope's.   **61** *House:* theatre audience.

62 *Lintot:* Bernard Lintot (1675–1736), bookseller, and publisher of Pope's *Homer* (1715–20, 1725–6).   **66** *go snacks:* share the profits.

69–72 *'Tis sung . . . burst:* "The Story is told by some of his Barber, but by *Chaucer* of his Queen. See Wife of Bath's Tale in *Dryden's* Fables" (Pope). Ovid, *Met.* xi. 146–93 and Persius, *Sat.* i. 121; Chaucer, *WBT*, ll. 952–78. Pope alludes satirically to George II, Queen Caroline, and her ally Walpole.

79 *Dunciad:* Pope's mock-heroic satire on folly (1728; 1742–3).

80 *Secret:* i.e. that his ass's ears can be seen.

The truth once told, (and wherefore shou'd we lie?)
The Queen of *Midas* slept, and so may I.
   You think this cruel? take it for a rule,
No creature smarts so little as a Fool.
85 Let Peals of Laughter, *Codrus!* round thee break,
Thou unconcern'd canst hear the mighty Crack.
Pit, Box, and Gall'ry in convulsions hurl'd,
Thou stand'st unshook amidst a bursting World.
Who shames a Scribler? break one cobweb thro',
90 He spins the slight, self-pleasing thread anew;
Destroy his Fib, or Sophistry; in vain,
The Creature 's at his dirty work again;
Thron'd in the Centre of his thin designs;
Proud of a vast Extent of flimzy lines.
95 Whom have I hurt? has Poet yet, or Peer,
Lost the arch'd eye-brow, or *Parnassian* sneer?
And has not *Colly* still his Lord, and Whore?
His Butchers *Henley*, his Free-masons *Moor*?
Does not one Table *Bavius* still admit?

85 *Codrus:* a bad Roman poet (Juvenal, *Sat.* i. 2); cf. l. 99.

86-8 *Thou unconcern'd . . . World:* a mock-heroic application, to the insensitive Codrus and the derisive theatre, of Horace's lines on the *iustum et tenacem . . . virum* (*Odes*, III. iii) as translated by Addison:

> Should the whole frame of nature round him break,
> In ruine and confusion hurl'd,
> He, unconcern'd, would hear the mighty crack,
> And stand secure amidst a falling world.

87 *Pit, Box, and Gall'ry:* the three parts of the theatre.

90 *He spins the . . . thread:* Cf. the allegory of the spider in Swift's *Battle of the Books.*

96 *Parnassian sneer:* an element in the expression of the "hero" of Pope's *Dunciad* (1729; ii. 5), Lewis Theobald.

97 *Colly:* Colley Cibber (1671–1757), actor, dramatist, and poet laureate; later to replace Theobald as "hero" of *The Dunciad.*

98 *Henley:* John Henley (1692–1756), a mountebank preacher who "set up his Oratory in Newport-Market, Butcher-Row". *Moor:* James Moore (see l. 23, note), a prominent freemason.

99 *Bavius:* a bad Roman poet (cf. Virgil, *Ecl.* iii. 90).

100 Still to one Bishop *Philips* seem a Wit?
     Still *Sapho*—"Hold! for God-sake—you 'll offend:
     No Names—be calm—learn Prudence of a Friend:
     I too could write, and I am twice as tall,
     But Foes like these!"—One Flatt'rer 's worse than all
105 Of all mad Creatures, if the Learn'd are right,
     It is the Slaver kills, and not the Bite.
     A Fool quite angry is quite innocent;
     Alas! 'tis ten times worse when they *repent*.
        One dedicates, in high Heroic prose,
110 And ridicules beyond a hundred foes;
     One from all *Grubstreet* will my fame defend,
     And, more abusive, calls himself my friend.
     This prints my Letters, that expects a Bribe,
     And others roar aloud, "Subscribe, subscribe".
115   There are, who to my Person pay their court,
     I cough like *Horace*, and tho' lean, am short,
     Ammon's great Son one shoulder had too high,
     Such *Ovid*'s nose, and "Sir! you have an *Eye*—"
     Go on, obliging Creatures, make me see
120 All that disgrac'd my Betters, met in me:
     Say for my comfort, languishing in bed,
     "Just so immortal *Maro* held his head:"

---

100 *Philips:* Ambrose Philips (?1675–1749), Pope's early rival in pastoral poetry; secretary to the Archbishop of Armagh (1724).

101 *Sapho:* the licentious Greek poetess of Lesbos; Pope's pseudonym for Lady Mary Wortley Montagu (see l. 305, note).

106 *Slaver:* saliva of a mad dog.

111 *Grubstreet:* a street near Moorfields in London frequented by literary hacks; the fraternity of such. See l. 378, note.

113 *This:* Curll (cf. l. 55), who printed some of Pope's letters without authority in 1726.

114 *Subscribe:* Subscription guaranteed a minimum sale and made it easier to get a book published.

116 *I cough . . . short:* Cf. Horace, *Sat.* I. ix. 32 and *Ep.* I. xx. 24.

117 *Ammon's great Son:* Alexander the Great, who claimed to be Jupiter Ammon's son. His head, says Plutarch, leant to the left.

122 *Maro:* Virgil.

And when I die, be sure you let me know
Great *Homer* dy'd three thousand years ago.
125   Why did I write? what sin to me unknown
Dipt me in Ink, my Parents', or my own?
As yet a Child, nor yet a Fool to Fame,
I lisp'd in Numbers, for the Numbers came.
I left no Calling for this idle trade,
130 No Duty broke, no Father dis-obey'd.
The Muse but serv'd to ease some Friend, not Wife
To help me thro' this long Disease, my Life,
To second, ARBUTHNOT! thy Art and Care,
And teach, the Being you preserv'd, to bear.
135   But why then publish? *Granville* the polite,
And knowing *Walsh*, would tell me I could write;
Well-natur'd *Garth* inflam'd with early praise,
And *Congreve* lov'd, and *Swift* endur'd my Lays;
The Courtly *Talbot, Somers, Sheffield* read,
140 Ev'n mitred *Rochester* would nod the head,

125 *Why did I write:* So Boileau, *Sat.* ix. 19-20: 'Quelle verve indis-crette . . . vous a rendu Poëte?' Cf. John ix. 2.

127-42 *As yet . . . more:* a recollection of childhood and friends on the model of Ovid, *Tristia*, IV. x. 19-64. "The enumeration of the choice spirits for whose praise the poet cared, gives effect by its contrast with the herd who decried him" (Pattison). Cf. conclusion of Horace, *Sat.* I. x.

135 *Granville:* George Granville, Lord Lansdowne (1667-1735), to whom Pope dedicated *Windsor Forest* (1713).

136 *Walsh:* William Walsh (1663-1708), poet, friend of Dryden and Pope; "the Muse's Judge" (Pope, *Essay on Criticism*, l. 729).

137 *Garth:* Samuel Garth (1661-1719), physician and poet, author of the mock-heroic *Dispensary* (1699).

138 *Congreve . . . Swift:* William Congreve (1670-1729), Restoration dramatist; and the satirist Jonathan Swift (1667-1745).

139 *The Courtly . . . Sheffield:* Charles Talbot, Earl of Shrewsbury (1660-1718); the Whig Lord Somers (1651-1716); John Sheffield, Earl of Mul-grave and Marquis of Normanby (1648-1721), Dryden's patron and author of *An Essay on Satire*.

140 *mitred Rochester:* Francis Atterbury, Bishop of Rochester (1662-1732) and, with Pope, a member of the Scriblerus Club; exiled for plotting to restore the Stuarts in 1723.

And *St. John*'s self (great *Dryden*'s friends before)
With open arms receiv'd one Poet more.
Happy my Studies, when by these approv'd!
Happier their Author, when by these belov'd!
145 From these the world will judge of Men and Books,
Not from the *Burnets*, *Oldmixons*, and *Cooks*.
     Soft were my Numbers, who could take offence
While pure Description held the place of Sense?
Like gentle *Fanny*'s was my flow'ry Theme,
150 A painted Mistress, or a purling Stream.
Yet then did *Gildon* draw his venal quill;
I wish'd the man a dinner, and sate still:
Yet then did *Dennis* rave in furious fret;
I never answer'd, I was not in debt:
155 If want provok'd, or madness made them print,
I wag'd no war with *Bedlam* or the *Mint*.
     Did some more sober Critic come abroad?
If wrong, I smil'd; if right, I kiss'd the rod.
Pains, reading, study, are their just pretence,
160 And all they want is spirit, taste, and sense.
Comma's and points they set exactly right,
And 'twere a sin to rob them of their Mite.

141 *St. John:* Henry St. John, Viscount Bolingbroke (1678–1751), Tory politician and Pope's neighbour; exiled as a Jacobite on George I's accession; returned in 1723 to oppose Walpole. "These are the persons to whose Account the Author charges the publication of his first pieces" (Pope).

146 *Burnets . . . Cooks:* "Authors of secret and scandalous History" (Pope): Thomas Burnet (1694–1753), son of the bishop-historian; John Oldmixon (1673–1742), author of the *Secret History of Europe* (1712); Thomas Cooke (see l. 49, note)—all critics or libellers of Pope.

149 *Fanny:* Lord Hervey (see l. 305, note).

151 *Gildon:* Charles Gildon (1655–1724), critic of Pope's *The Rape of the Lock*.

153 *Dennis:* John Dennis (1657–1734), one of the best critics of his time. He took offence at Pope's *Essay on Criticism*, and censured *The Rape of the Lock* and *Windsor Forest*. Pope's claim that he "never answer'd" Dennis is false.

156 *Bedlam or the Mint:* see ll. 4, 13, note.

Yet ne'r one sprig of Laurel grac'd these ribalds,
From slashing *Bentley* down to pidling *Tibalds*.
165 Each Wight who reads not, and but scans and spells,
Each Word-catcher that lives on syllables,
Ev'n such small Critics some regard may claim,
Preserv'd in *Milton*'s or in *Shakespear*'s name.
Pretty! in Amber to observe the forms
170 Of hairs, or straws, or dirt, or grubs, or worms;
The things, we know, are neither rich nor rare,
But wonder how the Devil they got there?
    Were others angry? I excus'd them too;
Well might they rage; I gave them but their due.
175 A man's true merit 'tis not hard to find,
But each man's secret standard in his mind,
That Casting-weight Pride adds to Emptiness,
This, who can gratify? for who can *guess?*
The Bard whom pilf'red Pastorals renown,
180 Who turns a *Persian* Tale for half a crown,
Just writes to make his barrenness appear,
And strains from hard-bound brains eight lines a-year:
He, who still wanting tho' he lives on theft,
Steals much, spends little, yet has nothing left:
185 And he, who now to sense, now nonsense leaning,
Means not, but blunders round about a meaning:
And he, whose Fustian 's so sublimely bad,
It is not Poetry, but Prose run mad:
All these, my modest Satire bad *translate*,
190 And own'd, that nine such Poets made a *Tate*.

164 *Bentley . . . Tibalds:* Richard Bentley (1662–1742), a great classical scholar who "slashed" Swift's patron Temple in the "Battle of the Books" and—with much less justification—"slashed" the text of *Paradise Lost*; Lewis Theobald (1688–1744), editor of Shakespeare (1734) and translator (see ll. 96–7 notes).

165 *Wight:* fellow; an obsolete word appropriate to antiquaries.

179–80 *The Bard:* Ambrose Philips, translator of *Persian Tales* (1714) and plagiarist from Theocritus, Virgil, &c.; see l. 100, note.

190 *Tate:* Nahum Tate (1652–1715), translator, poet laureate, and author (with Dryden) of the second Part of *Absalom and Achitophel*; versifier of the Psalms (1714).

How did they fume, and stamp, and roar, and chafe?
And swear, not *Addison* himself was safe.
   Peace to all such! but were there One whose fires
True Genius kindles, and fair Fame inspires,
195 Blest with each Talent and each Art to please,
And born to write, converse, and live with ease:
Shou'd such a man, too fond to rule alone,
Bear, like the *Turk*, no brother near the throne,
View him with scornful, yet with jealous eyes,
200 And hate for Arts that caus'd himself to rise;
Damn with faint praise, assent with civil leer,
And without sneering, teach the rest to sneer;
Willing to wound, and yet afraid to strike,
Just hint a fault, and hesitate dislike;
205 Alike reserv'd to blame, or to commend,
A tim'rous foe, and a suspicious friend,
Dreading ev'n fools, by Flatterers besieg'd,
And so obliging that he ne'er oblig'd;
Like *Cato*, give his little Senate laws,
210 And sit attentive to his own applause;
While Wits and Templers ev'ry sentence raise,
And wonder with a foolish face of praise.
Who but must laugh, if such a man there be?
Who would not weep, if *Atticus* were he!
215   What tho' my Name stood rubric on the walls?
Or plaister'd posts, with Claps in capitals?

192 *Addison:* Joseph Addison (1672–1719), Whig politician and journalist, and part author of the *Spectator* (1711–12). What lies behind the following portrait of Addison as "Atticus" (first sketched in 1715) is Pope's "consciousness of a deceptive friendship": Addison had encouraged Pope's rivals and critics. The portrait is historically accurate.

209 *Cato:* Caesar's opponent who set up a minor senate in Utica, and was the subject of a tragedy by Addison (1713).

211 *Templers:* lawyers.

214 *Atticus:* substituted for "Addison" in 1734; a Roman celebrated for moderation and friendship above party.

215 *stood rubric:* i.e. on red-letter title-pages stuck up outside bookshops as advertisement.

216 *Claps:* posters.

Or smoking forth, a hundred Hawkers load,
On Wings of Winds came flying all abroad?
I sought no homage from the Race that write;
220 I kept, like *Asian* Monarchs, from their sight:
Poems I heeded (now be-rym'd so long)
No more than Thou, great GEORGE! a Birth-day Song.
I ne'r with Wits or Witlings past my days,
To spread about the Itch of Verse and Praise;
225 Nor like a Puppy daggl'd thro' the Town,
To fetch and carry Sing-song up and down;
Nor at Rehearsals sweat, and mouth'd, and cry'd,
With Handkerchief and Orange at my side:
But sick of Fops, and Poetry, and Prate,
230 To *Bufo* left the whole *Castalian* State.
  Proud, as *Apollo* on his forked hill,
Sate full-blown *Bufo*, puff'd by ev'ry quill;
Fed with soft Dedication all day long,
Horace and he went hand in hand in song.
235 His Library, (where Busts of Poets dead
And a true *Pindar* stood without a head)
Receiv'd of Wits an undistinguish'd race,
Who first his Judgment ask'd, and then a Place:
Much they extoll'd his Pictures, much his Seat,
240 And flatter'd ev'ry day, and some days eat:
Till grown more frugal in his riper days,
He pay'd some Bards with Port, and some with Praise,
To some a dry Rehearsal was assign'd,
And others (harder still) he pay'd in kind.

222 *George:* George II, no admirer of poetry.
225 *daggl'd:* padded through mire.
228 *Orange:* to ward off smells and infection.
230 *Bufo:* the exemplar of a patron, characterised in ll. 231-48; based partly on the Earl of Halifax (1661-1715) and Bubb Dodington, Baron Melcombe (1691-1762), whom Welsted (see l. 49, note) hailed as a modern Maecenas. Bufo is more concerned with dead than with living writers. *Castalian:* of the Muses.   **232** *puff'd . . . quill:* flattered . . . pen.
236 *Pindar:* "ridicules the affectation of Antiquaries, who frequently exhibit the headless *Trunks* and *Terms* of Statues, for Plato, Homer, Pindar, &c." (Pope).

245 *Dryden* alone (what wonder?) came not nigh,
  Dryden alone escap'd this judging eye:
  But still the Great have kindness in reserve,
  He help'd to bury whom he help'd to starve.
   May some choice Patron bless each gray goose quill!
250 May ev'ry *Bavius* have his *Bufo* still!
  So, when a Statesman wants a Day's defence,
  Or Envy holds a whole Week's war with Sense,
  Or simple Pride for Flatt'ry makes demands;
  May Dunce by Dunce be whistled off my hands!
255 Blest be the *Great!* for those they take away,
  And those they left me—For they left me GAY,
  Left me to see neglected Genius bloom,
  Neglected die! and tell it on his Tomb;
  Of all thy blameless Life the sole Return
260 My Verse, and QUEENSB'RY weeping o'er thy Urn!
  Oh let me live my own! and die so too!
  ("To live and die is all I have to do:")
  Maintain a Poet's Dignity and Ease,
  And see what friends, and read what books I please.
265 Above a Patron, tho' I condescend
  Sometimes to call a Minister my Friend:
  I was not born for Courts or great Affairs,
  I pay my Debts, believe, and say my Pray'rs,
  Can sleep without a Poem in my head,
270 Nor know, if *Dennis* be alive or dead.
   Why am I ask'd, what next shall see the light?
  Heav'ns! was I born for nothing but to write?

248 *He help'd . . . starve:* probably a reference to Halifax's abortive plan to raise a monument to Dryden in Westminster Abbey.
 250 *Bavius:* see l. 99.
 254 *whistled off:* cast off, like falcons, by whistling; dismissed.
 256 GAY: John Gay (1685–1732), author of *The Beggar's Opera* (1728) and *Polly* (1729); taken into the patronage of Charles Douglas, Duke of Queensberry (1698–1778), when George II refused a licence to *Polly* (see l. 260); and commemorated by Queensberry in Westminster Abbey. Pope wrote the epitaph for his tomb.
 262 *"To live . . . do":* Sir John Denham, "Of Prudence", l. 94.

Has Life no Joys for me? or (to be grave)
Have I no Friend to serve, no Soul to save?
275 "I found him close with *Swift*"—"Indeed? no doubt"
(Cries prating *Balbus*) "something will come out."
'Tis all in vain, deny it as I will.
"No, such a Genius never can lye still,"
And then for mine obligingly mistakes
280 The first Lampoon Sir *Will.* or *Bubo* makes.
Poor guiltless I! and can I chuse but smile,
When ev'ry Coxcomb knows me by my *Style*?
   Curst be the Verse, how well soe'er it flow,
That tends to make one worthy Man my Foe,
285 Give Virtue scandal, Innocence a fear,
Or from the soft-ey'd Virgin steal a tear!
But he, who hurts a harmless neighbour's peace,
Insults fal'n Worth, or Beauty in distress,
Who loves a Lye, lame slander helps about,
290 Who writes a Libel, or who copies out:
That Fop whose pride affects a Patron's name,
Yet absent, wounds an Author's honest fame;
Who can your Merit selfishly approve,
And show the Sense of it, without the Love;
295 Who has the Vanity to call you Friend,
Yet wants the Honour injur'd to defend;
Who tells whate'er you think, whate'er you say,
And, if he lye not, must at least betray:
Who to the *Dean* and *silver Bell* can swear,
300 And sees at *Cannons* what was never there:

276 *Balbus:* Viscount Dupplin, son of the Earl of Kinnoull; noted for "incessant small talk".

280 *Sir Will:* Sir William Yonge (d. 1755), a poetaster and an instrument of Walpole's. *Bubo:* Bubb Dodington (see l. 230, note).

282 *knows . . . Style:* But cf. Ben Jonson, *Discoveries*, l. 2031: "*Language most shewes a man: speake that I may see thee*".

289-304 *Who loves . . . stead:* an imitation (first published by Pope in a newspaper, 1732) of Horace, *Sat.* I. iv. 81-5.

299-300 *to the Dean . . . never there:* Pope's denial of the charge that his account of Timon's chapel in *Moral Essays*, iv. 99-168, was based on the Duke of Chandos's house at Canons.

Who reads but with a Lust to mis-apply,
Make Satire a Lampoon, and Fiction, Lye.
A Lash like mine no honest man shall dread,
But all such babling blockheads in his stead.
305   Let *Sporus* tremble—"What? that Thing of silk,
Sporus, that mere white Curd of Ass's milk?
Satire or Sense alas! can *Sporus* feel?
Who breaks a Butterfly upon a Wheel?"
Yet let me flap this Bug with gilded wings,
310 This painted Child of Dirt that stinks and stings;
Whose Buzz the Witty and the Fair annoys,
Yet Wit ne'er tastes, and Beauty ne'er enjoys,
So well-bred Spaniels civilly delight
In mumbling of the Game they dare not bite.
315 Eternal Smiles his Emptiness betray,
As shallow streams run dimpling all the way.
Whether in florid Impotence he speaks,
And, as the Prompter breathes, the Puppet squeaks;
Or at the Ear of *Eve*, familiar Toad,
320 Half Froth, half Venom, spits himself abroad,
In Puns, or Politicks, or Tales, or Lyes,
Or Spite, or Smut, or Rymes, or Blasphemies.
His Wit all see-saw between *that* and *this*,
Now high, now low, now Master up, now Miss,
325 And he himself one vile Antithesis.
Amphibious Thing! that acting either Part,
The trifling Head, or the corrupted Heart!

305 *Sporus:* John, Baron Hervey of Ickworth (1696–1743), a supporter of
Walpole; formerly a friend of Pope's; author with Lady Mary Wortley
Montagu of a satiric attack on the poet (see Advertisement). Sporus was
Nero's "eunuch-love" (Suetonius, vi. 28). Pope echoes Thersites on
Patroclus, "thou idle immaterial skein of sleave silk . . ." (*Troilus and
Cressida*, V. i. 34) and Ben Jonson's epigram *On Court-worme*, "In silke . . .
first wrapt, and white as milke".

310 *painted Child:* Hervey used cosmetics.

314 *mumbling:* chewing softly (Hervey had no teeth).

318 *the Prompter:* Walpole.

319 *Eve:* Queen Caroline.

c

Fop at the Toilet, Flatt'rer at the Board,
Now trips a Lady, and now struts a Lord.

330 *Eve*'s Tempter thus the Rabbins have exprest,
A Cherub's face, a Reptile all the rest;
Beauty that shocks you, Parts that none will trust,
Wit than can creep, and Pride that licks the dust.
   Not Fortune's Worshipper, nor Fashion's Fool,

335 Not Lucre's Madman, nor Ambition's Tool,
Not proud, nor servile, be one Poet's praise
That, if he pleas'd, he pleas'd by manly ways;
That Flatt'ry, ev'n to Kings, he held a shame,
And thought a Lye in Verse or Prose the same:

340 That not in Fancy's Maze he wander'd long,
But stoop'd to Truth, and moraliz'd his song:
That not for Fame, but Virtue's better end,
He stood the furious Foe, the timid Friend,
The damning Critic, half-approving Wit,

345 The Coxcomb hit, or fearing to be hit;
Laugh'd at the loss of Friends he never had,
The dull, the proud, the wicked, and the mad;
The distant Threats of Vengeance on his head,
The Blow unfelt, the Tear he never shed;

350 The Tale reviv'd, the Lye so oft o'erthrown;
Th' imputed Trash, and Dulness not his own;
The Morals blacken'd when the Writings scape;
The libel'd Person, and the pictur'd Shape;
Abuse on all he lov'd, or lov'd him, spread,

355 A Friend in Exile, or a Father, dead;
The Whisper that to Greatness still too near,
Perhaps, yet vibrates on his SOVEREIGN's Ear—

330-1 *Eve's Tempter . . . rest:* Some medieval artists represent the Devil
as a serpent with a human head.

341 *stoop'd to Truth:* as a falcon swoops on its prey. A play on a technical
term.

343 *stood:* withstood.

349 *The Blow unfelt:* the thrashing which Pope was falsely said (probably by Lady Mary) to have been given.

355 *A Friend:* i.e. Atterbury; cf. l. 140, note.

Welcome for thee, fair Virtue! all the past:
For thee, fair Virtue! welcome ev'n the *last!*

360   "But why insult the Poor, affront the Great?"
A Knave 's a Knave, to me, in ev'ry State,
Alike my scorn, if he succeed or fail,
Sporus at Court, or *Japhet* in a Jayl,
A hireling Scribler, or a hireling Peer,

365   Knight of the Post corrupt, or of the Shire,
If on a Pillory, or near a Throne,
He gain his Prince's Ear, or lose his own.
    Yet soft by Nature, more a Dupe than Wit,
Sapho can tell you how this Man was bit:

370   This dreaded Sat'rist *Dennis* will confess
Foe to his Pride, but Friend to his Distress:
So humble, he has knock'd at *Tibbald*'s door,
Has drunk with *Cibber*, nay has rym'd for *Moor.*
Full ten years slander'd, did he once reply?

375   Three thousand Suns went down on *Welsted*'s Lye:
To please a *Mistress*, One aspers'd his life;
He lash'd him not, but let her be his *Wife:*
Let *Budgel* charge low *Grubstreet* on his quill,
And write whate'er he pleas'd, except his *Will;*

380   Let the *Two Curls* of Town and Court, abuse
His Father, Mother, Body, Soul, and Muse.

363 *Japhet:* the convicted forger Japhet Crook (1662–1734), sentenced to lose his ears.   **365** *Knight of the Post:* one hired to give false evidence.

369-73 *Sapho . . . Moor:* See notes on ll. 101; 153 ; 164, 97, 23.

375 *Welsted's Lye:* see l. 49, note. "This Man had the Impudence to tell in print, that Mr. P. had occasion'd a *Lady's death*" (Pope).

376-7 *To please . . . Wife:* William Windham may have been the collaborator of Lady Mary and Hervey in libelling Pope. His mistress Mary Howard, Countess of Deloraine, whom he later married (1744), was perhaps the angry Delia of Pope's epistle *To Fortescue* (1733), l. 81.

378-9 *Let Budgel . . . Will:* Eustace Budgell (1686–1737), a cousin of Addison's, was accused by *The Grubstreet Journal* of forging a will. In the "imagination" that Pope was responsible for the charge, "*Budgel* in a Weekly Pamphlet call'd the *Bee*, bestow'd much abuse on him" (Pope).

380 *Two Curls:* Edmund Curll (see l. 53, note) and Hervey (see l. 305, note).

Yet why? that Father held it for a rule
It was a Sin to call our Neighbour Fool,
That harmless Mother thought no Wife a Whore,—
385 Hear this! and spare his family, *James More!*
Unspotted Names! and memorable long,
If there be Force in Virtue, or in Song.
    Of gentle Blood (part shed in Honour's Cause,
While yet in *Britain* Honour had Applause)
390 Each Parent sprung— "What Fortune, pray?"—Their own,
And better got than *Bestia*'s from the Throne.
Born to no Pride, inheriting no Strife,
Nor marrying Discord in a Noble Wife,
Stranger to Civil and Religious Rage,
395 The good Man walk'd innoxious thro' his Age.
No Courts he saw, no Suits would ever try,
Nor dar'd an Oath, nor hazarded a Lye:
Un-learn'd, he knew no Schoolman's subtle Art,
No Language, but the Language of the Heart.
400 By Nature honest, by Experience wise,
Healthy by Temp'rance and by Exercise:
His Life, tho' long, to sickness past unknown,
His Death was instant, and without a groan.
Oh grant me thus to live, and thus to die!
405 Who sprung from Kings shall know less joy than I.
    O Friend! may each Domestick Bliss be thine!
Be no unpleasing Melancholy mine:
Me, let the tender Office long engage
To rock the Cradle of reposing Age,

385 *More:* See l. 23, note. "In some of *Curl*'s . . . Pamphlets, Mr. Pope's Father was said to be a Mechanic, a Hatter, a Farmer, nay a Bankrupt. . . . [He] was of a Gentleman's Family in *Oxfordshire*, the Head of which was the Earle of *Downe*" (Pope); an unjustified claim.

388 *Honour's Cause:* the cause of Charles I, in which one of Pope's maternal forbears was killed.

391 *Bestia:* probably the Duke of Marlborough. Calpurnius Bestia was a Roman consul who was bribed into making peace without honour.

397 *an Oath:* perhaps the oaths without which suspected papists could not ccept public employ.

410 With lenient Arts extend a Mother's breath,
     Make Languor smile, and smooth the Bed of Death,
     Explore the Thought, explain the asking Eye,
     And keep a while one Parent from the Sky!
     On Cares like these if Length of days attend,
415 May Heav'n, to bless those days, preserve my Friend,
     Preserve him social, chearful, and serene,
     And just as rich as when he serv'd a QUEEN!
     Whether that Blessing be deny'd, or giv'n,
     Thus far was right, the rest belongs to Heav'n.

417 *when he serv'd a* QUEEN: as physician to Queen Anne.

Soame Jenyns

THE MODERN FINE GENTLEMAN

USUALLY remembered only because of Johnson's brilliant review of his *Free Enquiry into the Nature and Origin of Evil* (1757), Soame Jenyns (1704-87) deserves a better fate. Boswell remarked that he "was possessed of lively talents, and a style eminently pure and easy, and could very happily play with a light subject, either in prose or verse" (*Life of Johnson*, ed. Hill and Powell, Oxford, 1934, i. 315). He published several satires, imitations of Horace, and numerous poems on miscellaneous subjects. The piece printed below is a lively example of a satiric "character" of a social type, compounded from Jenyns' experience of the climber, the fop, the would-be politician(Jenyns had been elected an M.P. in 1742), and the parasite, as well as from detailed observation of his social environment. *The Modern Fine Gentleman* (1746) forms part of the tradition which includes the portrait of the courtier in Donne's fourth *Satire* and Pope's "Sir Balaam" in the *Epistle to Bathurst*; in some respects we are reminded of Tom Rakewell in Hogarth's *Rake's Progress* and of the man of fashion *par excellence*, Sir Fopling Flutter, in Etherege's *Man of Mode*; but Jenyns' critical alertness to the concrete particulars of the life of his contemporaries is distinctively Augustan. The text is that of the first edition.

Just broke from School, pert, impudent, and raw,
Expert in Latin, more expert in Taw,
His Honour posts o're ITALY and FRANCE,
Measures ST. PETER's Dome, and learns to dance.
5 Thence having quick thro' various Countries flown,
Glean'd all their Follies, and expos'd his own,
He back returns, a Thing so strange all o'er,
As never Ages past produc'd before:
A Monster of such complicated Worth,
10 As no one single Clime could e're bring forth:
Half Atheist, Papist, Gamester, Bubble, Rook,
Half Fiddler, Coachman, Dancer, Groom, and Cook.
      Next, because Bus'ness now is all the Vogue,
And who'd be quite polite must be a Rogue,
15 In Parliament he purchases a Seat,
To make th' accomplish'd Gentleman compleat.
There safe in self-sufficient Impudence,
Without Experience, Honesty, or Sense,
Unknowing in her Int'rest, Trade, or Laws,
20 He vainly undertakes his Country's Cause:
Forth from his Lips, prepar'd at all to rail,
Torrents of Nonsense burst; like bottled Ale,
Tho' shallow, muddy, brisk, tho' mighty dull,
Fierce without Strength, o'erflowing, tho' not full.
25   Now quite a Frenchman in his Garb, and Air,
His Neck yok'd down with Bag and Solitaire.

2 *Taw:* a game played with marbles of variegated colours.

11 *Bubble:* a dupe or gull.   *Rook:* a swindler or card-sharper.

22-4 *like bottled . . . full:* Cf. Denham, *Cooper's Hill* (1642), ll. 191-2:

> Tho' deep, yet clear, tho' gentle yet not dull,
> Strong without rage, without overflowing full.

Jenyns may also have had in mind Pope's lines on Leonard Welsted, in *The Dunciad* (1728-43), iii. 169-72:

> Flow, Welsted, flow! like thine inspirer, Beer,
> Tho' stale, not ripe; tho' thin, yet never clear;
> So sweetly mawkish, and so smoothly dull;
> Heady, not strong; o'erflowing, tho' not full.

26 *Bag and Solitaire:* a bag-wig and a necktie of the kind worn by eighteenth-century gentlemen in imitation of a French fashion.

The Liberties of BRITAIN he supports,
And storms at Place-men, Ministers, and Courts;
Now in cropt greasy Hair, and leather Breeches,
30 He loudly bellows out his Patriot Speeches:
King, Lords, and Commons ventures to abuse,
Yet dares to shew those Ears, he ought to lose.
From hence to WHITE's our virtuous CATO flies,
There sits with Countenance erect, and wise,
35 And talks of Games at Whist, and pig-tail Pies.
Plays all the Night, nor doubts each Law to break,
Himself unknowingly has help'd to make,
Trembling, and anxious stakes his utmost Groat,
Peeps o'er his Cards, and looks as if he thought,
40 Next Morn disowns the Losses of the Night,
Because the Fool would fain be thought a Bite.
Devoted thus to Politicks, and Cards,
Nor Mirth, nor Wine, nor Women he regards,
So far is ev'ry Virtue from his Heart,
45 That not a gen'rous Vice can claim a Part;
Nay, lest one human Passion e're should move,
His Soul to Friendship, Tenderness, or Love,
To FIGG, and BRAUGHTON he commits his Breast,

---

28 *Place-men:* a pejorative term applied to men holding offices of profit under the Crown from motives of mere self-interest.

30 *Patriot:* defined in Johnson's *Dictionary* as "a factious disturber of the government".

32 *Yet dares . . . lose:* To lose one's ears as a punishment was prohibited by the Bill of Rights, 1689. Jenyns' allusion to the practice may have been prompted by the recent "War of Jenkin's Ear", 1739.

33 *White's:* the famous club and gaming house. *Cato:* the wise Roman consul and lawgiver (234–149 B.C.). But Jenyns may be alluding to Pope's "Atticus" portrait in the *Epistle to Dr. Arbuthnot* (1735), l. 209.

35 *pig-tail:* possibly a corruption of "pintail"—a species of duck or grouse.
41 *Bite:* a swindler.

48 *Figg:* James Figg (d. 1734) gave the young nobility instruction in boxing and swordsmanship at his "Academy" in Marylebone (cf. Pope, *The Fourth Satire of Dr. John Donne* (1735), l. 213). *Braughton*: John Broughton (1705–89), another noted pugilist and instructor.

To steel it to the fashionable Test.
50   Thus poor in Wealth he labours to no End,
      Wretched alone, in Crowds without a Friend;
      Insensible to all that's Good, or Kind,
      Deaf to all Merit, to all Beauty blind;
      For Love too busy, and for Wit too grave,
55   A harden'd, sober, proud, luxurious Knave,
      By little Actions striving to be Great,
      And proud to be, and to be thought a Cheat.
         And yet in this so bad is his Success,
      That as his Fame improves, his Rents grow less;
60   On Parchment Wings his Acres take their Flight,
      And his unpeopled Groves admit the Light;
      With his Estate his Int'rest too is done,
      His honest Borough seeks a warmer Sun,
      For him, now Cash, and Liquor flows no more,
65   His independent Voters cease to roar:
      And BRITAIN soon must want the great Defence
      Of all his Honesty, and Eloquence,
      But that the gen'rous Youth more anxious grown
      For publick Liberty, than for his own,
70   Marries some jointur'd antiquated Crone:
      And boldly, when his Country is at Stake,
      Braves the deep yawning Gulph, like CURTIUS, for its Sake.
         Quickly again distress'd for want of Coin,
      He digs no longer in th' exhausted Mine,

55 *luxurious:* self-indulgent, voluptuous.

60–61 *On Parchment . . . Light:* i.e. he has to mortgage his estate and sell his timber to raise money.

65 *His independent . . . roar:* i.e. the electors (in the "rotten borough") whose votes have been obtained through bribery no longer support him.

66 *want:* i.e. lack.

70 *Marries some . . . Crone:* i.e. he marries an aged, ugly widow whose wealth is independent of her deceased husband's estate. Cf. Hogarth, *Rake's Progress*, Plate no. V.

71–2 *And boldly . . . Sake:* Curtius was the brave young Roman knight who, to save his country, leaped into the chasm which suddenly opened in the Forum.

75 But seeks Preferement, as the last Resort,
    Cringes each Morn at Levee's, bows at Court,
    And, from the Hand he hates, implores Support:
    The Minister, well pleas'd at small Expence
    To silence so much rude Impertinence,
80 With Squeeze, and Whisper yields to his Demands,
    And on the venal List enroll'd he stands,
    A Ribband, and a Pension buy the Slave,
    This bribes the Fool about him, that the Knave.
        And now arriv'd at his meridian Glory,
85 He sinks apace, despis'd by Whig, and Tory;
    Of Independence now he talks no more,
    Nor shakes the Senate with his Patriot Roar,
    But silent votes, and with Court Trappings hung,
    Eyes his own glitt'ring Star, and holds his Tongue.
90 In Craft political a Bankrupt made,
    He sticks to Gaming, as the surer Trade;
    Turns downright Sharper, lives by sucking Blood,
    And grows in short the very Thing, he wou'd:
    Hunts out young Heirs, who have their Fortunes spent,
95 And lends them ready Cash at Cent per Cent,
    Lays Wagers on his own, and others Lives,
    Fights Uncles, Fathers, Grandmothers, and Wives,
    Till Death at length, indignant to be made
    The daily Subject of his Sport, and Trade,
100 Veils with his sable Hand the Wretch's Eyes,
    And groaning for the Betts, he loses by't, he dies.

FINIS

81 *venal List:* i.e. the list of paid supporters of the Government. Cf. Pope, *Epistle to Bathurst* (1733), l. 394: "And one more Pensioner St. Stephen gains."

89 *Star:* an ambiguous reference to his lofty ambitions and to the emblem of an order of chivalry.

Samuel Johnson

THE VANITY OF HUMAN WISHES.
THE TENTH SATIRE OF JUVENAL,
IMITATED

THIS poem was written—or at any rate completed—in 1748, "the first seventy lines" (says Johnson) "in the course of one morning" and "the whole number . . . composed before I committed a single couplet to writing". It was published by Dodsley in 1749, and reprinted with revisions in Dodsley's miscellany *Collection of Poems . . . by Several Hands* (1755; eighth edition, 1782). *The Vanity of Human Wishes* is a much freer imitation of Juvenal than Johnson's *London*, published in 1738—significantly with Juvenal's third Satire printed beneath the text; it is almost wholly independent of earlier versions of Juvenal, even of Dryden's, which is perhaps the high-water mark of Augustan translation. It is the most mature illustration of the eighteenth century ideal of imitation (see Introduction, pp. [14–15]), following closely enough the general theme—and sometimes the text—of its model, but providing modern examples of that theme, occasionally a highly personal interpretation of it, and a fully Christian conclusion. Juvenal writes like a public orator; vehemently, vividly, with a wealth of declamatory devices. Johnson's rhetoric is rather that of the Church: the slow, deliberate tempo; the parallelism and antithesis, and the massive structure of his paragraphs; the philosophical and verbal generalities; the thoughtful gravity.

The text is from Dodsley's *Collection* (1755), incorporating some holograph corrections recorded by Boswell. Two couplets were omitted in the 1755 edition; one of them, following l. 102, perhaps dropped accidentally:

> Turn'd by his nod the stream of honour flows,
> His smile alone security bestows.

Parts of the Latin text, and a translation, are provided; but the exercise of close comparison is left to the reader.

D. Iuni Iuvenalis Satura X

Omnibus in terris, quae sunt a Gadibus usque
Auroram et Gangen, pauci dinoscere possunt
vera bona atque illis multum diversa, remota
erroris nebula. quid enim ratione timemus
5   aut cupimus? quid tam dextro pede concipis ut te
conatus non paeniteat votique peracti?
evertere domos totas optantibus ipsis
di faciles. nocitura toga, nocitura petuntur
militia; torrens dicendi copia multis
10 et sua mortifera est facundia; viribus ille
confisus periit admirandisque lacertis;
sed plures nimia congesta pecunia cura
strangulat et cuncta exuperans patrimonia census,
quanto delphinis ballaena Britannica maior.

In all the lands that extend from Gades to the East and the Ganges, few men
(when the mist of ignorance has been removed) can distinguish between true
benefits and things quite different from them. For what do we rationally
fear or desire? (5) What do you undertake with such a confident step forward, that you do not repent of the attempt and of your wish when it is
accomplished? The indulgent gods have overthrown whole families by
granting their wishes. (8) Men seek harmful things, in peace and in war. A
rapid flow of speech, and their own eloquence, bring death to many men; he
who relied on his strength and his marvellous muscles perished. (12) But
money piled up with too much care strangles more, and so does property
that exceeds all patrimonies by as much as a British whale is bigger than
dolphins.

Let observation with extensive view,
Survey mankind, from China to Peru;
Remark each anxious toil, each eager strife,
And watch the busy scenes of crouded life;
5   Then say how hope and fear, desire and hate,
O'erspread with snares the clouded maze of fate,
Where wav'ring man, betray'd by vent'rous pride,
To tread the dreary paths without a guide,
As treach'rous phantoms in the mist delude,
10 Shuns fancied ills, or chases airy good;
How rarely reason guides the stubborn choice,
Rules the bold hand, or prompts the suppliant voice,
How nations sink, by darling schemes oppress'd,
When vengeance listens to the fool's request.
15 Fate wings with ev'ry wish th' afflictive dart,
Each gift of nature, and each grace of art,
With fatal heat impetuous courage glows,
With fatal sweetness elocution flows,
Impeachment stops the speaker's pow'rful breath,
20 And restless fire precipitates on death.

    But scarce observ'd, the knowing and the bold,
Fall in the gen'ral massacre of gold;
Wide-wasting pest! that rages unconfin'd,
And crouds with crimes the records of mankind;
25 For gold his sword the hireling ruffian draws,
For gold the hireling judge distorts the laws;
Wealth heap'd on wealth, nor truth nor safety buys,
The dangers gather as the treasures rise.

2 Cf. Sir William Temple, *Of Poetry*, 1690: "all Nations from *China* to *Peru*".

15-16 Every wish, natural gift, and cultivated grace serves to feather Fate's "afflictive dart".

20 *precipitates on:* i.e. drives the man of courage headlong to.

22 *of:* caused, wrought by.

15   temporibus diris igitur iussuque Neronis
     Longinum et magnos Senecae praedivitis hortos
     clausit et egregias Lateranorum obsidet aedes
     tota cohors; rarus venit in cenacula miles.
     pauca licet portes argenti vascula puri
20   nocte iter ingressus, gladium contumque timebis
     et mota ad lunam trepidabis harundinis umbra:
     cantabit vacuus coram latrone viator.
     prima fere vota et cunctis notissima templis
     divitiae, crescant ut opes, ut maxima toto
25   nostra sit arca foro. sed nulla aconita bibuntur
     fictilibus: tunc illa time, cum pocula sumes
     gemmata et lato Setinum ardebit in auro.
     iamne igitur laudas quod de sapientibus alter
     ridebat, quotiens de limine moverat unum
30   protuleratque pedem, flebat contrarius auctor?
     sed facilis cuivis rigidi censura cachinni:
     mirandum est unde ille oculis suffecerit umor.
     perpetuo risu pulmonem agitare solebat
     Democritus, /

In cruel times, therefore, and at Nero's command, a whole cohort surrounded Longinus and the great gardens of the excessively rich Seneca, and besieges the splendid homes of the Lateran family; a soldier rarely comes to a garret. (19) Although you carry a few little vessels of pure silver, as you travel at night, you'll be afraid of the sword and the spear, and shake at the shadow of a reed stirred in the moonlight. The empty-handed traveller will sing to a robber's face. (23) Usually our first prayers, and those commonest in all the temples, are that wealth—riches—may increase; that the greatest coffer in the whole forum may be ours. (25) But no poisons are drunk from earthen vessels; so fear poisons when you lift jewelled cups and the Setine wine sparkles in the wide golden bowl. (28) Don't you approve, therefore, of the fact that one of the philosophers laughed whenever he moved and thrust one foot over the threshold, and the other wept? (31) But the criticism of a rude laugh comes easily to anyone: what is astonishing is where that moisture came from for his eyes. (33) Democritus used to keep his lungs moving in perpetual laughter,

Let hist'ry tell where rival kings command,
30   And dubious title shakes the madded land,
When statutes glean the refuse of the sword,
How much more safe the vassal, than the lord;
Low sculks the hind beneath the rage of pow'r,
And leaves the wealthy traytor in the Tow'r,
35   Untouch'd his cottage, and his slumbers sound,
Tho' confiscation's vulturs hover round.

The needy traveller, serene and gay,
Walks the wild heath, and sings his toil away.
Does envy seize thee? crush th' upbraiding joy,
40   Increase his riches and his peace destroy;
Now fears in dire vicissitude invade,
The rustling brake alarms, and quiv'ring shade,
Nor light nor darkness brings his pain relief,
One shews the plunder, and one hides the thief.

45   Yet still one gen'ral cry the skies assails,
And gain and grandeur load the tainted gales;
Few know the toiling statesman's fear or care,
Th' insidious rival and the gaping heir.

Once more, Democritus, arise on earth,
50   With chearful wisdom and instructive mirth,
See motly life in modern trappings dress'd,
And feed with varied fools th' eternal jest:
Thou who couldst laugh where want enchain'd caprice,
Toil crush'd conceit, and man was of a piece;
55   Where wealth unlov'd without a mourner dy'd;
And scarce a sycophant was fed by pride;

30 *dubious:* in dispute. *madded:* enraged, violent.

33 *hind:* peasant.

47 *care:* anxiety.

49 *Democritus:* the ancient philosopher (d. 361 B.C.) who laughed continually at human folly (Juvenal, ll. 28-9).

51-2 *See . . . jest:* The metaphor is that of the court jester, in motley. So *varied:* (a) of different kinds; (b) variously coloured.

54 *conceit:* imagination.

/ quamquam non essent urbibus illis
35   praetextae trabeae fasces lectica tribunal.
quid si vidisset praetorem curribus altis
extantem et medii sublimem pulvere circi
in tunica Iovis et pictae Sarrana ferentem
ex umeris aulaea togae magnaeque coronae
40   tantum orbem, quanto cervix non sufficit ulla? . . .

ergo supervacua aut prope perniciosa petuntur,
55   propter quae fas est genua incerare deorum.
quosdam praecipitat subiecta potentia magnae
invidiae, mergit longa atque insignis honorum
pagina. descendunt statuae restemque sequuntur,
ipsas deinde rotas bigarum inpacta securis
60   caedit et inmeritis franguntur crura caballis.
iam strident ignes, iam follibus atque caminis
ardet adoratum populo caput et crepat ingens
Seianus, deinde ex facie toto orbe secunda
fiunt urceoli pelves sartago matellae.

although in these towns there were no togas, robes of state, fasces, no litter
or tribunal. What if he had seen the praetor, conspicuous in his lofty chariot,
high in the midst of the dusty circus, in Jove's tunic, wearing on his
shoulders the Tyrian tapestry of his embroidered gown, and such a ring of a
huge crown that one neck cannot support it? . . .

(54) So men seek those superfluous or pernicious things, for which they
must load the knees of the gods with wax tablets. Power, exposed to great
envy, drives some; a long and distinguished page of honours overwhelms
them. (58) The statues come down and follow the rope; the driven axe cuts
the very wheels of the double chariots, and the horses' legs are broken
undeservedly. (61) Already the fires roar, and the head once revered by the
people burns under the bellows and the furnace, and great Sejanus crackles;
then from the face, second only in the whole world, are made water-pots,
basins, frying-pans, and chamber-pots.

Where ne'er was known the form of mock debate,
Or seen a new-made mayor's unwieldy state;
Where change of fav'rites made no change of laws,
60   And senates heard before they judg'd a cause;
How wouldst thou shake at Britain's modish tribe,
Dart the quick taunt, and edge the piercing gibe?
Attentive truth and nature to descry,
And pierce each scene with philosophic eye.
65   To thee were solemn toys or empty shew,
The robes of pleasure and the veils of woe:
All aid the farce, and all thy mirth maintain,
Whose joys are causeless, or whose griefs are vain.

    Such was the scorn that fill'd the sage's mind,
70   Renew'd at ev'ry glance on humankind;
How just that scorn ere yet thy voice declare,
Search every state, and canvass ev'ry pray'r.

    Unnumber'd suppliants croud Preferment's gate,
Athirst for wealth, and burning to be great;
75   Delusive Fortune hears th' incessant call,
They mount, they shine, evaporate, and fall.
On ev'ry stage the foes of peace attend,
Hate dogs their flight, and insult mocks their end.
Love ends with hope, the sinking statesman's door
80   Pours in the morning worshiper no more;
For growing names the weekly scribbler lies,
To growing wealth the dedicator flies,
From every room descends the painted face,
That hung the bright Palladium of the place,
85   And smoak'd in kitchens, or in auctions sold,
To better features yields the frame of gold;

61 *modish:* in the present fashion (of behaviour as well as of dress and taste).

76 *They mount . . . and fall:* The metaphor is that of the meteor, or falling star, traditionally supposed to rise "from earthy Vapours, ere they shine in Skies" (Dryden).

81 *growing:* i.e. in reputation, power. *lies:* i.e. in the political journals.

84 *Palladium:* properly the image of the goddess Pallas, the defence of the citadel of Troy, saved from the burning of the city and brought to Rome.

65 pone domi laurus, duc in Capitolia magnum
    cretatumque bovem: Seianus ducitur unco
    spectandus, gaudent omnes. "quae labra, quis illi
    vultus erat. numquam, si quid mihi credis, amavi
    hunc hominem." "sed quo cecidit sub crimine? quisnam
70 delator quibus indicibus, quo teste probavit?"
    "nil horum; verbosa et grandis epistula venit
    a Capreis." "bene habet, nil plus interrogo." sed quid
    turba Remi? sequitur fortunam, ut semper, et odit
    damnatos. idem populus, si Nortia Tusco
75 favisset, si oppressa foret secura senectus
    principis, hac ipsa Seianum diceret hora
    Augustum. . . ."

87 "sed videant servi, ne quis neget et pavidum in ius
    cervice obstricta dominum trahat." hi sermones
    tunc de Seiano, secreta haec murmura vulgi.

Set laurels on your house, and lead a great ox whitened with chalk to the
capitol: Sejanus is dragged on a hook to be stared at; everyone rejoices.
"What lips, what a face he had! If you believe me at all, I never loved this
man." (69) "But what charge has he fallen under? Who was the informer,
and on what evidence, and with what witness has he proved it?" "It was
none of these; a long, wordy letter came from Capri." "That's good; I ask
no more." (72) But what of Remus's rabble? They follow fortune, as always,
and hate the condemned. If Nortia had favoured the Tuscan—if the secure
old age of the prince had been stamped out—the same people would at this
same hour have proclaimed Sejanus Augustus. . . ." (87) "But let our slaves
see us, lest any one deny it and drag his trembling master to law by his
fettered neck." These things were what they said about Sejanus, these the
secret mutterings of the mob.

For now no more we trace in ev'ry line
Heroic worth, benevolence divine:
The form distorted justifies the fall,
90   And detestation rids th' indignant wall.

But will not Britain hear the last appeal,
Sign her foes doom, or guard her fav'rites zeal;
Through Freedom's sons no more remonstrance rings,
Degrading nobles and controuling kings;
95   Our supple tribes repress their patriot throats,
And ask no questions but the price of votes;
With weekly libels and septennial ale,
Their wish is full to riot and to rail.
In full-blown dignity, see Wolsey stand,

100   Law in his voice, and fortune in his hand:
To him the church, the realm, their pow'rs consign,
Thro' him the rays of regal bounty shine,
Still to new heights his restless wishes tow'r,
Claim leads to claim, and pow'r advances pow'r;
105   Till conquest unresisted ceas'd to please,
And rights submitted, left him none to seize.
At length his sov'reign frowns—the train of state
Mark the keen glance, and watch the sign to hate.
Where-e'er he turns he meets a stranger's eye,
110   His suppliants scorn him, and his followers fly;
At once is lost the pride of aweful state,
The golden canopy, the glitt'ring plate,
The regal palace, the luxurious board,
The liv'ried army, and the menial lord.
115   With age, with cares, with maladies oppress'd,
He seeks the refuge of monastic rest.
Grief aids disease, remember'd folly stings,
And his last sighs reproach the faith of kings.

90 *rids th'* . . . *wall:* relieves the wall of the degrading portrait.

93 *remonstrance:* particularly the Grand Remonstrance to Charles I in 1641.

97 *septennial:* Parliaments were seven-yearly between 1716 and 1910.

99 *Wolsey:* Johnson has retained (ll. 83-90) some of the details in Juvenal's account of Sejanus; but his own exemplar of fallen power is Thomas Wolsey (1471–1530) who, in less than ten years, rose from a chaplaincy to become cardinal and Lord Chancellor, and died under indictment for high treason. Johnson's main model: the Shakespearian *Henry VIII.*

90 visne salutari sicut Seianus, habere
    tantundem, atque illi summas donare curules,
    illum exercitibus praeponere, tutor haberi
    principis angusta Caprearum in rupe sedentis
    cum grege Chaldaeo? vis certe pila cohortes
95 egregios equites et castra domestica, quidni
    haec cupias? . . .
    ergo quid optandum foret ignorasse fateris
    Seianum; nam qui nimios optabat honores
105 et nimias poscebat opes, numerosa parabat
    excelsae turris tabulata, unde altior esset
    casus et inpulsae praeceps inmane ruinae.
    quid Crassos, quid Pompeios evertit et illum,
    ad sua qui domitos deduxit flagra Quirites?
110 summus nempe locus nulla non arte petitus
    magnaque numinibus vota exaudita malignis.
    ad generum Cereris sine caede ac vulnere pauci
    descendunt reges et sicca morte tyranni.
        eloquium aut famam Demosthenis aut Ciceronis
115 incipit optare et totis quinquatribus optat
    quisquis adhuc uno parcam colit asse Minervam,
    quem sequitur custos angustae vernula capsae.

Do you want to be hailed as Sejanus was; to have as much wealth, and
bestow public bounty on one man; to set another in command of armies; to
be taken for the tutor of a prince, sitting on the narrow rock of Capri with a
flock of soothsayers? (94) Surely you wish to have javelins, cohorts, splendid
cavalry, a private camp; why wouldn't you want these things? (103) So
you say Sejanus did not know what ought to be wished for; he who wanted
too many honours, and asked for too much wealth, built the many floors of
a high tower; that his fall might be the higher, and the precipice of his
destruction the more frightful. What overturned the Crassi, the Pompeys
and him who tamed the subdued Romans to his whip? (110) A high position,
to be sure, sought with every art, and long prayers heard by malignant gods.
To Ceres's son-in-law few kings and tyrants go down without slaughter,
and wounds, and death without blood.

   (114) Whoever cultivates thrifty Minerva (eloquence) begins to wish for
the speech and renown of Demosthenes or Cicero, and prays for it throughout her five-day festival; the little slave follows him, guardian of his narrow
book-box.

Speak thou, whose thoughts at humble peace repine,
120 Shall Wolsey's wealth, with Wolsey's end be thine?
Or liv'st thou now, with safer pride content,
The wisest justice on the banks of Trent?
For why did Wolsey near the steeps of fate,
On weak foundations raise th' enormous weight?
125 Why but to sink beneath misfortune's blow,
With louder ruin to the gulphs below?

What gave great Villiers to th' assassin's knife,
And fix'd disease on Harley's closing life?
What murder'd Wentworth, and what exil'd Hyde,
130 By kings protected, and to kings ally'd?
What but their wish indulg'd in courts to shine,
And pow'r too great to keep, or to resign?

When first the college rolls receive his name,
The young enthusiast quits his ease for fame;
135 Through all his veins the fever of renown
Burns from the strong contagion of the gown;
O'er Bodley's dome his future labours spread,
And *Bacon's mansion trembles o'er his head.

127-30 *What gave . . . ally'd.* The modern Crassi and Pompeys are George
Villiers (1592–1628), Duke of Buckingham and favourite of Charles I,
assassinated by a discontented officer; Robert Harley (1661–1724), Queen
Anne's chief minister, imprisoned in the Tower for two years after his fall
from office in 1714; Thomas Wentworth (1593–1641), Earl of Strafford,
Charles I's close adviser at the end of his reign, executed on 12 May
1641; and Edward Hyde (1608–74), Earl of Clarendon, loyal servant to
Charles I, Charles II's Lord Chancellor, banished to France in 1667, and "to
kings ally'd" through his daughter's marriage to the future James II.

133-62 These lines have strong personal undertones. Reading the poem
aloud to friends, Johnson at this point "burst into a passion of tears" (Mrs.
Piozzi).

137 *Bodley's dome:* the Bodleian Library, Oxford, through which his
writings will spread.

138 *Bacon's mansion:* the gatehouse formerly on Folly Bridge, Oxford,
said to have been the house of the thirteenth-century philosopher Roger
Bacon. * *There is a tradition, that the study of friar Bacon, built on an arch
over the bridge, will fall when a man greater than Bacon shall pass under it.*

eloquio sed uterque perit orator, utrumque
largus et exundans leto dedit ingenii fons.
120   ingenio manus est et cervix caesa, necum quam
sanguine causidici maduerunt rostra pusilli.
"o fortunatam natam me consule Romam!"
Antoni gladios potuit contemnere, si sic
omnia dixisset. ridenda poemata malo
125   quam te, conspicuae divina Philippica famae,
volveris a prima quae proxima. /

But each orator perished by his eloquence; a full and abundant fountain of
genius gave both of them to death. On account of genius a hand and neck
are cut off; the rostrums have never been sprinkled with the blood of an
insignificant advocate. (122) "O fortunate Rome, redeemed by me, the
consul!" He could have despised Antony's swords, if all his speech had been
like that. I'd rather write poems to be laughed at, than write you, celebrated
and divine philippic, who are read second.

Are these thy views? proceed, illustrious youth,
140 And virtue guard thee to the throne of Truth!
Yet should thy soul indulge the gen'rous heat,
Till captive Science yields her last retreat;
Should Reason guide thee with her brightest ray,
And pour on misty Doubt resistless day;
145 Should no false Kindness lure to loose delight,
Nor Praise relax, nor Difficulty fright;
Should tempting Novelty thy cell refrain,
And Sloth effuse her opiate fumes in vain;
Should Beauty blunt on fops her fatal dart,
150 Nor claim the triumph of a letter'd heart;
Should no Disease thy torpid veins invade,
Nor Melancholy's phantoms haunt thy shade;
Yet hope not life from grief or danger free,
Nor think the doom of man revers'd for thee:
155 Deign on the passing world to turn thine eyes,
And pause awhile from letters, to be wise;
There mark what ills the scholar's life assail,
Toil, envy, want, the patron, and the jail.
See nations slowly wise, and meanly just,
160 To buried merit raise the tardy bust.
If dreams yet flatter, once again attend,
Hear Lydiat's life, and Galileo's end.

141 *gen'rous:* invigorating, fertilising.

142 *Science:* learning.

147 *refrain:* stay away from.

150 *triumph:* conquest (with suggestions of the Roman celebrations of victory).

158 *patron:* "commonly a wretch who supports with insolence, and is paid with flattery" (Johnson, *Dictionary*). The word replaced "Garret" in the 1755 edition, published just after Johnson wrote his celebrated letter on patronage to Chesterfield.

160 *the tardy bust:* the monuments erected in Westminster Abbey in the eighteenth-century to Shakespeare, Milton, and other seventeenth century poets.

162 *Lydiat:* a celebrated Oxford mathematician who died in poverty in 1646. *Galileo:* Copernican astronomer (1564–1642), imprisoned by the Inquisition and compelled to abjure his scientific beliefs.

/ saevus et illum
exitus eripuit, quem mirabantur Athenae
torrentem et pleni moderantem frena theatri.
dis ille adversis genitus fatoque sinistro,
130   quem pater ardentis massae fuligine lippus
a carbone et forcipibus gladiosque paranti
incude et luteo Vulcano ad rhetora misit.
    bellorum exuviae, truncis adfixa tropaeis
lorica et fracta de casside buccula pendens
135   et curtum temone iugum victaeque triremis
aplustre et summo tristis captivos in arcu
humanis maiora bonis creduntur. ad hoc se
Romanus Graiusque et barbarus induperator
erexit, causas discriminis atque laboris
140   inde habuit; tanto maior famae sitis est quam
virtutis. quis enim virtutem amplectitur ipsam,
praemia si tollas? patriam tamen obruit olim
gloria paucorum et laudis titulique cupido
haesuri saxis cinerum custodibus, ad quae
145   discutienda valent sterilis mala robora fici,
quandoquidem data sunt ipsis quoque fata sepulcris.

A cruel death also snatched away the man whom Athens admired—
eloquent, able to control the packed theatre; born with the gods and an
adverse fate against him; sent by his half-blind father from the smoke of the
burning mass, from the coal and tongs and the anvil making swords, to a
rhetorician.

(133) The spoils of war, the coat of mail fixed to tree-trunks as trophy, the
visor hanging from a splintered helmet, the chariot shorn of its beam, the
stern of a defeated galley, the sad captives on the high arch, are thought to
be greater than human blessings. For this the Roman, the Greek, the
barbarian commander exerted himself; from this he has learnt the causes of
danger and effort; the thirst for fame is so much stronger than that for
virtue. (141) For who embraces virtue herself, if you take away the rewards?
Yet once the glory of a few destroyed their fatherland—longing for praise,
and for an inscription to be set on their monuments as guardians of their
ashes; though the evil roots of a barren fig-tree can destroy them, for
calamity comes to sepulchres themselves.

Nor deem, when learning her last prize bestows,
The glitt'ring eminence exempt from foes;
165 See when the vulgar 'scape, despis'd or aw'd,
Rebellion's vengeful talons seize on Laud.
From meaner minds, tho' smaller fines content,
The plunder'd palace or sequester'd rent;
Mark'd out by dangerous parts he meets the shock,
170 And fatal Learning leads him to the block:
Around his tomb let Art and Genius weep,
But hear his death, ye blockheads, hear and sleep.

The festal blazes, the triumphal show,
The ravish'd standard, and the captive foe,
175 The senate's thanks, the gazette's pompous tale,
With force resistless o'er the brave prevail.
Such bribes the rapid Greek o'er Asia whirl'd,
For such the steady Romans shook the world;
For such in distant lands the Britons shine,
180 And stain with blood the Danube or the Rhine;
This pow'r has praise, that virtue scarce can warm,
Till fame supplies the universal charm.
Yet Reason frowns on War's unequal game,
Where wasted nations raise a single name,
185 And mortgag'd states their grandsires wreaths regret,
From age to age in everlasting debt;
Wreaths which at last the dear-bought right convey
To rust on medals, or on stones decay.

166 William Laud (1573–1645) was Bishop of Bath and Wells, Bishop of
London, Chancellor of Oxford, and Archbishop of Canterbury in Charles
I's reign; he was tried (pace Johnson) "for endeavouring to subvert the laws,
to overthrow the Protestant religion, and to act as an enemy to Parliament",
and executed on Tower Hill.

175 gazette: The first syllable is stressed.

181-2 This pow'r . . . charm: i.e. praise has this power, that even virtue
can hardly produce without seductive fame.

183 unequal: uneven, unjust (Lat. inaequalis).

expende Hannibalem: quot libras in duce summo
invenies? hic est quem non capit Africa Mauro
percussa oceano Niloque admota tepenti
150 rursus ad Aethiopum populos aliosque elephantos?
additur imperiis Hispania, Pyrenaeum
transilit. opposuit natura Alpemque nivemque:
diducit scopulos et montem rumpit aceto.
iam tenet Italiam, tamen ultra pergere tendit.
155 "actum" inquit "nihil est, nisi Poeno milite portas
frangimus et media vexillum pono Subura."
o qualis facies et quali digna tabella,
cum Gaetula ducem portaret belua luscum.
exitus ergo quis est? o gloria, vincitur idem
160 nempe et in exilium praeceps fugit atque ibi magnus
mirandusque cliens sedet ad praetoria regis,
donec Bithyno libeat vigilare tyranno.

Weigh Hannibal; how many pounds will you find in the supreme general?
(148) Is this the man whom Africa, pounded by the Moorish ocean and
reaching to the warm Nile, and to the Ethiopians and the other elephant
country, cannot hold? Spain is added to his conquests; he leaps across the
Pyrenees. (152) Nature set both the Alps and the snow against him; he splits
the rocks, and breaks asunder the mountain with vinegar. He holds Italy
now, but he decides to press further on. "Nothing is accomplished," he
says, "unless we burst the gates with our Punic army, and I set my standard
in the midst of Subura (in Rome)." (157) What a countenance; and worthy
of what a picture; when the Getulian elephant carried the one-eyed general!
What, then, is his end? (159) O, glory! This same man is defeated surely, and
flees headlong into exile; and there the great and marvellous vassal sits, at
the king's palace, until the Bithynian tyrant pleases to awake.

On what foundation stands the warrior's pride,
190 How just his hopes let Swedish Charles decide;
A frame of adamant, a soul of fire,
No dangers fright him, and no labours tire;
O'er love, o'er fear extends his wide domain,
Unconquer'd lord of pleasure and of pain;
195 No joys to him pacific scepters yield,
War sounds the trump, he rushes to the field;
Behold surrounding kings their pow'r combine,
And one capitulate, and one resign;
Peace courts his hand, but spreads her charms in vain;
200 "Think nothing gain'd", he cries, "till nought remain,
"On Moscow's walls till Gothic standards fly,
"And all be mine beneath the polar sky."
The march begins in military state,
And nations on his eye suspended wait;
205 Stern Famine guards the solitary coast,
And Winter barricades the realms of Frost;
He comes, not want and cold his course delay;—
Hide, blushing Glory, hide Pultowa's day:
The vanquish'd hero leaves his broken bands,
210 And shews his miseries in distant lands;
Condemn'd a needy suppliant to wait,
While ladies interpose, and slaves debate.

190 *Swedish Charles:* The modern Hannibal is Charles XII (1682–1718), who defeated Danish, Polish and Russian armies 1697–1706 (ll. 197-8), deposed Augustus II of Poland (l. 198), invaded Russia and was repulsed by the Czar at Pultowa in 1709 (l. 208).

210 *distant lands:* Turkish territory (1709–14).

212 *ladies:* especially Catherine the Great of Russia, when the Czar agreed (1711) not to prevent Charles's return home.

finem animae quae res humanas miscuit olim,
non gladii, non saxa dabunt nec tela, sed ille
165   Cannarum vindex et tanti sanguinis ultor
anulus. i demens et saevas curre per Alpes,
ut pueris placeas et declamatio fias.
unus Pellaeo iuveni non sufficit orbis,
aestuat infelix angusto limite mundi,
170   ut Gyarae clausus scopulis parvaque Seripho;
cum tamen a figulis munitam intraverit urbem,
sarcophago contentus erat. mors sola fatetur
quantula sint hominum corpuscula. creditur olim
velificatus Athos et quidquid Graecia mendax
175   audet in historia; constratum classibus isdem
suppositumque rotis solidum mare credimus, altos
defecisse amnes epotaque flumina Medo
prandente et madidis cantat quae Sostratus alis;
ille tamen qualis rediit Salamine relicta,
180   in corum atque eurum solitus saevire flagellis
barbarus Aeolio numquam hoc in carcere passos,
ipsum conpedibus qui vinxerat Ennosigaeum
(mitius id sane, quod non et stigmate dignum
credidit; huic quisquam vellet servire deorum?)
185   sed qualis rediit? nempe una nave, cruentis
fluctibus ac tarda per densa cadavera prora.
has totiens optata exegit gloria poenas.

Not swords, or stones, or spears will put an end to the life which once embroiled human affairs; but a (poisoned) ring, the avenger of Cannae and of so much blood. (166) Go, madman, and rush over the wild Alps, to please schoolboys and make a subject for an oration. One world is not enough for the Pellaean youth (Alexander); unhappy, he laments the narrow limit of the earth as if he were enclosed by little Serfo and the rocks of Gyaras: yet when he had entered the city (Babylon) fortified with brick, he was content with a tomb. (172) Death alone shows how fragile are the little bodies of men. It is believed that Athos was once circumnavigated—and whatever lying Greece dares to assert in history; we believe that the sea was covered with the same ships and like firm ground was put under wheels, that deep rivers failed and waters were drunk dry by the Mede as he dined—and the songs that Sostratus sings over his flowing cups. (179) Yet when he came back from abandoned Salamis what sort of a conqueror was he—that

THE VANITY OF HUMAN WISHES 93

But did not Chance at length her error mend?
Did no subverted empire mark his end?
215 Did rival monarchs give the fatal wound?
Or hostile millions press him to the ground?
His fall was destin'd to a barren strand,
A petty fortress, and a dubious hand;
He left the name, at which the world grew pale,
220 To point a moral, or adorn a tale.

All times their scenes of pompous woes afford,
From Persia's tyrant to Bavaria's lord.
In gay hostility, and barb'rous pride,
With half mankind embattled at his side,
225 Great Xerxes comes to seize the certain prey,
And starves exhausted regions in his way;
Attendant Flatt'ry counts his myriads o'er,
Till counted myriads sooth his pride no more;
Fresh praise is try'd till madness fires his mind,
230 The waves he lashes, and enchains the wind;
New pow'rs are claim'd, new pow'rs are still bestow'd,
Till rude resistance lops the spreading god;
The daring Greeks deride the martial show,
And heap their vallies with the gaudy foe;
235 Th' insulted sea with humbler thoughts he gains,
A single skiff to speed his flight remains;
Th' incumber'd oar scarce leaves the dreaded coast
Through purple billows and a floating host.

218 *a dubious hand:* It is uncertain whether Charles was killed by a cannon-ball during the siege of Frederikshald in 1718, or shot there by Siker, his aide.
222 *Bavaria's lord:* a modern supplement to Juvenal's exemplar, Xerxes; see l. 239, note.

---

barbarian who used to rage with scourges against the west wind and the east wind (in their Aeolian prison they who had bound Neptune the earthshaker himself with shackles never endured this); it was considerate, indeed, that he did not think Neptune also worthy of branding—which of the gods would be willing to serve him? But how did he come back? (185) Truly, through the bloody waves with one ship, its prow slow among the crowded corpses. Glory, so often desired, exacted these sacrifices.

"da spatium vitae, multos da, Iuppiter, annos"
hoc recto vultu, solum hoc et pallidus optas.
190 sed quam continuis et quantis longa senectus
plena malis. deformem et taetrum ante omnia vultum
dissimilemque sui, deformem pro cute pellem
pendentisque genas et talis aspice rugas
quales, umbriferos ubi pandit Thabraca saltus,
195 in vetula scalpit iam mater simia bucca.
plurima sunt iuvenum discrimina, pulchrior ille
hoc atque ille alio, multum hic robustior illo:
una senum facies. cum voce trementia membra
et iam leve caput madidique infantia nasi,
200 frangendus misero gingiva panis inermi;
usque adeo gravis uxori natisque sibique,
ut captatori moveat fastidia Cosso.
non eadem vini atque cibi torpente palato
gaudia. nam coitus iam longa oblivio . . .

210 nunc damnum alterius. nam quae cantante voluptas,

"Jupiter, give me length of life; give me many years": You may want this when your countenance is erect; you may want only this when you are sickly. But with what great ills a prolonged old age is filled! (191) Look, above all, at the misshapen and hideous face unlike itself, the ugly hide for a skin, the flabby cheeks, and wrinkles like those a mother-ape now scrapes on her old cheek where Tabraca extends its shady groves. (195) There are many differences among young men; this one is fairer than that and he than another, this one much sturdier than that: old men have one face. Their limbs tremble with their voice; their head is bald now, and their nose runs like an infant's; bread has to be broken for the wretch with his toothless gum, such a nuisance to wife, and children, and to himself, that he would provoke loathing in the legacy-hunter Cossus. (203) When the palate is sluggish there isn't the same pleasure in wine and food. Now there is a long forgetfulness of sexual intercourse. . . . (209) Look now at the loss of another faculty; for what delight has he in the singing

The bold Bavarian, in a luckless hour,
240 Tries the dread summits of Cesarean pow'r,
With unexpected legions bursts away,
And sees defenceless realms receive his sway;
Short sway! fair Austria spreads her mournful charms,
The queen, the beauty, sets the world in arms;
245 From hill to hill the beacons rousing blaze
Spreads wide the hope of plunder and of praise;
The fierce Croatian, and the wild Hussar,
And all the sons of ravage croud the war;
The baffled prince in honour's flatt'ring bloom
250 Of hasty greatness finds the fatal doom,
His foes derision, and his subjects blame,
And steals to death from anguish and from shame.

Enlarge my life with multitude of days,
In health, in sickness, thus the suppliant prays;
255 Hides from himself his state, and shuns to know,
That life protracted is protracted woe.
Time hovers o'er, impatient to destroy,
And shuts up all the passages of joy:
In vain their gifts the bounteous seasons pour,
260 The fruit autumnal, and the vernal flow'r,
With listless eyes the dotard views the store,
He views, and wonders that they please no more;
Now pall the tastless meats, and joyless wines,
And Luxury with sighs her slave resigns.
265 Approach, ye minstrels, try the soothing strain,
Diffuse the tuneful lenitives of pain;

239 *The bold Bavarian:* Charles Albert, Elector of Bavaria, who invaded Austria and Bohemia and had himself crowned emperor in 1742. But his sovereignty was nominal, and his hereditary territories were overrun. He died disgraced in 1745.

244 *The Queen:* Maria Theresa.

247 *Hussar:* Hungarian cavalry-man.

258 *passages of joy:* senses.

266 *tuneful lenitives:* music, believed by classical and Renaissance theorists to have curative properties.

sit licet eximius, citharoedo sive Seleuco
et quibus aurata mos est fulgere lacerna?
quid refert, magni sedeat qua parte theatri
qui vix cornicines exaudiet atque tubarum
215 concentus? clamore opus est, ut sentiat auris
quem dicat venisse puer, quot nuntiet horas.
praeterea minimus gelido iam in corpore sanguis
febre calet sola, circumsilit agmine facto
morborum omne genus, quorum si nomina quaeras,
220 promptius expediam quot amaverit Oppia moechos,
quot Themison aegros autumno occiderit uno. . . .

                                         sed omni
membrorum damno maior dementia, quae nec
nomina servorum nec vultum agnoscit amici
235 cum quo praeterita cenavit nocte, nec illos
quos genuit, quos eduxit. nam codice saevo
heredes vetat esse suos, bona tota feruntur
ad Phialen; tantum artificis valet halitus oris,
quod steterat multis in carcere fornicis annis.

ministrel—though he is supremely good—or in the harper Seleucus, and those whose habit it is to shine in a gold-braided mantle? (213) What does it matter where he sits in the great theatre, when he can hardly hear the horn-players and the trumpets' concord? Who is said by his boy to have arrived, or what hour he makes it, has to be roared out that his ear may pick it up. (217) Moreover, only a fever now warms the very thin blood in his chill body; every kind of disease rushes around him in close order—if you ask their names, I could more quickly count how many adulterers Oppia loved, how many sick men Themison killed off in one autumn. . . . (232) But worse than all this damage to the body is mental weakness; he knows neither the servants' names nor the face of a friend with whom he dined the night before, nor those he fathered or brought up. (236) For by a harsh codicil he keeps his own children from being his heirs; his property is all conveyed to Phiale, so strong is the breath of her artful mouth that had survived many years in a brothel-prison.

No sounds alas would touch th' impervious ear,
Though dancing mountains witness'd Orpheus near;
Nor lute nor lyre his feeble pow'rs attend,
270 Nor sweeter musick of a virtuous friend,
But everlasting dictates croud his tongue,
Perversely grave, or positively wrong.
The still returning tale, and ling'ring jest,
Perplex the fawning niece and pamper'd guest,
275 While growing hopes scarce awe the gath'ring sneer,
And scarce a legacy can bribe to hear;
The watchful guests still hint the last offence,
The daughter's petulance, the son's expence,
Improve his heady rage with treach'rous skill,
280 And mould his passions till they make his will.

Unnumber'd maladies his joints invade,
Lay siege to life and press the dire blockade;
But unextinguish'd Av'rice still remains,
And dreaded losses aggravate his pains;
285 He turns, with anxious heart and cripled hands,
His bonds of debt, and mortgages of lands;
Or views his coffers with suspicious eyes,
Unlocks his gold, and counts it till he dies.

But grant, the virtues of a temp'rate prime
290 Bless with an age exempt from scorn or crime;
An age that melts with unperceiv'd decay,
And glides in modest Innocence away;
Whose peaceful day Benevolence endears,
Whose night congratulating Conscience cheers;
295 The gen'ral fav'rite as the gen'ral friend:
Such age there is, and who shall wish its end?

269 *attend:* pay heed to.

278 *expence:* extravagance.

279 *Improve:* increase.

289–96 *But grant . . . its end?:* This passage, according to Johnson's friend, Mrs. Piozzi, is in part a memorial of his mother.

295 *The gen'ral . . . friend:* as much everyone's favourite as everyone's friend.

D

240   ut vigeant sensus animi, ducenda tamen sunt
       funera natorum, rogus aspiciendus amatae
       coniugis et fratris plenaeque sororibus urnae.
       haec data poena diu viventibus, ut renovata
       semper clade domus multis in luctibus inque
245   perpetuo maerore et nigra veste senescant.
       rex Pylius, magno si quidquam credis Homero,
       exemplum vitae fuit a cornice secundae. . . .

       festino ad nostros et regem transeo Ponti
       et Croesum, quem vox iusti facunda Solonis
275   respicere ad longae iussit spatia ultima vitae.
       exilium et carcer Minturnarumque paludes
       et mendicatus victa Carthagine panis
       hinc causas habuere; quid illo cive tulisset
       natura in terris, quid Roma beatius umquam,
280   si circumducto captivorum agmine et omni
       bellorum pompa animam exhalasset opimam,
       cum de Teutonico vellet descendere curru? . . .

       formam optat modico pueris, maiore puellis
290   murmure, cum Veneris fanum videt, anxia mater
       usque ad delicias votorum. "cur tamen," inquit

Though his mental faculties are vigorous, yet the funerals of his children have to be seen to; he has to look at the funeral pile of his dear wife, and his brother, and the urn filled with his sisters' ashes. (243) This is the punishment given to the long-lived: that as the destruction of their family is constantly resumed they must grow old in great sorrow, in continual grief and black weeds. The Pylian king (Nestor)—if you believe great Homer at all—exemplified a life close to that of a crow. . . . (273) I hurry on to examples of our own, and pass over the king of Pontus, and Croesus, whom Solon's fluent voice ordered to look at the last stages of a long life. Here were the causes of (Marius's) exile and imprisonment, and the marshes of Minturnae, and the begging of bread in conquered Carthage. (278) What had nature ever borne in the earth—what had Rome ever had—more blessed than that citizen, if he had breathed out his splendid life when he dismounted from his Teutonic chariot surrounded by a throng of captives and in all the pomp of wars? . . . (289) When she looks at the shrine of Venus the anxious mother wishes beauty for her boys in a quiet whisper, and more loudly for her girls, all through her fond prayers. "But why," she says,

Yet ev'n on this her load Misfortune flings,
To press the weary minutes flagging wings:
New sorrow rises as the day returns,
300 A sister sickens, or a daughter mourns.
Now kindred Merit fills the sable bier,
Now lacerated Friendship claims a tear.
Year chases year, decay pursues decay,
Still drops some joy from with'ring life away;
305 New forms arise, and diff'rent views engage,
Superfluous lags the vet'ran on the stage,
Till pitying Nature signs the last release,
And bids afflicted worth retire to peace.

But few there are whom hours like these await,
310 Who set unclouded in the gulphs of fate.
From Lydia's monarch should the search descend,
By Solon caution'd to regard his end,
In life's last scene what prodigies surprise,
Fears of the brave, and follies of the wise?
315 From Marlb'rough's eyes the streams of dotage flow,
And Swift expires a driv'ler and a show.

The teeming mother, anxious for her race,
Begs for each birth the fortune of a face:
Yet Vane could tell what ills from beauty spring;
320 And Sedley curs'd the form that pleas'd a king.
Ye nymphs of rosy lips and radiant eyes,
Whom Pleasure keeps too busy to be wise,
Whom Joys with soft varieties invite,
By day the frolick, and the dance by night,
325 Who frown with vanity, who smile with art,
And ask the latest fashion of the heart,

302 *lacerated:* maimed, mangled.

311 *Lydia's monarch:* Croesus (*fl.* 550 B.C.). His contemporary Solon was the law-giver of Athens.

315-16 *Marlb'rough:* John Churchill (1650-1722), first Duke, the greatest soldier in Europe in his day, who suffered two paralytic strokes towards the end of his life. *Swift:* "grew more violent; and his mental powers declined. ... His madness was compounded of rage and fatuity" (Johnson, *Life of Swift*).

319-20 *Vane ... Sedley:* Anne Vane (1705-36), mistress to Frederick Prince of Wales; and Catherine Sedley (1657-1717), only daughter of the Restoration wit, and mistress to James Duke of York (James II).

"corripias? pulchra gaudet Latona Diana."
sed vetat optari faciem Lucretia qualem
ipsa habuit, cuperet Rutilae Verginia gibbum
295 accipere atque suum Rutilae dare. filius autem
corporis egregii miseros trepidosque parentes
semper habet; rara est adeo concordia formae
atque pudicitiae. sanctos licet horrida mores
tradiderit domus ac veteres imitata Sabinos,
300 praeterea castum ingenium vultumque modesto
sanguine ferventem tribuat natura benigna
larga manu (quid enim puero conferre potest plus
custode et cura natura potentior omni?)
non licet esse viro. nam prodiga corruptoris
305 improbitas ipsos audet temptare parentes;
tanta in muneribus fiducia. . . .

nil ergo optabunt homines? si consilium vis,
permittes ipsis expendere numinibus quid
conveniat nobis rebusque sit utile nostris.
nam pro iucundis aptissima quaeque dabunt di.
350 carior est illis homo quam sibi. nos animorum

"do you blame me? Latona delights in her lovely Diana." But Lucretia
forbids wishing for such a face as she herself had; Virginia would want
to take Rutila's hump-back, and give her own beauty to Rutila. (295)
Yet a youth with a handsome form has always unhappy and trembling
parents. The conjunction of beauty and chastity is so rare. Though a rude
cottage communicates holy virtues and imitates the old Sabines—though
liberal nature, with generous hand, gives a chaste temperament and a face
glowing with a modest blush (for what more can nature, more powerful
than her guardian, and than all caution, give a boy?)—he is not allowed to
become a man. For the extravagant wickedness of the seducer dares to
tempt the parents themselves; such is their confidence in bribes. . . . (346)
Shall men then wish for nothing? If you want advice, you should leave the
gods themselves to determine what is right for us and profitable to our
affairs. For the gods will give what is best, instead of what is pleasant. (350)
Man is dearer to them than he is to himself. We, led on by the

What care, what rules your heedless charms shall save,
Each nymph your rival, and each youth your slave?
Against your fame with fondness hate combines,
330   The rival batters, and the lover mines.
With distant voice neglected Virtue calls,
Less heard and less, the faint remonstrance falls;
Tir'd with contempt, she quits the slipp'ry reign,
And Pride and Prudence take her seat in vain.
335   In croud at once, where none the pass defend,
The harmless Freedom, and the private Friend.
The guardians yield, by force superior ply'd;
By Int'rest, Prudence; and by Flatt'ry, Pride.
Now Beauty falls betray'd, despis'd, distress'd,
340   And hissing Infamy proclaims the rest.

Where then shall Hope and Fear their objects find?
Must dull Suspence corrupt the stagnant mind?
Must helpless man, in ignorance sedate,
Roll darkling down the torrent of his fate?
345   Must no dislike alarm, no wishes rise,
No cries attempt the mercies of the skies?
Enquirer, cease, petitions yet remain,
Which heav'n may hear, nor deem religion vain.
Still raise for good the supplicating voice,
350   But leave to heav'n the measure and the choice;
Safe in his pow'r, whose eyes discern afar
The secret ambush of a specious pray'r.

341-66 *When then . . . does not find:* Johnson rejects Juvenal's pagan Stoicism. "Real alleviation of the loss of friends," he wrote in the *Idler* (No. 41, 1759), "and rational tranquillity in the prospect of our own dissolution, can be received only from the promises of [God] and from the assurance of another and better state."

343 *sedate:* passive, unmoved.

344 *darkling:* in the dark; but taken in the *Dictionary* to be a participle.

inpulsu et caeca magnaque cupidine ducti
coniugium petimus partumque uxoris, at illis
notum qui pueri qualisque futura sit uxor.
ut tamen et poscas aliquid voveasque sacellis
355   exta et candiduli divina tomacula porci,
orandum est ut sit mens sana in corpore sano.
fortem posce animum mortis terrore carentem,
qui spatium vitae extremum inter munera ponat
naturae, qui ferre queat quoscumque labores.
360   nesciat irasci, cupiat nihil et potiores
Herculis aerumnas credat saevosque labores
et venere et cenis et pluma Sardanapalli.
monstro quod ipse tibi possis dare, semita certe
tranquillae per virtutem patet unica vitae.
365   nullum numen habes si sit prudentia, nos te,
nos facimus, Fortuna, deam caeloque locamus.

impulse of our minds and by a blind and powerful desire, seek marriage
and the delivery of our wife; but what the boys and the wife may turn out
to be is known to the gods alone. And yet, so that you may ask something,
and vow entrails and the sacred puddings of a white pig to their shrines,
you must pray for a sound mind in a healthy body. (357) Ask for a brave
spirit, without fear of death, that puts the last stage of life among nature's
gifts; that is able to endure any hardships. (360) Do not let it know how
to be angry; let it desire nothing, and let it think the toils and violent
labours of Hercules better than love, and gluttony, and the feather-beds of
Sardanapalus. (363) I show you what you, yourself, can give yourself; the
only path, indeed, to a peaceful life is revealed through virtue. If there is
wisdom, Fortune, then you have no divinity; but we, we ourselves, make
you a goddess and give you a place in heaven.

Implore his aid, in his decisions rest,
Secure whate'er he gives, he gives the best.
355 Yet when the sense of sacred presence fires,
And strong devotion to the skies aspires,
Pour forth thy fervours for a healthful mind,
Obedient passions, and a will resign'd;
For love, which scarce collective man can fill;
360 For patience sov'reign o'er transmuted ill;
For faith, that panting for a happier seat,
Counts death kind Nature's signal of retreat:
These goods for man the laws of heav'n ordain,
These goods he grants, who grants the pow'r to gain;
365 With these celestial wisdom calms the mind,
And makes the happiness she does not find.

354 *Secure:* tranquil, confident that (Lat. *securus*).
356 *devotion:* prayer.

359 *scarce collective man can fill:* all mankind can hardly satisfy, absorb.

Charles Churchill

THE AUTHOR

CHURCHILL (1732–64), an indigent Anglican priest and schoolmaster who first took to poetry to help support his family, and became an able and devoted supporter of John Wilkes, made the last considerable contributions to the tradition of political satire inaugurated by Dryden. *The Author* (1763), though one of his minor and less strident satires, is a good illustration of his plain, hard style which (as Hopkins said of Dryden's verse) exposes "the naked thew and sinew of the English language". He is sometimes diffusely rhetorical (cf. ll. 51–92, 127–44, 185–210); but his best writing is close and firm (cf. ll. 13–30, 93–106, 245–62, 307–26, and especially 357–66), effective in mass rather than in isolated detail. He has, too, some of Dryden's skill in paragraphing. Though he continues the Drydenian tradition of exemplary "character", he is markedly less interested in personality and appearance than in conduct. In *The Author*, the *personality* of John Kidgell alone is fully realised (ll. 357–82): Churchill doubtless found Kidgell's clerical hypocrisy peculiarly offensive. Though he can, on occasion, step from vituperation and complaint into irony, he has little talent for—and probably no interest in—Dryden's "fine Raillery": he takes a simple, solid moral stance on the Christian virtues and the classical principle of moral responsibility in writing (cf. ll. 211–14, 341–56, 391–8).

> Accurs'd the man, whom fate ordains, in spite,
> And cruel parents teach, to Read and Write!
> What need of letters? Wherefore should we spell?
> Why write our names? A mark will do as well.
>
> 5   Much are the precious hours of youth misspent,
> In climbing Learning's rugged steep ascent;
> When to the top the bold advent'rer 's got,
> He reigns, vain monarch, o'er a barren spot,
> Whilst in the *vale of Ignorance* below,
> 10 FOLLY and VICE to rank luxuriance grow;
> Honours and wealth pour in on ev'ry side,
> And proud Preferment rolls her golden tide.
>   O'er crabbed authors life's gay prime to waste,
> To cramp wild genius in the chains of taste,

14 *To cramp ... taste:* by a study of the critics, to subject imagination, energy, and originality to judgment, decorum, and convention. Cf. Young, quoted *supra*, p. 15.

15 To bear the slavish drudgery of schools,
    And tamely stoop to ev'ry pedant's rules,
    For seven long years debarr'd of lib'ral ease,
    To plod in college trammels to *degrees*,
    Beneath the weight of solemn toys to groan,
20 Sleep over books, and leave mankind unknown,
    To praise each senior blockhead's thread-bare tale,
    And laugh till reason blush, and spirits fail,
    Manhood with vile submission to disgrace,
    And *cap* the fool, whose merit is his Place;
25 VICE CHANCELLORS, whose knowledge is but small,
    And CHANCELLORS, who nothing know at all,
    Ill-brook'd the gen'rous Spirit, in those days
    When Learning was the certain road to praise,
    When Nobles, with a love of Science bless'd,
30 Approv'd in others what themselves possess'd.

    But *Now*, when DULLNESS rears aloft her throne,
    When LORDLY Vassals her wide Empire own,
    When Wit, seduc'd by Envy, starts aside,
    And basely leagues with Ignorance and Pride,
35 What *Now* should tempt us, by false hopes misled,
    Learning's unfashionable paths to tread;
    To bear those labours, which our Fathers bore,
    That Crown with-held, which They in triumph wore?

    When with much pains this boasted Learning 's got,
40 'Tis an affront to those who have it not.
    In some it causes hate, in others fear,
    Instructs our Foes to rail, our Friends to sneer.

17 *seven long years:* the qualifying period for the master's degree.

18 *trammels:* hobbles to keep a horse from kicking or straying.

24 *cap:* doff the cap to, out of respect.

27 *Ill-brook'd:* barely tolerated.

31 DULLNESS *rears . . . throne:* The sovereignty of Dullness became a satiric theme in Dryden's *Mac Flecknoe*, and received final expression in Pope's *Dunciad*.

With prudent haste the worldly-minded fool,
Forgets the little which he learn'd at School;
45 The Elder Brother, to vast fortunes born,
Looks on all Science with an Eye of Scorn;
Dependent Breth'ren the same features wear,
And younger Sons are stupid as the Heir.
In Senates, at the Bar, in Church and State,
50 Genius is vile, and Learning out of date.
Is this—O Death to think! is this the Land
Where Merit and Reward went hand in hand,
Where Heroes, Parent-like, the Poet view'd?—
By whom they saw their glorious deeds renew'd;
55 Where Poets, true to Honour, tun'd their lays,
And by their Patrons sanctify'd their praise?
Is this the Land, where, on our SPENCER's tongue,
Enamour'd of his voice, Description hung;
Where JOHNSON rigid gravity beguil'd,
60 Whilst Reason thro' her Critic fences smil'd;
Where NATURE list'ning stood, whilst SHAKESPEAR play'd,
And wonder'd at the Work herself had made?
Is this the Land, where, mindful of her charge
And Office high, fair Freedom walk'd at large;
65 Where, finding in our Laws a sure defence,
She mock'd at all restraints, but those of Sense;
Where, health and honour trooping by her side,
She spread her sacred empire far and wide;
Pointed the Way, Affliction to beguile,
70 And bade the Face of Sorrow wear a smile,
Bade those, who dare obey the gen'rous call,
Enjoy her blessings, which GOD meant for all?
Is this the Land, where, in some Tyrant's reign,
When a *weak, wicked Ministerial* train,
75 The tools of pow'r, the slaves of int'rest, plann'd
Their Country's ruin, and with bribes unman'd

46 *Science:* learning.
57 SPENCER: Edmund Spenser (1552?–99), the Elizabethan poet.
58 *Description:* i.e. the spirit of pictorial and narrative poetry.
59 JOHNSON: Ben Jonson (1572–1637), dramatist and critic.

Those wretches, who, ordain'd in Freedom's cause,
Gave up our liberties, and sold our laws;
When Pow'r was taught by Meanness where to go,
80 Nor dar'd to love the Virtue of a foe;
When, like a lep'rous plague, from the foul head
To the foul heart her sores Corruption spread,
Her iron arm when stern Oppression rear'd,
And Virtue, from her broad base shaken, fear'd
85 The scourge of Vice; when, impotent and vain,
Poor Freedom bow'd the neck to Slav'ry's chain;
Is this the Land, where, in those worst of times,
The hardy Poet rais'd his honest rimes
To dread rebuke, and bade controulment speak
90 In guilty blushes on the villain's cheek,
Bade Pow'r turn pale, kept mighty rogues in awe,
And made them fear the Muse, who fear'd not Law?

How do I laugh, when men of narrow souls,
Whom folly guides, and prejudice controuls;
95 Who, one dull drowsy track of business trod,
Worship their Mammon, and neglect their God;
Who, breathing by one musty set of rules,
Dote from the birth, and are by system fools;
Who, form'd to dullness from their very youth,
100 Lies of the day prefer to Gospel truth,
Pick up their little knowledge from Reviews,
And lay out all their stock of faith in news:
How do I laugh, when Creatures, form'd like these,
Whom Reason scorns, and I should blush to please,
105 Rail at all lib'ral arts, deem verse a crime,
And hold not Truth, as Truth, if told in rime?

74-8 *When a weak . . . laws:* a reference to the decision of both houses of parliament, in November 1763, that parliamentary privilege did not extend to the publication of seditious libels.

88 *The hardy Poet:* possibly a specific reference to the Whig satirist Andrew Marvell (1621–78).

96 *Mammon . . . God:* Matt. vi. 24.

101 *Reviews:* periodicals.

How do I laugh, when PUBLIUS, hoary grown
In zeal for SCOTLAND's welfare, and his own,
By slow degrees, and course of office, drawn
110   In mood and figure at the helm to yawn,
Too mean (the worst of curses Heav'n can send)
To have a foe, too proud to have a friend,
Erring by form, which Blockheads sacred hold,
Ne'er making new faults, and ne'er mending old,
115   Rebukes my Spirit, bids the daring Muse
Subjects more equal to her weakness chuse;
Bids her frequent the haunts of humble swains,
Nor dare to traffick in ambitious strains;
Bids her, indulging the poetic whim
120   In quaint-wrought Ode, or Sonnet pertly trim,
Along the Church-way path complain with GRAY,
Or dance with MASON on the first of May?
"All sacred is the name and pow'r of Kings,
"All States and Statesmen are those mighty Things
125   "Which, howsoe'er they out of course may roll,
"Were never made for Poets to controul."

Peace, Peace, thou Dotard, nor thus vilely deem
Of Sacred Numbers, and their pow'r blaspheme;
I tell thee, Wretch, search all Creation round,
130   In Earth, in Heav'n, no Subject can be found

107 PUBLIUS: probably the Scottish novelist and journalist, Tobias
Smollett (1721–71), editor of the *Critical Review* (which was to give *The
Author* a laudatory notice). Churchill had earlier, in *The Apology* (1761),
reviled Smollett as dishonourable, "bitter as gall, and sharper than the
sword" in criticism, inconsistently "holding forth against Abuse".

110 *In mood . . . yawn:* to be, in style and attitude, a disdainful and irre-
sponsible editor.

111 *mean:* insignificant, contemptible.

120-1 *quaint-wrought Ode . . . Church-way path:* Thomas Gray's odes—
notably *The Progress of Poesy* and *The Bard* (1757)—and his *Elegy Written in
a Country Churchyard* (1750).

122 MASON: William Mason (1724–97), Gray's friend; writer of odes,
imitative elegies, and classical dramas.

(Our God alone except) above whose weight
The Poet cannot rise, and hold his State.
The blessed Saints above in numbers speak
The praise of God, tho' there all praise is weak;
135   In Numbers here below the Bard shall teach
Virtue to soar beyond the Villain's reach;
Shall tear his lab'ring lungs, strain his hoarse throat,
And raise his voice beyond the trumpet's note,
Should an afflicted Country, aw'd by men
140   Of slavish principles, demand his pen.
This is a great, a glorious point of view,
Fit for an English Poet to pursue,
Undaunted to pursue, tho', in return,
His writings by the common Hangman burn.

145   How do I laugh, when men, by fortune plac'd
Above their Betters, and by rank disgrac'd,
Who found their pride on titles which they stain,
And, mean themselves, are of their Fathers vain,
Who would a bill of privilege prefer,
150   And treat a Poet, like a Creditor,
The gen'rous ardour of the Muse condemn,
And curse the storm they know must break on them?
"What, shall a reptile Bard, a wretch unknown,
"Without one badge of merit, but his own,
155   "Great Nobles lash, and *Lords*, like common men,
"Smart from the vengeance of a Scribbler's pen?"

      What's in this name of *Lord*, that we should fear
To bring their vices to the public ear?
Flows not the honest blood of humble swains
160   Quick as the tide which swells a Monarch's veins?

131 *Our God alone except:* On the inadequacy of religious poetry, see
Johnson, *Lives of the English Poets*, ed. G. B. Hill, 1905, i. 292.
      144 *His writings . . . burn:* A mob had just prevented (3 December 1763)
the burning of the *North Briton* by the hangman on the order of Parliament.
      149 *a bill of privilege:* Peers were protected by privilege from arrest in civil
actions. Sixteen peers protested (29 November 1763) against parliament's
decision on seditious libels (see ll. 74-8, note).

Monarchs, who wealth and titles can bestow,
Cannot make Virtues in succession flow.
Would 'st Thou, Proud Man, be safely plac'd above
The censure of the Muse, deserve her Love,
165 Act as thy Birth demands, as Nobles ought;
Look back, and by thy worthy Father taught,
Who *earn'd* those Honours, Thou wert *born* to wear,
Follow his steps, and be his Virtue's heir.
But if, regardless of the road to Fame,
170 You start aside, and tread the paths of shame,
If such thy life, that should thy Sire arise,
The sight of such a Son would blast his eyes,
Would make him curse the hour which gave Thee birth,
Would drive him, shudd'ring, from the face of earth
175 Once more, with shame and sorrow, 'mongst the dead
In endless night to hide his rev'rend head;
If such thy life, tho' Kings had made thee more
Than ever King a scoundrel made before,
Nay, to allow thy pride a deeper spring,
180 Tho' God in vengeance had made Thee a King,
Taking on Virtue's wing her daring flight,
The Muse should drag thee trembling to the light,
Probe thy foul wounds, and lay thy bosom bare
To the keen question of the searching air.

185   Gods! with what pride I see the titled slave,
Who smarts beneath the stroke which Satire gave,
Aiming at ease, and with dishonest art
Striving to hide the feelings of his heart!
How do I laugh, when, with affected air,
190 (Scarce able thro' despite to keep his chair,
Whilst on his trembling lip pale anger speaks,
And the chaf'd blood flies mounting to his cheeks)
He talks of Conscience, which good men secures
From all those evil moments guilt endures,

175-6 *with shame . . . head:* cf. Gen. xlii. 38.

187-96 *with dishonest art . . . bard:* Cf. Dryden's account of Buckingham,
satirised as "Zimri", *supra*, Introduction, pp. 11-12.

195 And seems to laugh at those, who pay regard
  To the wild ravings of a frantic bard.
   "SATIRE, whilst envy and ill-humour sway
  "The mind of man, must always make her way,
  "Nor to a bosom, with discretion fraught,
200 "Is all her malice worth a single thought.
  "The Wise have not the will, nor Fools the pow'r
  "To stop her headstrong course; within the hour,
  "Left to herself, she dies; opposing Strife,
  "Gives her fresh vigour, and prolongs her life.
205 "All things her prey, and ev'ry man her aim,
  "I can no patent for exemption claim,
  "Nor would I wish to stop that harmless dart
  "Which plays around, but cannot wound my heart:
  "Tho' pointed at myself, be SATIRE free;
210 "To Her 'tis pleasure, and no pain to Me."

   Dissembling Wretch! hence to the Stoic school,
  And there amongst thy breth'ren play the fool,
  There, unrebuk'd, these wild, vain doctrines preach;
  Lives there a Man, whom SATIRE cannot reach?
215 Lives there a Man, who calmly can stand by,
  And see his conscience ripp'd with steady eye?
  When SATIRE flies abroad on Falshood's wing,
  Short is her life indeed, and dull her sting;
  But when to Truth allied, the wound she gives
220 Sinks deep, and to remotest ages lives.
  When in the tomb thy pamper'd flesh shall rot,
  And e'en by friends thy mem'ry be forgot,
  Still shalt Thou live, recorded for thy crimes,
  Live in her page, and stink to after-times.

225 Hast Thou no feeling yet? Come, throw off pride,
  And own those passions which Thou shalt not hide.

211 *the Stoic school:* the Athenian philosophers who sought fulfilment in
the mastery of passion.

216 *ripp'd:* slashed skilfully, as by a butcher.

224 *Live . . . and stink:* Churchill fuses the images of death and literary
immortality in a paradox.

S——, who, from the moment of his birth,
Made human Nature a reproach on earth,
Who never dar'd, nor wish'd behind to stay,
230 When Folly, Vice, and Meanness led the way,
Would blush, should he be told, by Truth and Wit,
Those actions, which he blush'd not to commit;
Men the most infamous are fond of fame,
And those who fear not guilt, yet start at shame.

235   But whither runs my zeal, whose rapid force,
Turning the brain, bears Reason from her course,
Carries me back to times, when Poets, bless'd
With courage, grac'd the Science they profess'd;
When They, in Honour rooted, firmly stood
240 The bad to punish, and reward the good;
When, to a flame by Public Virtue wrought,
The foes of Freedom They to justice brought,
And dar'd expose those slaves, who dar'd support
A Tyrant plan, and call'd themselves a Court.

245 Ah! What are Poets now? as slavish those
Who deal in Verse, as those who deal in Prose.
Is there an Author, search the Kingdom round,
In whom true worth, and real Spirit 's found?
The Slaves of Booksellers, or (doom'd by Fate
250 To baser chains) vile pensioners of State;
Some, dead to shame, and of those shackles proud
Which Honour scorns, for slav'ry roar aloud,
Others, *half-palsied* only, mutes become,

227 *S——:* John Montagu (1718–92), fourth Earl of Sandwich, a profligate who betrayed his friend Wilkes by laying Wilkes's *Essay on Woman*
(see l. 357, note) before the Lords on 15 November 1763.

241-4 *When . . . a Court:* Probably another reference to the Whig
satirists of Charles II's reign (cf. ll. 87-92).

250-3 *vile pensioners . . . half-palsied:* specifically Dr. Johnson, who
suffered from convulsions and who had accepted a pension from George
III in 1762 despite his own definition of "pensioner" as "a slave of state hired
by a stipend to obey his master" (*Dictionary*, 1755). Cf. Churchill's *Ghost*,
iii (1763), 819, "He damns the *Pension* which he takes".

And what makes SMOLLETT write, makes JOHNSON dumb.
255 Why turns yon villain pale? why bends his eye
Inward, abash'd, when MURPHY passes by?
Dost Thou sage MURPHY for a blockhead take,
Who wages war with vice for Virtue's sake?
No, No—like other *Worldlings*, you will find
260 He shifts his sails, and catches ev'ry wind.
His soul the shock of int'rest can't endure,
Give him a pension then, and sin secure.

With laurell'd wreaths the flatt'rer's brows adorn,
Bid Virtue crouch, bid Vice exalt her horn,
265 Bid Cowards thrive, put honesty to flight,
MURPHY shall prove, or try to prove it right.
Try, thou State-Juggler, ev'ry paltry art,
Ransack the inmost closet of my heart,
Swear Thou 'rt my Friend; by that base oath make way
270 Into my breast, and flatter to betray;
Or, if those tricks are vain, if wholesome doubt
Detects the fraud, and points the Villain out,
Bribe those who daily at my board are fed,
And make them take my life who eat my bread;
275 On Authors for defence, for praise depend;
Pay him but well, and MURPHY is thy friend.
He, He shall ready stand with venal rimes
To varnish guilt, and consecrate thy crimes,
To make corruption in false colours shine,
280 And damn his own good name, to rescue thine.

But, if thy niggard hands their gifts with-hold,
And Vice no longer rains down show'rs of gold,

254 SMOLLETT: a supporter of Bute's administration (but not as a state pensioner) in *The Briton* (1762–3).

256 *Murphy:* the dramatist Arthur Murphy (1727–1805), paid supporter of Bute's administration in *The Auditor* (1762–3).

264 *exalt her horn:* a biblical gesture of strength and pride; e.g. 1 Sam. ii. 10, Ps. lxxv. 4–5.

282 *rains ... gold:* as Jove seduced Danaë by coming to her as a shower of gold.

Expect no mercy; facts, well grounded, teach,
MURPHY, if not rewarded, will impeach.

285   What tho' each man of nice and juster thought,
Shunning his steps, decrees, by Honour taught,
He ne'er can be a Friend, who stoops so low
To be the base betrayer of a foe;
What tho', with thine together link'd, his name

290   Must be with thine transmitted down to shame,
To ev'ry manly feeling callous grown,
Rather than not blast thine, he'll blast his own.

To ope the fountain, whence Sedition springs,
To slander Government, and libel Kings,

295   With Freedom's name to serve a present hour,
Tho' born, and bred to arbitrary pow'r,
To talks of WILLIAMS with insidious art,
Whilst a vile STUART 's lurking in his heart,
And, whilst mean Envy rears her loathsome head,

300   Flatt'ring the living, to abuse the dead,
Where is SHEBBEARE? O, let not foul reproach,
Travelling thither in a City-Coach,
The Pill'ry date to name; the whole intent
Of that Parade was Fame, not Punishment,

305   And that old, staunch Whig BEARDMORE standing by,
Can in full Court give that report the lye.

With rude unnat'ral jargon to support,
Half *Scotch*, half *English*, a declining Court,
To make most glaring contraries unite,

310   And prove, beyond dispute, that black is white,

284 *not rewarded, will impeach:* According to Gray, Murphy thought himself ill-paid and threatened to expose those who employed him.

285 *nice:* discriminating.

296 *arbitrary pow'r:* which the Whigs had accused Charles II and James II of seeking, and was now said to be the ambition of Bute (cf. l. 301, note).

297 WILLIAMS: William III and the "Protestant succession".

301 SHEBBEARE: John Shebbeare (1709–88), a Jacobite pamphleteer who was sentenced to the pillory in 1758 and driven there in a City coach by the under-sheriff, Arthur Beardmore, and protected from the crowd. He was pensioned by Bute, and defended Bute's administration in the *Moderator*.

To make firm Honour tamely league with shame,
Make Vice and Virtue differ but in name,
To prove that Chains and Freedom are but one,
That to be sav'd must mean to be undone,
315 Is there not GUTHRIE? Who, like him, can call
All Opposites to proof, and conquer all?
He calls forth living waters from the rock;
He calls forth children from the barren stock;
He, far beyond the springs of Nature led,
320 Makes Women bring forth after they are dead;
He, on a curious, new, and happy plan,
In *Wedlock*'s sacred bands joins Man to Man;
And, to complete the whole, most strange, but true,
By some rare magic, makes them fruitful too,
325 Whilst from their loins, in the due course of years,
Flows the rich blood of GUTHRIE's *English Peers*.

Dost Thou contrive some blacker deed of shame,
Something which Nature shudders but to name,
Something which makes the Soul of man retreat,
330 And the life-blood run backward to her seat?
Dost Thou contrive, for some base private end,
Some selfish view, to hang a trusting friend,
To lure him on, e'en to his parting breath,
And promise life, to work him surer death?
335 Grown old in villainy, and dead to grace,
Hell in his heart, and TYBURNE in his face;
Behold, a Parson at thy Elbow stands,
Low'ring damnation, and with open hands

315 GUTHRIE: William Guthrie (1708–70), Scottish Jacobite historian; the first, says Boswell, "who had recourse to . . . the Parliamentary Journals"; "such was the power of his political pen, that . . . Government thought it worth while to keep it quiet by a pension" (*Life of Johnson*, ed. Hill-Powell, 1934, i. 117).

317-18 *He calls forth . . . stock:* like Moses (Num. xx. 7-11). Churchill ridicules Guthrie's *History of the English Peerage*, 1763.

337 *a Parson:* Philip Francis (1708?-73), tutor to Charles James Fox, translator of Horace, and traducer of Pitt after his resignation in 1761.

Ripe to betray his Saviour for reward;
340   The Atheist Chaplain of an Atheist Lord.

Bred to the Church, and for the gown decreed,
'Ere it was known that I should learn to read;
Tho' that was nothing, for my Friends, who knew
What mighty Dullness of itself could do,
345   Never design'd me for a working Priest,
But hop'd, I should have been a DEAN at least;
Condemn'd (like many more, and worthier men,
To whom I pledge the service of my pen),
Condemn'd (whilst proud, and pamper'd Sons of Lawn,
350   Cramm'd to the throat, in lazy plenty yawn)
In pomp of *rev'rend begg'ry* to appear,
To pray, and starve on forty pounds a year;
My Friends, who never felt the galling load,
Lament that I forsook the Packhorse road,
355   Whilst Virtue to my conduct witness bears
In throwing off that gown, which FRANCIS wears.

What Creature 's that, so very pert and prim;
So very full of foppery, and whim;
So gentle, yet so brisk; so wond'rous sweet,
360   So fit to prattle at a Lady's feet,
Who looks, as he the Lord's rich vineyard trod,
And by his Garb appears a man of God?
Trust not to looks, nor credit outward show;
The villain lurks beneath the *cassock'd* Beau;
365   That 's an Informer; what avails the name?

349 *Sons of Lawn:* bishops.

350 *Cramm'd to the throat:* Dryden's phrase, in his translation of Lucretius, "Against the Fear of Death", l. 131.

352 *starve on forty pounds a year:* Goldsmith's parson was "passing rich" on this stipend (*The Deserted Village*, 1770, l. 142).

357 *Creature:* John Kidgell, rector of several Suffolk and Surrey parishes and chaplain to the libertine Earl of March (later the Duke of Queensberry, "Old Q"). He procured a copy of Wilkes's *Essay on Woman* for Sandwich (see l. 227, note), and described its contents with ill-disguised relish in his *Narrative of a Scandalous, Obscene, and exceedingly Profane Libel*, which obstructed his preferment.

Suffice it that the wretch from SODOM came.

His tongue is deadly—from his presence run,
Unless thy rage would wish to be undone.
No ties can hold him, no affection bind,
370 And Fear alone restrains his coward mind;
Free him from that, no Monster is so fell,
Nor is so sure a blood-hound found in hell.
His silken smiles, his hypocritic air,
His meek demeanour, plausible and fair,
375 Are only worn to pave Fraud's easier way,
And make gull'd Virtue fall a surer prey.
Attend his Church—his plan of doctrine view—
The Preacher is a Christian, dull but true;
But when the hallow'd hour of preaching 's o'er,
380 That plan of doctrine 's never thought of more;
CHRIST is laid by neglected on the shelf,
And the vile Priest is Gospel to himself.

By CLELAND tutor'd, and with BLACOW bred,
(BLACOW, whom by a brave resentment led,
385 OXFORD, if OXFORD had not sunk in fame,
Ere this, had damn'd to everlasting shame)
Their steps he follows, and their crimes partakes,
To Virtue lost, to Vice alone he wakes,
Most lusciously declaims 'gainst luscious themes,
390 And, whilst he rails at blasphemy, blasphemes.

Are these the Arts, which Policy supplies?
Are these the steps, by which grave Churchmen rise?
Forbid it, Heav'n; or, should it turn out so,
Let Me, and Mine, continue mean and low.
395 Such be their Arts, whom Interest controuls;
KIDGELL and I have free and honest souls.
We scorn Preferment which is gain'd by Sin,
And will, tho' poor without, have peace within.

383 CLELAND: John Cleland (1709–89), author of *Fanny Hill, or, The Memoirs of a Woman of Pleasure* (1750), and a government pensioner. Richard BLACOW (d. 1760) informed against students who created a Jacobite riot in the streets of Oxford in 1747. He became a canon of Windsor in 1754.

Oliver Goldsmith

RETALIATION

"DR. GOLDSMITH belonged to a Club of Beaux Esprits, where Wit sparkled sometimes at the Expence of Good-nature. It was proposed to write Epitaphs on the Doctor; his Country, Dialect and Person, furnished Subjects of Witticism.—The Doctor was called on for Retaliation, and at their next Meeting produced the following Poem. . . ." (Preface to *Retaliation*, 19 April 1774.) Composed (partly at least) in February 1774, the poem was read out at the St. James's Coffee House not long before Goldsmith's death on 3 April. It was unfinished; some lines, allegedly by Goldsmith but now believed to be the work of Caleb Whitefoord, wine-merchant and rhymester, are not printed here; nor are others (on William and Richard Burke) which were sent by Whitefoord to Edmund Burke, *c.* 5 May 1774. (See *The Correspondence of Edmund Burke*, ed. Lucy S. Sutherland, ii (1960), 536.)

Garrick's extempore epitaph spoken at the Club was the famous couplet:

> Here lies NOLLY Goldsmith, for shortness call'd Noll,
> Who wrote like an angel, but talk'd like poor Poll.

He and his associates were effectively answered by Goldsmith's humane satire. The dominant mood of the poem is good-humoured; but this should not blind the reader to its intelligent organization, the occasional sharpness (as on the unrealistic characters in Cumberland's plays, or Garrick's conceit), and Goldsmith's ability (as in the portrait of Burke) to express memorably in a single couplet an essential feature of a personality. He is also capable of neat ambiguity, as in the rejoinder to Garrick's couplet:

> "But peace to his spirit, wherever it flies,
> To act as an angel, and mix with the skies"—

where the second line wittily echoes Garrick's own words. But above all, Goldsmith shrewdly assesses his friends' characters without rancour; he writes intimately, playing with nicknames and personal eccentricities; and the poem shows that the tone of satire can be good-natured as well as venomous.

The text is (with one minor exception) taken from the third edition; footnotes which appear in inverted commas are taken from that edition.

Of old, when Scarron his companions invited,
Each guest brought his dish, and the feast was united;
If our landlord supplies us with beef, and with fish,
Let each guest bring himself, and he brings the best dish:
5 Our Dean shall be venison, just fresh from the plains;
Our Burke shall be tongue, with a garnish of brains;
Our Will shall be wild fowl, of excellent flavour,
And Dick with his pepper, shall heighten their savour:
Our Cumberland's sweet-bread, its place shall obtain,
10 And Douglas is pudding, substantial and plain:
Our Garrick's a sallad, for in him we see
Oil, vinegar, sugar, and saltness agree:
To make out the dinner, full certain I am,
That Ridge is anchovy, and Reynolds is lamb:

1 *Scarron:* Paul Scarron (1610–60); Goldsmith's translation of his *Roman Comique* appeared in 1776.

3 *landlord:* "The Master of St. James's Coffee-house, where the Doctor, and the Friends he has characterized in this Poem, held an occasional Club."

5 *Dean:* Dr. Thomas Barnard (1728–1806), Dean of Derry.

6 *Burke:* Edmund Burke (1729–97), the Whig politician and writer. He was a fellow-undergraduate with Goldsmith at Trinity College, Dublin, and "one of the greatest orators in this country".

7 *Will:* William Burke (d. 1798), a relative of Edmund, and a distinctly reckless individual.

8 *Dick:* Richard Burke (1733–94), Edmund's brother; he was on leave from the West Indies where he was Collector of Customs at Grenada. His connection with the West Indies gave rise to his nickname of "Pepper" (see *The Letters of David Garrick*, ed. Little and Kahrl, (1963), ii. 476).

9 *Cumberland:* Richard Cumberland (1732–1811), author of sentimental comedies; his best-known play was *The West Indian* (1771).

10 *Douglas:* Dr. John Douglas (1721–1807), then canon of Windsor, later (1791) bishop of Salisbury.

11 *Garrick:* David Garrick (1717–79), dramatist and famous actor-manager at Drury Lane. His nickname was "Vinegar" (see *Letters*, ed. Little and Kahrl, ii. 749).

14 *Ridge:* "Counsellor John Ridge, a gentleman belonging to the Irish bar, the relish of whose agreeable and pointed conversation is admitted, by all his acquaintance, to be very properly compared to the above sauce." Ridge (*c.* 1728–76) was Burke's lawyer in Ireland.   *Reynolds:* "Sir Joshua Reynolds [1723–92], President of the Royal Academy."

15   That Hickey's a capon, and by the same rule,
      Magnanimous Goldsmith, a goosberry fool:
      At a dinner so various, at such a repast,
      Who'd not be glutton, and stick to the last:
      Here, waiter, more wine, let me sit while I'm able,
20   'Till all my companions sink under the table;
      Then with chaos and blunders encircling my head,
      Let me ponder, and tell what I think of the dead.
         Here lies the good Dean, re-united to earth,
      Who mixt reason with pleasure, and wisdom with mirth:
25   If he had any faults, he has left us in doubt,
      At least, in six weeks, I could not find 'em out;
      Yet some have declar'd, and it can't be denied 'em,
      The sly-boots was cursedly cunning to hide 'em.
         Here lies our good Edmund, whose genius was such,
30   We scarcely can praise it, or blame it too much;
      Who, born for the Universe, narrow'd his mind,
      And to party gave up, what was meant for mankind.
      Thro' fraught with all learning, yet straining his throat,
      To persuade Tommy Townsend to lend him a vote;
35   Who, too deep for his hearers, still went on refining,

15 *Hickey:* Thomas Hickey (d. 1794), an Irish lawyer, "whose hospitality and good humour have acquired him, in this Club, the title of 'honest Tom Hickey'".

16 *goosberry fool:* Apparently this dish was a fairly recent innovation; *O.E.D.*'s earliest quotation is from 1747.

32 *And to . . . mankind:* A neat statement—which became almost a cliché among anti-Burke writers—of the view that Burke's literary and philosophical abilities were dissipated by his labours for the Rockingham Whigs.

34 *Townsend:* Thomas Townsend (1733-1800), M.P. for Whitchurch, later Viscount Sydney. Boswell maintained that this reference was in retaliation for Townsend's parliamentary opposition to the granting of a pension to Johnson (*Life of Johnson*, ed. Hill-Powell, (1934), iv. 318).

35-6 *Who, too . . . dining:* Lecky argues that, despite his faults, Burke's oratory on important occasions had "a wonderful power upon his hearers" (*History of England in the 18th Century*, 1892, iii. 392). Nevertheless these defects—a tendency to "wind himself into his subject" and too readily to assume a profound interest among his listeners—sometimes drove M.P.'s out of the House and earned Burke the nickname of "the Dinner Bell".

And thought of convincing, while they thought of dining;
Tho' equal to all things, for all things unfit,
Too nice for a statesman, too proud for a wit:
For a patriot too cool; for a drudge, disobedient,
40 And too fond of the *right* to pursue the *expedient*.
In short, 'twas his fate, unemploy'd, or in place, Sir,
To eat mutton cold, and cut blocks with a razor.
  Here lies honest William, whose heart was a mint,
While the owner ne'er knew half the good that was in't;
45 The pupil of impulse, it forced him along,
His conduct still right, with his argument wrong;
Still aiming at honour, yet fearing to roam,
The coachman was tipsy, the chariot drove home;
Would you ask for his merits, alas! he had none,
50 What was good was spontaneous, his faults were his own.
  Here lies honest Richard, whose fate I must sigh at,
Alas, that such frolic should now be so quiet!
What spirits were his, what wit and what whim,
Now breaking a jest, and now breaking a limb;
55 Now wrangling and grumbling to keep up the ball,
Now teazing and vexing, yet laughing at all!
In short so provoking a Devil was Dick,
That we wish'd him full ten times a day at Old Nick,
But missing his mirth and agreeable vein,
60 As often we wish'd to have Dick back again.
  Here Cumberland lies having acted his parts,
The Terence of England, the mender of hearts;
A flattering painter, who made it his care
To draw men as they ought to be, not as they are.

---

42 *To . . . cold:* a possible reference to Burke's recurring financial problems.

54 *Now breaking . . . limb:* "This gentleman having slightly fractured one of his arms and legs, at different times, the Doctor has rallied him upon those accidents, as a kind of *retributive justice* for breaking jests upon other people."

55 *to keep . . . ball:* to sustain the conversation.

62 *Terence:* Latin comic playwright (195-159 B.C.)

65 His gallants are all faultless, his women divine,
    And comedy wonders at being so fine;
    Like a tragedy queen he has dizen'd her out,
    Or rather like tragedy giving a rout.
    His fools have their follies so lost in a croud
70 Of virtues and feelings, that folly grows proud,
    And coxcombs alike in their failings alone,
    Adopting his portraits are pleas'd with their own.
    Say, where has our poet this malady caught,
    Or wherefore his characters thus without fault?
75 Say was it that vainly directing his view,
    To find out men's virtues and finding them few,
    Quite sick of pursuing each troublesome elf,
    He grew lazy at last and drew from himself?
        Here Douglas retires from his toils to relax,
80 The scourge of impostors, the terror of quacks:
    Come all ye quack bards, and ye quacking divines,
    Come and dance on the spot where your tyrant reclines,
    When Satire and Censure encircl'd his throne,
    I fear'd for your safety, I fear'd for my own;
85 But now he is gone, and we want a detector,
    Our Dodds shall be pious, our Kenricks shall lecture;

65-6 *His gallants . . . fine:* In the preface to *The Good Natur'd Man* (1768) Goldsmith attacked "elevated and sentimental" comedy which had banished "humour and character" from French drama and was in danger of doing so from the English.

67 *dizen'd:* i.e. adorned with finery.

68 *rout:* a fashionable reception.

80 *The scourge . . . quacks:* Douglas had exposed William Lauder's Miltonic forgeries in 1750, and proved Archibald Bower, author of *A History of the Popes* (1748–66), a secret member of the Roman Catholic Church. They were both Scotsmen (see l. 89).

86 *Dodds:* Rev. Dr. William Dodd (1729–77) was struck off the list of royal chaplains (in 1774) for improperly soliciting preferment from the Lord Chancellor; he was later executed for forgery.

86 *Kenricks:* Dr. William Kenrick (1725?–79), a journalist who had attacked Goldsmith in *The Monthly Review*, 1759, but recanted in 1762 with a favourable review of *The Citizen of the World*. In 1774 he was giving a series of lectures on "The School of Shakespeare".

Macpherson write bombast, and call it a style,
Our Townshend make speeches, and I shall compile;
New Lauders and Bowers the Tweed shall cross over,
90 No countryman living their tricks to discover;
Detection her taper shall quench to a spark,
And Scotchman meet Scotchman and cheat in the dark.
    Here lies David Garrick, describe me who can,
An abridgment of all that was pleasant in man;
95 As an actor, confest without rival to shine,
As a wit, if not first, in the very first line,
Yet with talents like these, and an excellent heart,
The man had his failings, a dupe to his art;
Like an ill-judging beauty, his colours he spread,
100 And beplaistered with rouge his own natural red.
On the stage he was natural, simple, affecting,
'Twas only that, when he was off, he was acting:
With no reason on earth to go out of his way,
He turn'd and he varied full ten times a-day;
105 Tho' secure of our hearts, yet confoundedly sick
If they were not his own by finessing and trick,
He cast off his friends, as a huntsman his pack,
For he knew when he pleas'd he could whistle them back.
Of praise a mere glutton, he swallow'd what came,
110 And the puff of a dunce, he mistook it for fame;
'Till his relish grown callous, almost to disease,
Who pepper'd the highest, was surest to please.
But let us be candid, and speak out our mind,
If dunces applauded, he paid them in kind.

87 *Macpherson:* James Macpherson (1736–96), author of the allegedly Ossianic poems, *Fingal* (1762), and *Temora* (1763).

93-124 *Here lies . . . above:* There is a dualism in Goldsmith's assessment of Garrick; some admiration is evident but it is offset by an acerbity of tone. This may have sprung not only from an almost instinctive animosity between the two men, but also from Garrick's part in preventing Goldsmith's election as Secretary of the Royal Society as well as his reluctance to stage *The Good Natur'd Man.*

115   Ye Kenricks, ye Kellys, and Woodfalls so grave,
       What a commerce was yours, while you got and you gave!
       How did Grub-street re-echo the shouts that you rais'd,
       While he was beroscius'd, and you were beprais'd!
       But peace to his spirit, wherever it flies,
120   To act as an angel, and mix with the skies;
       Those poets, who owe their best fame to his skill,
       Shall still be his flatterers, go where he will.
       Old Shakespeare, receive him, with praise and with love,
       And Beaumonts and Bens be his Kellys above.

125   Here Hickey reclines, a most blunt, pleasant creature,
       And slander itself must allow him good-nature:
       He cherish'd a friend, and he relish'd a bumper;
       Yet one fault he had, and that one was a thumper:
       Perhaps you may ask if the màn was a miser?
130   I answer, no, no, for he always was wiser;
       Too courteous, perhaps, or obligingly flat:
       His very worst foe can't accuse him of that.
       Perhaps he confided in men as they go;
       And so was too foolishly honest; ah, no.
135   Then what was his failing? come tell it, and burn ye,
       He was, could he help it? a special attorney.
          Here Reynolds is laid, and, to tell you my mind,
       He has not left a better or wiser behind;

115 *Kellys:* Hugh Kelly (1739–77), an Irish playwright. His vapid sentimental comedy, *False Delicacy* (1768), was staged by Garrick at Drury Lane
in preference to Goldsmith's *Good Natur'd Man*.

115 *Woodfalls:* William Woodfall (1746–1803), dramatic critic.

118 *beroscius'd:* i.e. ranked with the famous Roman actor Roscius Gallus
(d. *c.* 62 B.C.). "Our English Roscius" was a term freely applied to Garrick
by his contemporaries.

123-4 *Old Shakespeare . . . above:* Garrick was famous as a Shakespearean
actor, especially as Richard III and Hamlet; his repertoire also included plays
by Francis Beaumont and Ben Jonson (particularly *The Alchemist* in which
he played Abel Drugger).

131 *flat:* i.e. deferential.

136 *special attorney:* a lawyer with power to act in a specific case or court
(in contrast to Attorney-General).

His pencil was striking, resistless and grand,
140 His manners were gentle, complying and bland;
Still born to improve us in every part,
His pencil our faces, his manners our heart:
To coxcombs averse, yet most civilly steering,
When they judg'd without skill he was still hard of hearing:
145 When they talked of their Raphaels, Corregios and stuff,
He shifted his trumpet, and only took snuff.

146 *He shifted . . . snuff:* "Sir Joshua Reynolds is so remarkably deaf as to be under the necessity of using an ear-trumpet in company; he is, at the same time, equally remarkable for taking a great quantity of snuff."

[According to Goldsmith's nineteenth-century biographer, Prior, the manuscript of the poem finished with the incomplete line: "By flattery unspoiled...."]

Robert Burns

HOLY WILLIE'S PRAYER

THE Scottish poet Burns (1759–96) wrote this satiric monologue early in 1785, after the presbytery judgment described in the "Argument". The poem "alarmed the kirk-Session so much", Burns said in a letter, "that they held three several meetings to look over their holy artillery, if any of it was pointed againt profane Rhymers". The destructive monologue is an old satiric device, related to the burlesque confession and the mock-testament of medieval literature. The *Prayer* is primarily, but not merely, personal satire: Burns exposes the hypocrisy and malice of Holy Willie and, at a deeper level, the grotesque distortion of Calvinist doctrine by which he justifies himself. The poem is written in the absurd mixture of spoken Scots and Biblical English associated with the Covenanters (cf. Scott's *Old Mortality*) and the eighteenth-century Presbyterian evangelicals. Burns makes the impropriety of this language comically explicit; linguistic contrasts support satiric oppositions of attitude and theme. Thus the anxious vernacular confessions of ll. 31–2, 37, and 43–8 are set in a scriptural framework, ironically twisted (ll. 25–30, 34–6, 39–40, 49–54); ll. 61–4 and 67–70 are blended with the scriptural ll. 65–6 and 71–2; and the agonised recollection of defeat in ll. 79–84 is a foil (as well as, psychologically, a gloss) to the Biblical invocations in ll. 73–8 and 85–90. The *Prayer* takes the conventional Protestant form: (*a*) invocation and praise (ll. 1–6, 7–30)—here entirely self-centred, addressed to a deity whose power has been splendidly expressed in the creation and election of Willie Fisher; (*b*) confession and penitence (ll. 31–54)—here confined to sexual sin, with which Willie (responsible, as an elder, for the sexual discipline of the parish) is obsessed, and which inspires fear (ll. 39–40) rather than guilt and (incredibly) a sense of divine purpose (ll. 49–54; the echo of St. Paul is a master-stroke); (*c*) intercession, here characteristically brief (ll. 55–6); and (*d*) petition (ll. 57–96), here mainly for vengeance.

Holy Willie's Prayer is printed from Burn's holograph in the Glenriddell MSS, a collection made for his friend Robert Riddell in 1791. The *Epitaph on Holy Willie*, probably written about 1785, was first published in 1801.

> *And send the Godly in a pet to pray—*
>
> Pope

ARGUMENT

Holy Willie was a rather oldish batchelor Elder in the parish of Mauchline, and much and justly famed for that polemical chattering which ends in tippling Orthodoxy, and for that Spiritualized Bawdry which refines to Liquorish Devotion.—In a Sessional process with a gentleman in Mauchline, a Mr Gavin Hamilton, Holy Willie, and his priest, father Auld, after full hearing in the Presbytry of Ayr, came off but second best; owing partly to the oratorical powers of Mr Robt Aiken, Mr Hamilton's Counsel; but chiefly to Mr Hamilton's being one of the most irreproachable and truly respectable characters in the country.—On losing his Process, the Muse overheard him at his devotions as follows—

> O Thou that in the Heavens does dwell!
> Wha, as it pleases best thysel,
> Sends ane to heaven and ten to h—ll,
>   A' for thy glory!

Epigraph: from *The Rape of the Lock*, iv. 64.

1-2 *O Thou . . . thysel:* Ps. cxv. 3, cxxiii. 1.

3-4 *Sends ane . . . glory:* the Calvinist doctrine of double predestination. "Neither are any redeemed by Christ . . . but the elect only. The rest of mankind God was pleased . . . to pass by" (Westminster Confession, 1643, iii). Cf. ll. 15-18.

5   And no for ony gude or ill
            They've done before thee—

I bless and praise thy matchless might,
When thousands thou hast left in night,
That I am here before thy sight,
10   For gifts and grace,
A burning and a shining light
            To a' this place.—

What was I, or my generation,
That I should get such exaltation?
15 I, wha deserv'd most just damnation,
            For broken laws,
Sax thousand years ere my creation,
            Thro' Adam's cause!

When from my mother's womb I fell,
20 Thou might hae plunged me deep in hell,
To gnash my gooms, and weep, and wail,
            In burning lakes,
Where damned devils roar and yell
            Chain'd to their stakes.—

25 Yet I am here, a chosen sample,
To shew thy grace is great and ample:
I'm here, a pillar o' thy temple

5-6 *no for ony gude . . . thee:* "Good works are only such as God hath commanded in His holy Word. . . . Works done by unregenerate men . . . cannot please God" (Westminster Confession, xvi).

8 *thousands . . . left in night:* Cf. 1 Thess. v. 5.

10 *gifts and grace:* Cf. Rom. xii. 6.

11-12 *a burning . . . place:* John v. 35.

13 *generation:* family, line (Biblical sense).

14 *exaltation:* Cf. Ps. lxxxix. 19-20.

17 *Sax thousand years:* the traditional dating of the creation.

18 *Adam's cause:* Cf. Rom. v. 12-19.

19-24 *When . . . stakes:* Cf. Isa. xlix. 5, xlviii. 8; on hell, Matt. xiii. 41-2, Rev. xx. 10 and xix. 20.

27 *a pillar o' thy temple:* Rev. iii. 12.

Strong as a rock,
A guide, a ruler and example
30   To a' thy flock.—

But yet—O L—d—confess I must—
At times I'm fash'd wi' fleshly lust;
And sometimes too, in warldly trust
        Vile Self gets in;
35 But thou remembers we are dust,
        Defil'd wi' sin.—

O L—d—yestreen—thou kens—wi' Meg—
Thy pardon I sincerely beg!
O may 't ne'er be a living plague,
40   To my dishonor,
And I'll ne'er lift a lawless leg
        Again upon her.—

Besides, I farther maun avow,
Wi' Leezie's lass, three times—I trow—
45 But L—d, that Friday I was fou
        When I cam near her;
Or else, thou kens, thy servant true
        Wad never steer her.—

Maybe thou lets this fleshly thorn
50 Buffet thy servant e'en and morn,

31, 37 The flow of Biblical rhetoric dries up as Willie begins to face facts.
32 *fash'd:* troubled. *fleshly lust:* Cf. Ephes. ii. 3, 1 Peter ii. 11, 2 Peter ii. 10.

33 *warldly trust:* Willie's responsibilities as valuer and arbitrator in parish farming.

35-6 *thou remembers . . . sin:* Ps. ciii. 14. The elect may, by their sins, "fall under God's fatherly displeasure"; but "they can never fall from the state of justification" (Westminster Confession, xi, xviii).

37 *yestreen:* last night.

39-40 *O may 't . . . dishonor:* i.e. through pregnancy; a practical and cowardly reading of Prov. vi. 32-3.

43 *maun avow:* must confess.   **45** *fou:* drunk.
48 *Wad never steer:* would never have roused.
49-50 *thou lets . . . morn:* Cf. 2 Cor. xii. 7-9.

Lest he o'er high and proud should turn,
        That he 's sae gifted;
If sae, thy hand maun e'en be borne
        Untill thou lift it.—

55 L—d bless thy Chosen in this place,
For here thou hast a chosen race:
But G—d, confound their stubborn face,
        And blast their name,
Wha bring thy elders to disgrace
60   And open shame.—

L—d mind Gaun Hamilton's deserts!
He drinks, and swears, and plays at cartes,
Yet has sae mony taking arts
        Wi' Great and Sma',
65 Frae G—d's ain priest the people's hearts
        He steals awa'.—

And when we chasten'd him therefore,
Thou kens how he bred sic a splore,
As set the warld in a roar
70   O' laughin at us:
Curse thou his basket and his store,
        Kail and potatoes.—

L—d hear my earnest cry and prayer
Against that Presbytry of Ayr!
75 Thy strong right hand, L—d, make it bare
        Upon their heads!

55 *thy Chosen:* Cf. Ps. xxxiii. 12; Mark xiii. 20. "I am," Burns wrote in a letter, "in perpetual warfare with that doctrine of our Reverend Priesthood . . . a kind of Spiritual Filtration or rectifying process called effectual Calling."

58 *blast:* wither, disgrace. Cf. 2 Sam. xxii. 16, Job iv. 9.

65-6 *the people's hearts . . . awa':* Cf. 2 Sam. xv. 6.

68 *bred sic a splore:* provoked such merriment.

71-2 *Curse thou his . . . potatoes:* a base version of Jehovah's curse on the wicked, Deut. xxviii. 15-19.

73 *hear my . . . prayer:* Cf. 2 Chron. vi. 19, 1 Kings viii. 28.

75 *Thy strong right hand:* Cf. Isa. lii. 10.

E

L—d visit them, and dinna spare,
　　　For their misdeeds!

O L—d my G—d, that glib-tongu'd Aiken!
80　My very heart and flesh are quaking
　To think how I sat, sweating, shaking,
　　　And p-ss'd wi' dread,
　While Auld wi' hingin lip gaed sneaking
　　　And hid his head!

85　L—d, in thy day o' vengeance try him!
　L—d visit him that did employ him!
　And pass not in thy mercy by them,
　　　Nor hear their prayer;
　But for thy people's sake destroy them,
90　　　And dinna spare!

But L—d, remember me and mine
Wi' mercies temporal and divine!
That I for grace and gear may shine,
　　　Excell'd by nane!
95　And a' the glory shall be thine!
　　　AMEN! AMEN!

77 *visit:* punish. Cf. Jer. xiv. 10.　　*dinna:* do not.
80 *My very heart . . . quaking:* an ironic adaptation of Ps. lxxxiv. 2.
83 *gaed:* went.　　**87** *pass not . . . by them:* Cf. Amos vii. 8-9, viii. 2.
93 *I for grace . . . may shine:* Cf. Phil. ii. 15; ll. 9-12 *supra.* Willie shows a
concern for property characteristic of Presbyterians but not authorised by
Calvin.　　　　　　　　　　　**94** *nane:* none.
95 *a' the glory . . . thine:* the conversion of a pious promise into a bribe.

EPITAPH ON HOLY WILLIE

Here Holy Willie's sair worn clay
　Taks up its last abode;
His saul has ta'en some other way,
　I fear, the left-hand road.

1 *sair:* sorely.　　　**2, 3** *taks, ta'en:* takes, taken.
4 *left-hand:* "sinister", leading to hell.

5   Stop! there he is as sure 's a gun,
        Poor silly body see him;
     Nae wonder he 's as black 's the grun,
        Observe wha 's standing wi' him.

     Your brunstane devilship I see
10   Has got him there before ye;
     But ha'd your nine-tail cat a wee,
        Till ance you've heard my story.

     Your pity I will not implore,
        For pity ye have nane;
15   Justice, alas! has gi'en him o'er,
        And mercy's day is gane.

     But hear me, Sir, de'il as ye are,
        Look something to your credit;
     A coof like him wou'd stain your name,
20   If it were kent ye did it.

6 *silly:* hapless, pitiful.
7 *grun:* ground, earth.
9 *brunstane:* brimstone.
11 *ha'd:* hold, withhold.   *nine-tail cat:* i.e. cat-o'-nine-tails; a whip
with knotted lashes.   *a wee:* for a moment.
12 *ance:* once.
15 *gi'en:* given.
16 *gane:* gone.
17 *de'il:* devil.
19 *coof:* fool, clown.
20 *kent:* known.

Peter Pindar

A POETICAL AND CONGRATULATORY EPISTLE TO JAMES BOSWELL ESQ. ON HIS JOURNAL OF A TOUR TO THE HEBRIDES WITH THE CELEBRATED DOCTOR JOHNSON

FEW journalistic satirists have achieved greater fame in their own lifetime than John Wolcot (1738–1819), who wrote under his *nom de guerre* "Peter Pindar". (For some details of his life see the notes to Gifford's *Epistle to Peter Pindar*, pp. 160–8.) Notorious through his personal eccentricities, the scandals (exaggerated by his enemies) of his private life, and his readiness to attack in verse any public figure—from the King or Tom Paine to the President of the Royal Society—Wolcot became a national institution. After 1782, when he first used his pseudonym on a major work, no item of public gossip was immune from his attention. George III's discovery of a louse on his dinner-plate, or the jealousies of Boswell and Mrs. Thrale over their friendship with Johnson, equally provided subject-matter for his verses. The public could not be indifferent to him—"I swear to you that my flesh creeps at his name", Coleridge remarked; they found in him a pleasure like that excited by the political caricaturists of his day, Gilray and Rowlandson.

The *Epistle to Boswell* (1786), which went through ten impressions in three years, was the first of Wolcot's literary criticisms. Johnson had been dead only two years; Boswell's *Journal*, giving a host of details about "Ursa Major" on tour in Scotland and the Hebrides (that "most dolorous country"), was published in 1785; and Wolcot, with an observant eye for sycophancy and false pride, detected a situation he could readily exploit. He was also able to give critical respectability to his attack on Boswell. Implicitly he accuses him of pandering to the taste for trivia (the indiscriminate use of which, in biography, Johnson had condemned in *Rambler* No. 60); of satisfying a love of scandal (a charge which Wordsworth later made against the *Life of Johnson*); and therefore of failing to achieve the homiletic purpose which the eighteenth century associated with biography. Made by Wolcot, of course, the indictment was hypocritical. Nevertheless, through a shrewd, tendentious selection from the trivialities which abound in Boswell's *Journal*, and a fluent, deflating sprightliness, Wolcot manages to diminish Boswell's (and the King's) claims to serious interest. The parody of Johnsonian prose in the "Postcript" is a further merit.

The text is printed from *The Works of Peter Pindar Esq.* (1824). The notes in quotation marks are Wolcot's own.

O Boswell, Bozzy, Bruce, what'er thy name,
Thou mighty shark for anecdote and fame;
Thou jackall, leading lion Johnson forth,
To eat M'Pherson 'midst his native North;
5 To frighten grave professors, with his roar,
And shake the Hebrides, from shore to shore—
All hail!—At length, ambitious Thane, thy rage,
To give one spark to Fame's bespangled page,
Is amply gratified—a thousand eyes
10 Survey thy books with rapture and suprize!
Loud, of thy Tour, a thousand tongues have spoken,
And wondered—that thy bones were never broken!
    Triumphant, thou through Time's vast gulf shalt sail,
The pilot of our literary whale;
15 Close to the classic Rambler, shalt thou cling,
Close, as a supple courtier to a king!
Fate shall not shake thee off, with all its power,
Stuck, like a bat, to some old ivied tower.
Nay, though thy Johnson ne'er had blessed thy eyes,
20 Paoli's deeds had raised thee to the skies!
Yes! his broad wing had raised thee, (no bad hack)
A tom-tit, twittering on an eagle's back.
    Thou, curious scrapmonger, shalt live in song,
When death hath stilled the rattle of thy tongue;

1 *Bruce:* Boswell claimed that, through his descent from Alexander, Earl of Kincardine, "the blood of *Bruce* flows in [his] veins" (*Johnson's Journey to the Western Islands of Scotland and Boswell's Journal of a Tour to the Hebrides with Samuel Johnson, LL.D.*, ed. R. W. Chapman (Oxford, 1930)—hereafter cited as *Journal*—p. 175, note).

4 *M'Pherson:* James Macpherson. See *supra*, p. 123, l. 87, note.

5 *To frighten . . . roar:* Johnson was alleged to have achieved this feat at the University of St. Andrews. See *Journal*, pp. 199–202.

15 *Rambler:* Boswell frequently referred to Johnson as "the Rambler", in reference to his famous series of essays (cf. *Journal*, pp. 240, 253).

20 *Paoli:* The Corsican patriot-leader, General Pasquale Paoli (1725–1807), whom Boswell celebrated in his *Account of Corsica* (1768). Boswell was "known at Edinburgh by the name of Paoli" (*Journal*, p. 237) long before his association with Johnson.

25 Even future babes to lisp thy name shall learn,
    And Bozzy join with Wood, and Tommy Hearn,
    Who drove the spiders from much prose and rhyme,
    And snatched old stories from the jaws of time.
        Sweet is thy page, I ween, that doth recite,
30 How thou and Johnson, arm in arm, one night,
    Marched through fair Edinburgh's Pactolian showers,
    Which Cloacina bountifully pours;
    Those gracious showers, that, fraught with fragrance, flow,
    And gild, like gingerbread, the world below.
35 How sweetly grumbled, too, was Sam's remark,
    "I smell you, master Bozzy, in the dark!"
    Alas! historians are confounded dull,
    A dim Boeotia reigns in every skull;
    Mere beasts of burden, broken-winded, slow,
40 Heavy as dromedaries, on they go;
    Whilst thou, a Will-o'-wisp, art here, art there,
    Wild darting coruscations every where.
        What tasteless mouth can gape, what eye can close,
    What head can nod, o'er thy enlivening prose?
45 To others' works, the works of *thy* inditing
    Are downright diamonds, to the eyes of whiting.
    Think not I flatter thee, my flippant friend;
    For well I know, that flattery would offend:
    Yet honest praise, I'm sure, thou wouldst not shun,
50 Born with a stomach to digest a tun!

26 *Wood:* Anthony à Wood (1632–95), antiquary and historian.

26 *Hearn:* Thomas Hearne (1678–1735), antiquary and editor of early English chronicles, etc.

29-34 *Sweet is . . . below:* Boswell records his embarrassment at "the evening effluvia of Edinburgh" which "assailed" Johnson's nostrils when he arrived in the capital at the beginning of their Scottish tour. The city had "no covered sewers" (*Journal*, p. 173). *Pactolian:* i.e. golden, relating to the golden sands of the Lydian river Pactolus. *Cloacina:* the Roman goddess of the sewer.

36 *I smell . . . dark:* See *Journal*, p. 173.

38 *Boeotia:* a country in central Greece which had given rise to the term "Boeotian", meaning dull-witted.

Who can refuse a smile, that reads thy page,
Where surly Sam, inflamed with Tory rage,
Nassau bescoundrels, and with anger big,
Swears, Whigs are rogues, and every rogue a Whig?
55 Who will not, too, thy pen's *minutiæ* bless,
That gives posterity the Rambler's dress?
Methinks I view his full, plain suit of brown,
The large grey bushy wig, that graced his crown;
Black worsted stockings, little silver buckles;
60 And shirt, that had no ruffles for his knuckles.
I mark the brown great-coat of cloth he wore,
That two huge Patagonian pockets bore,
Which Patagonians (wondrous to unfold!)
Would fairly both his Dictionaries hold.
65 I see the Rambler, on a large bay mare,
Just like a Centaur, every danger dare;
On a full gallop dash the yielding wind;
The colt and Bozzy scampering close behind.
        Of Lady Lochbuy, with what glee we read,
70 Who offered Sam, for breakfast, cold sheep's head;
Who, pressed and worried by this dame so civil,
Wished the sheep's head, and woman's, at the devil.
        I see you sailing both in Buchan's pot—
Now storming an old woman and her cot,

53 *Nassau bescoundrels:* "that scoundrel, king William [III]" (*Journal* p. 331).

54 *Swears, Whigs . . . Whig:* See *Journal*, pp. 342, 388.

57-64 *Methinks I . . . hold: Ibid.*, p. 171.

62 *Patagonian:* i.e. gigantic, alluding to the Indian race inhabiting southern Patagonia, said by seventeenth- and eighteenth-century travellers to be of giant size.

64 *both his Dictionaries:* Johnson's *Dictionary* was published in two folio volumes (in 1755).

65-8 *I see . . . behind:* See *Journal*, p. 363.

69-72 *Of Lady . . . devil: Ibid.*, p. 391.

73 *I see . . . pot: Ibid.*, pp. 222-3. ("Buchan's pot" was "a circular bason [formed in the rocky east coast near Slain's Castle] of large extent, surrounded with tremendous rocks".)

75   Who, terrified at each tremendous shape,
     Deemed you two demons, ready for a rape:
     I see all marvelling at M'Leod's together,
     On Sam's remarks on whey, and tanning leather:
     At Corrichatachin's, the Lord knows how,
80   I see thee, Bozzy, drunk as David's sow,
     And begging, with raised eyes and lengthened chin,
     Heaven not to damn thee for the deadly sin:
     I see, too, the stern moralist regale,
     And pen a Latin ode to Mrs. Thrale.
85   I see, without a night-cap on his head,
     Rare sight! bald Sam, in the Pretender's bed:
     I hear (what's wonderful!) unsought by studying,
     His classic dissertation upon pudding:
     Of provost Jopp, I mark the marvelling face,
90   Who gave the Rambler's freedom with a grace:
     I see, too, travelling from the *Isle* of *Egg*,
     The humble servant of a horse's leg;
     And Snip, the tailor, from the *Isle* of *Muck*,
     Who stitched in *Sky* with tolerable luck:
95   I see the horn, that drunkards must adore;
     The horn, the mighty horn of Rorie More;
     And bloody shields, that guarded hearts in quarrels,
     Now guard from rats the milk and butter barrels.

74-6 *Now storming . . . rape:* A reference to Boswell's amusing account of the travellers' visit to a peasant-hut on the side of Loch Ness (*Journal*, pp. 243-4).

77-8 *I see . . . leather:* See *Journal*, p. 324.

79-82 *At Corrichatachin's . . . sin: Ibid.*, pp. 333-4.

83-4 *I see . . . Thrale: Ibid.*, p. 261. (Hester Lynch Thrale (1741-1821), a close friend of Johnson.)

85-6 *I see . . . bed: Ibid.*, pp. 280-1.

87-8 *I hear . . . pudding: Ibid.*, pp. 397-8.

89-90 *Of provost . . . grace: Ibid.*, p. 216.

91-4 *I see . . . luck: Ibid.*, p. 310. ("The humble servant" was a blacksmith.)

95-6 *I see . . . More: Ibid.*, p. 300. ("Rorie More" was Sir Roderick Macleod.)

97-8 *And bloody . . . barrels: Ibid.*, p. 300.

Methinks, the Caledonian dame I see,
100 Familiar sitting on the Rambler's knee,
Charming, with kisses sweet, the chuckling sage;
Melting, with sweetest smiles, the frost of age;
Like Sol, who darts, at times, a cheerful ray,
O'er the wan visage of a winter's day.
105 "Do it again, my dear," I hear Sam cry,
"See, who first tires, (my charmer!) you or I."
I see thee stuffing, with a hand uncouth,
An old dried whiting in thy Johnson's mouth;
And lo! I see, with all his might and main,
110 Thy Johnson spit the whiting out again.
Rare anecdotes! 'tis anecdotes like these,
That bring thee glory, and the million please!
On these, shall future times delighted stare,
Thou charming haberdasher of small ware!
115 Stewart and Robertson from thee shall learn
The simple charms of history to discern:
To thee, fair history's palm, shall Livy yield,
And Tacitus, to Bozzy, leave the field!
Joe Miller's self, whose page such fun provokes,
120 Shall quit his shroud, to grin at Bozzy's jokes!
How are we all with rapture touched, to see,
Where, when, and at what hour, you swallowed tea!
How, once, to grace this Asiatic treat,
Came haddocks, which the Rambler could not eat!
125   Pleased, on thy book thy sovereign's eye-balls roll,
Who loves a gossip's story from his soul!

99-106 *Methinks, the . . . I: Ibid.*, p. 336.

107-110 *I see . . . again: Ibid.*, p. 194.

115 *Stewart:* apparently the drunken Scottish historian, editor of *The Edinburgh Magazine*, and reviewer, Gilbert Stuart (1742–86).

115 *Robertson:* William Robertson (1721–93), Scottish historian.

117, 118 *Livy, Tacitus:* Roman historians: Livy (59 B.C.–A.D. 17); Tacitus (b. *c.* A.D. 55).

119 *Miller:* Joseph Miller (1684–1738), an actor whose jest-book, *Joe Miller's Jests* (1739), gave rise to the term "a Joe Miller", meaning a stale joke.

125 *thy sovereign:* George III (whom Wolcot frequently satirised).

Blessed with the memory of the Persian king,
He every body knows, and every thing;
Who's dead, who's married, what poor girl beguiled,
130   Hath lost a paramour and found a child;
Which gardener hath most cabbages and peas,
And which old woman hath most hives of bees;
Which farmer boasts the most prolific sows,
Cocks, hens, geese, turkies, goats, sheep, bulls, and cows;
135   Which barber best the ladies' locks can curl;
Which house in Windsor sells the finest purl;
Which chimney-sweep best beats, in gold array,
His brush and shovel, on the first of May;
Whose dancing dogs, in rigadoons excel;
140   And whose the puppet-show, that bears the bell:
Which clever smith, the prettiest man-trap makes,
To save from thieves the royal ducks and drakes,
The Guinea hens and peacocks with their eggs,
And catch his loving subjects by the legs.
145   O! since the prince of gossips reads thy book,
To what high honours may not Bozzy look?
The sunshine of his smile may soon be thine—
Perchance, in converse thou may'st hear him shine:
Perchance, to stamp thy merit through the nation,
150   He begs of Johnson's Life, thy dedication;
Asks questions of thee, O thou lucky elf,
And kindly answers every one himself.

127 *Persian king:* Cyrus (d. 529 B.C.)

136 *purl:* gold or silver thread used for embroidery.

137-8 *chimney-sweep . . . May:* "May day" was the sweeps' traditional holiday. (See Dickens's "The First of May" in *Sketches by Boz*.)

139 *rigadoon:* i.e. a lively and rather complicated dance.

141 *man-trap:* "His majesty hath planted a number of these trusty guardians around his park at Windsor, for the benefit of the public."

150 *Johnson's Life:* Boswell had made it known in the *Journal* (cf. pp. 215 n., 242 n., 370) that he would write the biography of Johnson which he subsequently published in 1791.

151-2 *Asks questions . . . himself:* Wolcot cites Johnson's alleged comment on George III after his interview with him: "His majesty indeed was *multifarious* in his *questions;* but, thank God, he answered them all *himself.*"

Blessed with the classic learning of a college,
Our king is not a miser in his knowledge:
155 Nought in the storehouse of his brains turns musty:
No razor-wit, for want of use, grows rusty:
Whate'er his head suggests, whate'er he knows,
Free as election beer from tubs it flows!
Yet, ah! superior far!—it boasts the merit
160 Of never fuddling people with the spirit!
Say, Bozzy, when to bless our anxious sight,
When shall thy volume burst the gates of light?
O! clothed in calf, ambitious brat be born—
Our kitchins, parlours, libraries, adorn!
165 My fancy's keen anticipating eye,
A thousand charming anecdotes can spy:
I read, I read of George the learned display
On Lowth's and Warburton's immortal fray:
Of George, whose brain, if right the mark I hit,
170 Forms one huge Cyclopaedia of wit:
That holds the wisdom of a thousand ages,
And frightens all his workmen, and his pages!
O Bozzy, still thy tell-tale plan pursue:
The world is wondrous fond of something new:
175 And, let but Scandal's breath embalm the page,
It lives a welcome guest from age to age.
Not only say who breathes an arrant knave,
But who hath sneaked a rascal to his grave:
Make o'er his turf (in Virtue's cause) a rout,
180 And, like a damned good Christian, pull him out.
Without a fear on families harangue,
Say who shall lose their ears, and who shall hang;

162 *thy volume:* the projected *Life of Johnson*.

167-8 *I read . . . fray:* "His majesty's commentary on that quarrel, in which the bishop [Robert Lowth, 1710–87] and the doctor [William Warburton, 1698–1779] pelted one the other with dirt so gracefully, will be a treasure to the lovers of literature! Mr. B. hath as good as promised it to the public [*Journal*, p. 238 and note], and, we hope, means to keep his word." Boswell gave a brief account of the controversy in the *Life of Johnson* (ed. Hill-Powell, ii. 37).

Publish the demireps, and punks—nay more,
Declare what virtuous wife will be a whore.
185   Thy brilliant brain, conjecture can supply,
To charm through every leaf the eager eye.
The blue-stocking society describe,
And give thy comment on each joke and gibe:
Tell what the women are, their wit, their quality,
190   And dip them in thy streams of immortality!
Let Lord M'Donald threat thy breech to kick,
And o'er thy shrinking shoulders shake his stick;
Treat with contempt the menace of this lord,
'Tis History's province, Bozzy, to record.
195   Though Wilkes abuse thy brain, that airy mill,
And swear poor Johnson murdered by thy quill;
What's that to thee? Why, let the victim bleed—
Thy end is answered, if the nation read.
The fiddling knight, and tuneful Mrs. Thrale,
200   Who frequent hobbed or nobbed with Sam, in ale,
Snatch up the pen (as thirst of fame inspires!)
To write his jokes and stories by their fires;
Then why not thou, each joke and tale enrol,
Who like a watchful cat before a hole,

183 *Demireps and punks:* i.e. women of doubtful reputation, and prostitutes.

187 *blue-stocking society:* "A club, mostly composed of learned ladies, to which Mr. B. was admitted." (Cf. *Life of Johnson*, iv. 108.)

191-2 *Let Lord . . . stick:* "A letter of severe remonstrance was sent to Mr. B. who, in consequence, omitted, in the second edition of his Journal, what is so generally pleasing to the public, *viz.* the scandalous passages relative to this nobleman [Sir Alexander Macdonald]." (See *Journal*, pp. 254-5.)

195 *Wilkes:* John Wilkes (1727–97), notorious radical politician vigorously distrusted by Johnson.

199-202 *The fiddling . . . fires:* "Sir John Hawkins, who (as well as Mrs. Thrale, now Madame Piozzi) threatens us with the life of the late lexicographer." Hawkins (1719–98) published his *Life of Johnson* in 1787, and Mrs. Thrale (Piozzi) her *Anecdotes of the late Samuel Johnson* in 1786. (Wolcot's satire entitled, *Bozzy and Piozzi; or, the British Biographers* appeared in 1786.)

205 Full twenty years (inflamed with lettered pride)
    Didst mousing sit, before Sam's mouth so wide,
    To catch as many scraps as thou wert able—
    A very Lazarus at the rich man's table?
    What though against thee porters bounce the door,
210 And bid thee hunt for secrets there no more;
    With pen and ink so ready at thy coat,
    Exciseman-like, each syllable to note,
    That given to printers' devils (a precious load!)
    On wings of print comes flying all abroad?
215 Watch then the venal valets—smack the maids,
    And try with gold to make them rogues and jades:
    Yet should their honesty thy bribes resent;
    Fly to thy fertile genius, and invent:
    Like old Voltaire, who placed his greatest glory,
220 In cooking up an entertaining story;
    Who laughed at truth, whene'er her simple tongue
    Would snatch amusement from a tale or song.
        O! whilst amid the anecdotic mine,
    Thou labour'st hard to bid thy hero shine,
225 Run to Bolt Court, exert thy Curl-like soul,
    And fish for golden leaves from hole to hole:
    Find when he ate, and drank, and coughed, and sneezed—
    Let all his motions in thy book be squeezed:
    On tales, however strange, impose thy claw;
230 Yes, let thy amber lick up every straw;
    Sam's nods, and winks, and laughs, will form a treat;
    For all that breathes of Johnson must be great!

208 *Lazarus:* See Luke, xvi. 20-21.

209 *What though . . . door:* "This is literally true—Nobody is at home.—
Our great people want the taste to relish Mr. Boswell's vehicles to immortality. Though in London, poor Bozzy is in a desert."

219 *Voltaire:* French philosopher, historian and critic (1694-1778).

225 *Bolt Court:* "In Fleet Street, where the doctor lived [from 1776] and died."

225 *Curl:* Edmund Curll (1675-1747), "the bookseller, frequently bribed people to hunt the temples of Cloacina, for Pope's and Swift's letters." He had an infamous reputation for publishing scandal.

Blessed be thy labours, most adventurous Bozzy,
Bold rival of Sir John, and Dame Piozzi;
235 Heavens! with what laurels shall thy head be crowned!
A grove, a forest, shall thy ears surround!
Yes! whilst the Rambler shall a comet blaze,
And gild a world of darkness with his rays,
Thee too, that world, with wonderment, shall hail,
240 A lively, bouncing cracker at his tail!

POSTSCRIPT

As Mr. Boswell's Journal has afforded such universal pleasure by the
relation of minute incidents, and the great moralist's opinion of men
and things, during his northern tour; it will be adding greatly to the
anecdotical treasury, as well as making Mr. B. happy, to communi-
5 cate part of a dialogue that took place between Dr. Johnson, and the
author of this congratulatory epistle, a few months before the doctor
paid the great debt of nature. The doctor was very cheerful that
day; had on a black coat and waistcoat, a black plush pair of breeches,
and black worsted stockings; a handsome grey wig, a shirt, a muslin
10 neck-cloth, a black pair of buttons in his shirt sleeves, a pair of shoes,
ornamented with the very identical little buckles that accompanied
the philosopher to the Hebrides; his nails were very neatly pared,
and his beard fresh shaved with a razor fabricated by the ingenious
Mr. Savigny.

15 P.P. Pray, doctor, what is your opinion of Mr. Boswell's literary
powers?

Johnson. Sir, my opinion is, that whenever Bozzy expires, he will
create no *vacuum* in the region of literature—he seems strongly
affected by the *cacoëthes scribendi;* wishes to be thought a *rara avis;* and
20 in truth so he is—your knowledge in ornithology, Sir, will easily
discover, to what species of bird I allude. [*Here the doctor shook his
head and laughed.*]

P.P. What think you, Sir, of his account of Corsica?—of his
character of Paoli?

14 *Savigny:* John H. Savigny published his *Treatise on the use and manage-
ment of a Razor* in 1786 (?).

Johnson. Sir, he hath made a mountain of a wart. But Paoli has   25
virtues. The account is a farrago of disgusting egotism and pompous
inanity.

P.P. I have heard it whispered, doctor, that should you die before
him, Mr. B. means to write your life.

Johnson. Sir, he cannot mean me so irreparable an injury.—Which   30
of us shall die first, is only known to the Great Disposer of events;
but were I sure that James Boswell would write *my* life, I do not
know whether I would not anticipate the measure, by taking *his*.

[*Here he made three or four strides across the room, and returned to his
chair with violent emotion.*]   35

P.P. I am afraid that he means to do you the favour.

Johnson. He dares not—he would make a scarecrow of me. I give
him liberty to fire his blunderbuss in *his own* face, but not to murder
me. Sir, I heed not his αὐτός ἔφα—Boswell write my life! whythe
fellow possesses not abilities for writing the life of an *ephemeron*.   40

28 *I have . . . ephemeron:* See l. 150 n. Boswell claimed (*Journal*, p. 370 n.)
that, Johnson knew of his intention to write the *Life* and had "communi-
cated to [him] . . . many particulars of his life, which probably could not
otherwise have been preserved."

39 αὐτὸς ἔφα: *ipse dixit*, assertion of authority.

John Courtenay

A POETICAL AND PHILOSOPHICAL ESSAY ON
THE FRENCH REVOLUTION ADDRESSED TO
THE RIGHT HON. EDMUND BURKE

COURTENAY (1741–1816), Member of Parliament for Tamworth and well
known in the Commons for his ironic wit, was an ardent opponent of
despotism wherever he saw it. This accounted for his part in the proceedings
against Warren Hastings on the one hand; on the other, for his fervent
support of the French revolutionaries. His sympathy with them—first

expressed in *Philosophical Reflections on the late Revolution in France* (1790)—brought him into conflict with Edmund Burke, whose *Reflections on the Revolution in France* (1790) savagely denounced the Revolution, its philosophy, and the significance which had been claimed for it as an example to Britain. Courtenay, in his *Poetical and Philosophical Essay* (1793), was one of the seventy or more writers who published their replies to Burke's *Reflections* in the three years following its appearance (see James T. Boulton, *The Language of Politics in the Age of Wilkes and Burke*, 1963).

The poem from which an extract is printed below is prefaced by a prose statement of Courtenay's faith in the revolutionists and his conviction that "the freedom of mankind" depended on the success of their armies. The poem itself is valuable evidence of the survival of the Augustan manner in satire at the end of the century. Courtenay writes fluently in the heroic couplet; with an irony sharpened by his radical views he links Burke with a long tradition of alleged obscurantism (embracing Laud, Filmer, Sacheverell, and the Roman Catholic Church); and, very effectively, he uses a detailed knowledge of Burke's *Reflections* to pillory the political philosophy and the literary manner of that book.

> Ye Nuns and Capuchins, begin the song,
> In EDMUND's praise, your sweetest notes prolong;
> EDMUND, whom whiggish strains delight no more,
> Your ravish'd joys now labours to restore:
> 5   Mitres and thrones again with lustre shine,
> And George and Louis rule by right divine.
> No more in tropes sublime with patriot spleen,
> He *hurls* a Monarch, shoves aside a Queen:
> When *phantom-struck*, he view'd with frantic air,
> 10   A Lawyer's seal usurp the regal Chair.

1-2 *Ye Nuns . . . prolong:* A mock invocation to representatives of the obscurantism with which Courtenay identifies Burke.

3 *Edmund, whom . . . more:* There had been a split among the Whigs; the "old Whigs" led by the Duke of Portland abandoned the "new Whigs" led by Fox, and joined the Government; and Burke, in 1792, formally took his seat on the Government benches (cf. l. 107 below).

7-10 *No more . . . Chair:* a reference to Burke's apparent inhumanity in his remarks on George III's insanity at the time of the Regency crisis, 1788-89, and to his strident opposition to an "elective" (as distinct from an hereditary) monarchy.

8 *hurls:* i.e. throws (as in wrestling).

Ye Tories, hear your new Sacheverel preach,
And a whole People for their crimes impeach;
Exulting read what the old Whig indites;
"In arms we're ready to abjure our rights;
15 Sceptres from royal hands, no more we'll sever,
But kneel and cry—tho' tyrants, reign for ever!"
Cashiering Kings is treason by *that* law,
Which gave the Crown to Brunswick and Nassau:
And lest posterity assert their claim,
20 We boldly here renounce it in their name.
    To Nobles, Priests, ye People bow the head,
Tho' spurn'd by those, who by your toils are fed:
Ye rich and great, who weep your fancy'd woes,
Look up to Heav'n, and give your souls repose.
25 Releas'd from sin, you'll reach your kindred skies,
As sea-born vapours drop their salts and rise.
Worn down by pleasure, impotent with pain,
Spurn the frail flesh, and Paradise regain.
Sudden as Quixote's balsam, mystic grace,

11 *Sacheverel:* Dr. Henry Sacheverell (1674–1724), the high Anglican whose virulent support for the Established Church and opposition to the Dissenters earned him the support of the Tories and the enmity of the Whigs.

14-20 *In arms . . . name:* Dr. Richard Price whose sermon, on 4 November 1789, provided the immediate impetus for Burke's *Reflections,* claimed that the English nation had the right to choose their own governors and "to cashier them for misconduct". Burke's reply was that the nation rejected Price's "bill of rights" and would "resist the practical assertion of it with their lives and fortunes". Furthermore, "So far is it from being true, that we acquired a right by the [1688] Revolution to elect our kings, that if we had possessed it before, the English nation did at that time most solemnly renounce and abdicate it, for themselves, and for all their posterity for ever" (*Reflections,* Everyman edn., 1910, pp. 14, 18).

18 *Brunswick and Nassau:* George I and William of Orange.

29 *Quixote's balsam:* Cervantes' *Don Quixote* was a fruitful source of satiric jibes at Burke's veneration of chivalry, among writers' who denounced the *Reflections* (cf. l. 35 below, "your Knight-Errant"). Quixote carried "an earthen jar of precious balsam" as a protection against wounds received on his chivalric missions.

30 Will terrors, whims, and mental pangs efface;
    Since earthly joys you're doom'd to taste no more,
    In faith's balloon to brighter regions soar;
    To sated appetite an edge supply,
    And beg celestial manna, from *on high*.

35 To sooth vain sorrows, your Knight-Errant flies,
    With real grief he scorns to sympathise;
    Dramatic woe in splendid fiction's dress,
    He bodies forth—to weep at the distress!
    Of pomps and vanities bewails the loss,

40 Cries o'er the Ribband, and adores the Cross.
    Ye poor and wretched, suffer and be dumb,
    And wait for happiness in worlds to come;
    With meekness, patience, your sad duties fill,
    What's cold and hunger to ideal ill?

45   When vice is gross, he owns 'tis mean and base,
    But polish'd vice assumes bright Virtue's grace;
    By Dovey's art, as spurious diamonds shine,

32 *faith's balloon:* probably an allusion to recent aeronautical experiments, which culminated in the Channel flight in a balloon by Blanchard and Jeffries in 1785.

36-8 *With real . . . distress:* Paine, among others, makes a similar charge: that Burke lavished attention on the miseries of Marie Antoinette—"a tragedy-victim expiring in show"—but ignored "the real prisoner of misery" dying in jail. In the *Reflections*, according to Paine, "facts are manufactured for the sake of show, and accommodated to produce, through the weakness of sympathy, a weeping effect" (*Rights of Man*, Everyman edn., 1906, pp. 24, 22).

41-4 *Ye poor . . . ill?:* Cf. Burke, *Reflections:* "[The body of the people] must labour to obtain what by labour can be obtained; and when they find, as they commonly do, the success disproportioned to the endeavour, they must be taught their consolation in the final proportions of eternal justice" (pp. 240-1).

45-6 *When vice . . . grace:* Cf. Burke, *Reflections:* "It is gone, that sensibility of principle, that chastity of honour . . . which ennobled whatever it touched, and under which vice itself lost half its evil, by losing all its grossness" (p. 73).

47 *Dovey:* A Goldsmith named Richard Dovey entered his trademark in the Assay Office at Goldsmiths' Hall in March 1773.

And boast the splendour of Golconda's mine.
Vice decks a Lord, but ill becomes a Swain;
50 Charming at Court, but odious on the Plain:
As poisons scented with nice chymic skill,
Delight the sense, and lose their pow'r to kill:
Such EDMUND's logic, such his moral page!
Fit for the bar, the pulpit, and the stage.
55   But lo! he burns with more than priestly zeal,
To prove the Church preserves the Commonweal;
Search the historic page—the Church, we find,
"The first, the last, the midst in every mind."
By blood, by crimes, and theologic hate,
60 She proudly rose, the MOLOC of the State.
By Superstition's aid pursu'd her plan,
The bane of reason, and the foe of man.
Above the clouds, she rests her starry throne,
Yet humbly makes this vale of tears her own.
65 Around the State her harlot arms she flings,
Exhausts its strength, relaxes all its springs:
The palm's rich juice, thus savage Indians drain,
And leave it withering on the desert plain.
She wafts contagion by her venom'd breath,
70 And widely spreads the principle of death.

48 *Golconda:* the old name for Hyderabad, formerly celebrated for its diamonds; thus synonymous with great wealth.

50 *Charming at . . . Plain:* Courtenay subtly identifies Burke with the world of aristocratic pretensions through allusions to the language used by "Papillia" in Pope's *Epistle to a Lady* (1735), ll. 37-40.

51 *chymic:* i.e. alchemic.

54 *Fit for . . . stage:* Cf. Pope, *Epilogue to the Satires* (1738), Dialogue II, 1. 210: "Safe from the Bar, the Pulpit, and the Throne". The substitution of "stage" for "Throne" harmonises with Courtenay's attack on Burke's "dramatic" devices (see above, l. 37).

58 *The first . . . mind:* Cf. Burke, *Reflections:* "our church establishment . . . is first, and last, and midst in our minds" (pp. 88-9).

The poison'd vest o'er all mankind she throws,
A fatal gift pregnant with human woes.
—But *here*, she rears her mitr'd front with grace,
While Court and Parliament admire her face.
75 Exacts her tythes, her right divine of spoil,
To tax hard industry, and check the soil:
And waits till vain philosophy expires,
With the law's torch to light up Smithfield's fires.
     With due encomium, saintly EDMUND tells,
80 How cloyster'd sages dignify their cells;
Quibble on oaths, prevaricate by rule,
To guard the system of their gothic school;
Lest innovation shed a baneful light,
And spoil the darkness of their monkish night.
85   Behold *his* puff'd Divine with pompous air,
Drives the pert youngster, round the world to stare
At pictures, ladies, statues, saints and kings,
And form his morals by such charming things.
At length the pilgrim hears his pupil call,
90 Thou faithful servant—lo, a Bishop's stall!
A solemn Swiss round whom the rabble gape,
Thus leads about a brisk fantastic ape,

71 *poison'd vest:* The shirt of Nessus was infected by the poisoned arrow with which Hercules killed him; later the wearing of this shirt caused Hercules' own death.

73-4 *But here . . . face:* Cf. Burke, *Reflections:* "we have not relegated religion (like something we are ashamed to show) to obscure municipalities, or rustic villages. No! we will have her to exalt her mitred front in courts and parliaments" (p. 100).

78 *Smithfield:* the open space outside the City of London where heretics were burned in the sixteenth century.

79-82 *With due . . . school:* For Burke's apology for monastic landlords see the *Reflections*, pp. 156-9.

85-8 *Behold his . . . things:* A satiric reference to the aristocratic "Grand Tour" and to Burke's statement: "when our youth, leaving schools and universities, . . . visit other countries, instead of old domestics whom we have seen as governors to principal men from other parts, three-fourths of those who go abroad with our young nobility and gentlemen are ecclesiastics" (*Reflections*, p. 96).

With phyz demure, contrasts his comrade's play,
Till countless pence his social toils repay.
95   His clinquant trade the dazzling Sophist plys,
And bids exploded themes with lustre rise.
O'er FILMER's dirt a brilliant hue he flings,
The meteor gilds the bog from whence it springs:
With specious art refines his spurious ore,
100 And gives it colour, but he gives no more.
Splendid perversions fancy's rays supply,
As light refracted paints a wat'ry sky.
Soaring in mystic prose, 'bove flights in rhyme,
Th' obscure he proves one source of the sublime.
105 Imagination's dupe from earliest youth,
His glittering page was never dull'd by truth.
Himself a host;—now from his party fled,
Mambrino's helmet blazing on his head;
He views thro' chivalry's prophetic eye,
110 Ten thousand swords by vital instinct fly,
To guard his Saint; for love's chaste star had shed
A holy radiance round her royal head.

95 *clinquant:* i.e. glittering.

97 *Filmer:* Sir Robert Filmer (d. 1653); to the radical mind he was the archetypal apologist for the divine right of kings in his *Patriarcha* (1680).

98 *The meteor . . . bog:* Cf. *The Vanity of Human Wishes*, p. 81, l. 76, note.

104 *Th' obscure . . . sublime.* Cf. Burke, *A Philosophical Enquiry into . . . the Sublime and Beautiful*, (ed. J. T. Boulton, 1958, p. 58): "terror is in all cases whatsoever . . . the ruling principle of the sublime"; "to make any thing very terrible, obscurity seems in general to be necessary".

108 *Mambrino:* the pagan king, in *Orlando Furioso*, whose magic helmet is acquired by Rinaldo. Courtenay was probably alluding to the incident in *Don Quixote* where the hero mistakes the brass basin on the barber's head for Mambrino's helmet, and gets possession of it.

109-12 *He views . . . head:* An allusion to possibly the most famous passage in the *Reflections*, the "apostrophe" to Marie Antoinette; there, with quasi-religious fervour, Burke recalls seeing her in 1774 and laments her present defenceless plight. "I thought ten thousand swords must have leaped from their scabbards to avenge even a look that threatened her with insult. But the age of chivalry is gone" (p. 73).

In these degenerate days, how vain his hope,
Can he revive Don Quixote and the Pope?
115 Yet in his ear fame's trumpet seems to sound,
And still with LAUD, he treads on holy ground;
O'er thrones polluted flings a beam of glory,
In faith a Zealot, and in Creed a Tory. . . .

116 *Laud:* the seventeenth-century archbishop William Laud(1573–1645), who would be repugnant to Courtenay for his unyielding support for Divine Right and the Anglican Church.

From

THE ANTI-JACOBIN; OR, WEEKLY EXAMINER

SOME of the most assured satire of a political kind between Pope and Byron appeared in the weekly numbers of *The Anti-Jacobin* (1797–8). It was written in the main by William Gifford (the editor), George Canning, and John Hookham Frere. The poems—which include imitations of Horace, parodies (of Southey, Payne Knight and Erasmus Darwin), and the serious work (of 465 lines) *New Morality*, among others—were sometimes written jointly; all the writers mentioned contributed to *New Morality*. What united them was their detestation of "Jacobinism"; any sign of sympathy with the French revolutionists or the "philosophes", or any evidence of what they considered unrestrained emotionalism, provided targets for their satire.

Parody was a favourite weapon. Its purpose was twofold, as suggested by the editor's introductory remarks: "we shall select from time to time, from among those effusions of the *Jacobin* Muse which happen to fall in our way, such pieces as may serve to illustrate some one of the principles, on which the poetical, as well as the political doctrine of the NEW SCHOOL is established . . . accompanying [some prefatory remarks] with an humble production of our own, in Imitation of the Poem itself, and in further illustration of its principle." The parody had, then, a poetical and a political object: to ridicule bad writing (as well as giving pleasure through the parodist's literary ingenuity) and to censure wrong principles. *New Morality*

—from which an extract is printed below—is explicit about these objectives in its opening lines:

> From mental mists to purge a nation's eyes;
> To animate the weak, unite the wise;
> To trace the deep infection, that pervades
> The crowded town, and taints the rural shades;
> To mark how wide extends the mighty waste
> O'er the fair realms of Science, Learning, Taste;
> To drive and scatter all the brood of lies,
> And chase the varying falsehood as it flies;
> The long arrears of ridicule to pay,
> To drag reluctant Dullness back to day.

In their rhythm and phrasing, as well as through specific reference, the poets acknowledge their debt to Pope; their vigour, trenchant irony, and verbal control enable them to pay it handsomely.

The texts are printed from the original *Anti-Jacobin*; significant variations in the text as reprinted in *Poetry of the Anti-Jacobin*, 1799, are recorded. Notes shown in quotation marks are the authors' own.

I

(Imitation)

Sapphics

The Friend of Humanity and the Knife-Grinder

[In Robert Southey's *Poems* (1797) there appeared the following piece, entitled "The Widow, Sapphics".

> Cold was the night wind, drifting fast the snow fell,
> Wide were the downs and shelterless and naked,
> When a poor wanderer struggled on her journey,
>   Weary and way-sore.
>
> Dreary were the downs, more dreary her reflections;
> Cold was the night-wind, colder was her bosom:
> She had no home, the world was all before her,
>   She had no shelter.
>
> Fast o'er the heath a chariot rattled by her,
> "Pity me!" feebly cried the lonely wanderer.
> "Pity me, strangers! lest with cold and hunger
>   Here I should perish.

"Once I had friends, but they have all forsook me!
Once I had parents—they are now in heaven!
I had a home once—I had once a husband—
    Pity me, strangers!

"I had a home once—I had once a husband—
I am a widow poor and broken-hearted!"
Loud blew the wind, unheard was her complaining,
    On drove the chariot.

Then on the snow she laid her down to rest her;
She heard a horseman—"Pity me!" she groaned out;
Loud was the wind, unheard was her complaining,
    On went the horseman.

Worn out with anguish, toil and cold and hunger,
Down sunk the wanderer, sleep had seized her senses,
There did the traveller find her in the morning;
    God had released her.

The parody that follows, by George Canning and John Hookham Frere,
was published in No. 2 of *The Anti-Jacobin*, 27 November 1797.]

THE FRIEND OF HUMANITY AND THE KNIFE-GRINDER

FRIEND OF HUMANITY

"Needy Knife-grinder! whither are you going?
Rough is the road, your Wheel is out of order—
Bleak blows the blast;—your hat has got a hole in't,
    So have your breeches.

5   "Weary Knife-grinder! little think the proud ones,
Who in the coaches roll along the turnpike—
—road, what hard work 'tis crying all day "Knives and
    Scissars to grind O!"

"Tell me, Knife-grinder, how you came to grind knives?
10 Did some rich man tyrannically use you?
Was it the 'Squire? or Parson of the Parish?
    Or the Attorney?

"Was it the 'Squire for killing of his Game? or
Covetous Parson for his Tythes distraining?
15 Or roguish Lawyer made you lose your little
    All in a law-suit?

"(Have you not read the Rights of Man, by TOM PAINE?)
Drops of compassion tremble on my eye-lids,
Ready to fall, as soon as you have told your
20   Pitiful story."

KNIFE-GRINDER

"Story! God bless you! I have none to tell, Sir,
Only last night a-drinking at the Chequers,
This poor old hat and breeches, as you see, were
                                          Torn in a scuffle.

25   "Constables came up for to take me into
Custody; they took me before the Justice;
Justice OLDMIXON put me in the Parish—
                                          -stocks for a Vagrant.

"I should be glad to drink your Honour's health in
30   A Pot of Beer, if you will give me Sixpence;
But for my part, I never love to meddle
                                          With Politics, Sir."

FRIEND OF HUMANITY

"*I* give thee Sixpence! I will see thee damn'd first—
Wretch! whom no sense of wrongs can rouse to vengeance–
35   Sordid, unfeeling, reprobate, degraded,
                                          Spiritless outcast!"

(*Kicks the Knife-grinder, overturns his Wheel, and exit in a transport of republican enthusiasm and universal philanthropy.*)

The Friend of Humanity: a nickname given to George Tierney (1761–1830), M.P. for Southwark.

17 *Have you . . . Paine:* Thomas Paine (1737–1809) published his *Rights of Man* (Part I, 1791; Part II, 1792) in reply to Burke's *Reflections on the Revolution in France* (1790). Its popularity was immediate and T. J. Mathias (*Pursuits of Literature,* 1797). observed that "our peasantry now read the *Rights of Man* on mountains, and moors, and by the wayside".

II

NEW MORALITY

[In the following extract ll. 119–57 are by Canning; ll. 158–67 by Frere; and ll. 168–248 by Canning.]

> . . . Sweet SENSIBILITY, that dwells enshrin'd
120 In the fine foldings of the feeling mind;—
> With delicate *Mimosa's* sense endu'd,
> That shrinks instinctive from a hand too rude;
> Or, like the *Pimpernel*, whose prescient flow'r
> Shuts her soft leaves at evening's chilly hour.
125 Sweet Child of sickly fancy—Her of yore
> From her lov'd *France* ROUSSEAU to exile bore;
> And while midst lakes and mountains wild he ran
> Full of himself, and shunn'd the haunts of Man,
> Taught her o'er each lone vale and Alpine steep
130 To lisp the stories of his wrongs, and weep;
> Taught her to cherish still in either eye,
> Of tender tears a plentiful supply,
> And pour them in the brooks that babbled by—
> Taught her to mete by rule her feelings strong,
135 False by degrees, and delicately wrong.
> For the crush'd Beetle, *first*—the widow'd Dove,
> And all the warbled sorrows of the grove.
> *Next* for poor suff'ring *Guilt*—and, *last* of all,
> For Parents, Friends, a King and Country's fall.

123 *Pimpernel*] *anagallis 1799*
124 soft leaves . . . hour] soft petals at the approaching shower *1799*
134 Taught her . . . her] Taught by nice scales to mete her *1799*
135 delicately] exquisitely *1799*

---

126 *Rousseau:* Jean-Jacques Rousseau (1712–78), the French philosopher who went to Switzerland to escape prosecution after the publication of *Émile* (1762). His philosophy gave prominence to sentiment, the individual, sensibility, and sympathy with Nature.
134 *mete:* i.e. measure.

140   Mark her fair Votaries—Prodigal of Grief,
          With cureless pangs, and woes that mock relief,
          Droop in soft sorrow o'er a faded flow'r;
          O'er a dead Jack-Ass pour the pearly show'r—
          But hear unmov'd of *Loire's* ensanguin'd flood,
145   Choak'd up with slain;—of *Lyons* drench'd in blood;
          Of Crimes that blot the Age, the World with shame,
          Foul crimes, but sicklied o'er with Freedom's name;
          Altars and Thrones subverted, social life
          Trampled to earth—the Husband from the Wife,
150   Parent from Child, with ruthless fury torn—
          Of Talents, Honour, Virtue, Wit, forlorn,
          In friendless exile—of the wise and good
          Staining the daily Scaffold with their blood—
          Of savage cruelties, that scare the mind—
155   The rage of madness with Hell's lust combin'd—
          Of Hearts torn reeking from the mangled breast,
          They hear—and hope that ALL IS FOR THE BEST.

          FOND hope!—but JUSTICE sanctifies the pray'r—
          JUSTICE—Here Satire strike, 'twere sin to spare—
160   Not She in British Courts that takes her stand,
          The dawdling balance dangling in her hand,
          Adjusting punishments to Fraud and Vice
          With scrup'lous quirks, and disquisition nice—

143 *O'er a . . . show'r:* "Vide [Sterne's] Sentimental Journey." (See sections entitled "The Bidet" and "Nampont".)

144-7 *But hear . . . name:* Here and in the lines that follow, the reference is to the bloodshed during the period of "The Terror", 1793-4. At Nantes about 4,000 people were killed in four months, some by being sent out on the Loire in a boat which was deliberately sunk; mass executions were carried out at Lyons.

152 *wise and good:* Cf. Milton, Sonnet XII, l. 12: "who loves [Liberty] must first be wise and good".

157 *All is . . . best:* An ironic reference to the "optimistic" philosophy associated with the names of Leibnitz, Shaftesbury and Pope (in the *Essay on Man*), and ridiculed by Voltaire in *Candide* (1759).

163 *quirk:* "subtilty; nicety; artful distinction" (Johnson).

But firm, erect, with keen reverted glance
165 Th' avenging Angel of regen'rate *France*,
Who visits antient sins on modern times,
And punishes the POPE for CÆSAR's crimes.
Such is the lib'ral Justice which presides
In these our days, and modern Patriots guides—
170 Justice, whose blood-stain'd Book one sole Decree,
One Statute fills—"the People shall be Free."
Free by what means?—by folly, madness, guilt,
By boundless rapines, blood in oceans spilt;
By Confiscation, in whose sweeping toils
175 The poor Man's pittance with the rich Man's spoils,
Mix'd in one common mass, are swept away—
To glut the short-liv'd Tyrant of the day.
By Laws, Religion, Morals all o'erthrown,
—Rouse then, ye Sov'reign People, claim your own—
180 The License that enthrals, the Truth that blinds,
The Wealth that starves you, and the Pow'r that grinds.
—So Justice bids—'twas her enlighten'd doom,
LOUIS, thy head devoted to the tomb—
'Twas Justice claim'd, in that accursed hour,
185 The fatal forfeit of too lenient pow'r.
Mourn for the Man we may—but for the King—
Freedom, oh! Freedom's such a charming thing.

183 thy head] thy holy head *1799*

---

167 *And punishes . . . crimes:* "The Manes of VERCENGETORIX are supposed to have been very much gratified by the Invasion of Italy and the Plunder of the Roman Territory. The defeat of the Burgundians is to be revenged on the modern inhabitants of Switzerland.—But the Swiss were a Free People, defending their Liberties against a Tyrant. Moreover, they happened to be in Alliance with France at the time. No matter, *Burgundy* is since become a Province of France, and the French have acquired a property in all the injuries and defeats which the People of that Country may have sustained, together with a title to revenge and retaliation to be exercised in the present, or any future centuries, as may be found most glorious and convenient."

183 *Louis:* Louis XVI of France, executed 21 January 1793.

"MUCH may be said on both sides."—Hark! I hear
A well-known voice that murmurs in my ear—
190   The voice of CANDOUR—Hail! most solemn Sage,
Thou driv'ling Virtue of this Moral Age,
Candour, which softens Party's headlong rage.
Candour—which spares its foes—nor e'er descends
With bigot zeal to combat for its friends.
195   Candour—which loves in see-saw strain to tell
Of acting foolishly, but meaning well:
Too nice to praise by wholesale, or to blame,
Convinc'd that all men's motives are the same;
And finds, with keen discriminating sight,
200   BLACK's not *so* black—nor WHITE *so very* white.

"Fox, to be sure, was vehement and wrong—
"But then PITT's words, you'll own, were *rather* strong.
"Great Men will have their foibles—'twas just so
"With FOX and PITT full forty years ago.
205   "So WALPOLE, PULTENEY—Factions in all times
"Have had their follies, Ministers their crimes."

GIVE me th' avow'd, th' erect, the manly Foe
Bold I can meet—perhaps may turn his blow;

203 Great Men . . . 'twas] Both must be blamed, both pardon'd;—'twas
1799

---

188 *Much may . . . sides:* Cf. Addison, *Spectator* No. 122: "Sir Roger told them . . . that much might be said on both sides."

190 *Candour:* "sweetness of temper, kindness" (Johnson). (Cf. Johnson, *Preface to Shakespeare:* "that bigotry which sets candour higher than truth".)

201 *Fox:* Charles James Fox (1749–1806), prominent Whig politician who sympathised with the French revolutionists and frequently disputed Pitt's policy towards France.

202 *Pitt:* William Pitt (1759–1806), Prime Minister, 1783–1801.

204 *With Fox . . . ago:* Henry Fox (1705–74) and William Pitt, 1st Earl of Chatham (1708–78), political rivals in the 1750's.

205 *Walpole:* Sir Robert Walpole (1676–1745), Prime Minister, 1721–42.

205 *Pulteney:* William Pulteney, Earl of Bath (1684–1764), anti-Walpole politician; in the 1720's he led the group of discontented Whigs called "the patriots".

But of all plagues, good Heav'n, thy wrath can send,
210 Save, save, oh! save me from the *Candid* Friend!

"Barras loves plunder—Merlin takes a bribe—
"What then?—Shall Candour these good men proscribe?
"No! ere we join the loud-accusing throng,
"Prove—not the facts—but that *they thought them wrong*.

215 "Why hang O'Quigley?—he, misguided man,
"In sober thought his Country's weal *might* plan.
"And, though his deep-laid Treason sapp'd the Throne,
"*Might* act from *taste in morals*, all his own."

Peace to such Reasoners—let them have their way,
220 Shut their dull eyes against the blaze of day—
Priestley's a Saint, and Stone a Patriot still;
And La Fayette a Hero, if they will.

I Love the bold uncompromising mind,
Whose principles are fix'd, whose views defin'd:
225 Who, sick of modern cant, discredits quite
All *taste* in morals, innate sense of right,

217 And, though . . . Treason] And, while his deep-wrought Treason *1799*
225 Who, sick . . . quite] Who scouts and scorns, in canting Candour's spite *1799*

---

211 *Barras:* Vicomte de Barras (1755–1829), a French revolutionary leader alleged to have adopted revolutionary politics as a means of escaping from his debts.

211 *Merlin:* not identified.

215 *O'Quigley:* James O'Coigly (otherwise Quigley) who was tried for treasonable correspondence with the enemy in May 1798, and executed (see *State Trials*, ed. T. J. Howell, 1819, Vol. 26).

221 *Priestley:* Joseph Priestley (1733–1804), theologian, scientist, and political radical. His crime in the eyes of *The Anti-Jacobin* would be his out-spoken support of the French Revolution.

221 *Stone:* Francis Stone (1738–1813), Unitarian controversialist; he too advocated the French cause, and, like Priestley, published an attack on Burke's *Reflections on the Revolution in France*.

222 *La Fayette:* Marquis de La Fayette (1757–1834), prominent in the early stages of the Revolution as commander of the National Guard and a prime mover of the "Declaration of the Rights of Man".

And Nature's impulse, all uncheck'd by art,
And feelings fine, that float about the heart.
Content for good men's guidance, bad men's awe,
230   On moral truth to rest, and gospel law;
Who owns, when Traitors feel th' avenging rod,
Just retribution, and the hand of God—
Who hears the groans through *Olmutz* roofs that ring,
Of him who chain'd, and who betray'd his King—
235   Hears unappall'd—though Freedom's Zealots preach—
Unmov'd, unsoften'd by F–TZP–TR–K's Speech;
That Speech on which the melting Commons hung
"While truths divine came mended from his tongue"—

234 him who . . . his] him who mock'd, misled, betray'd his *1799*
235 Freedom's] factious *1799*

225-8 *Who, sick . . . heart.* Sympathisers with the French Revolution made similar protests against Burke's alleged reliance on an intuitive sense of rightness in his *Reflections.* Cf. Mary Wollstonecraft: "A kind of mysterious instinct is *supposed* to reside in the soul, that instantaneously discerns truth, without the tedious labour of ratiocination. This instinct . . . has been termed *common sense,* and more frequently, *sensibility;* it has been *supposed* . . . to reign paramount over the other faculties of the mind, and to be an authority from which there is no appeal (*A Vindication of the Rights of Man,* 1790, p. 64).

233-7 *Who hears . . . hung.* "The speech of General Fitzpatrick, on his motion for an Address of the House of Commons to the Emperor of Germany [on 16 December 1796], to demand the deliverance of M. La Fayette from the prison of Olmutz, was one of the most dainty pieces of oratory that ever drew tears from a crowded gallery, and the clerks at the table. It was really quite moving to hear the General talk of religion, conjugal fidelity, and 'such branches of learning'. There were a few who laughed indeed, but that was thought hard-hearted and immoral, and irreligious, and God knows what. Crying was the *order of the day.* Why will not the Opposition try these topics again? La Fayette indeed (the more's the pity) is out. But why not a motion for a general gaol-delivery of all State Prisoners throughout Europe?" (*Poetry of the Anti-Jacobin*). General Richard Fitzpatrick (1747–1813) was a close friend of Fox and a leading author of *The Rolliad,* a collection of Whig satires (1784–95) aimed at ridiculing Pitt and his supporters.

238 *"While truths . . . tongue"*: Pope, *Eloisa to Abelard,* l. 66.

How loving Husband clings to duteous Wife—
240　How pure Religion soothes the ills of life—
How Popish Ladies trust their pious fears
And naughty actions in their Chaplain's ears—
Half Novel and half Sermon on it flow'd,
With pious zeal the Opposition glow'd;
245　And as o'er each the soft infection crept,
Sigh'd as he whin'd, and as he whimper'd, wept—
E'en C–w–n dropt the sentimental tear,
And stout St. A–dr–w yelp'd a softer "Hear!". . .

247 *E'en C–w–n . . . tear:* "Now all the while did not this stony-hearted *Cur* shed one tear. MERCHANT OF VENICE." ["Yet did not this cruel-hearted cur shed one tear", *Two Gentlemen of Verona*, II, iii.] John Christian Curwen (*c.* 1756–1828), M.P. for Carlisle, was a vociferous member of the Opposition; his name frequently appears in Pitt's reports to George III (see *The Later Correspondence of George III*, ed. A. Aspinall (Cambridge, 1963), Vol. II).

248 *And stout . . . Hear:* The Hon. St. Andrew St. John (1759–1817), M.P. for Bedfordshire, 1780–1805.

William Gifford

EPISTLE TO PETER PINDAR

THE quarrel which led to the publication of this poem was a *cause célébre* involving two of the most notorious and abusive satirists at the end of the century. Gifford (1756–1826) was known for *The Baviad* (1791), which attacked the "Della Cruscan" group of poetasters in an effort to "check the inundation of absurdity that was bursting upon us from a thousand springs"; and for *The Maeviad* (1795), directed at the same group's efforts in drama. He edited *The Anti-Jacobin; or Weekly Examiner* (see p. 150) and, later, *The Quarterly Review*. In November 1799 the *Anti-Jacobin Review and Magazine* printed an attack on John Wolcot ("Peter Pindar") for his volume of poems, *Nil Admirari: or A Smile at the Bishop*. Wolcot (wrongly) believed Gifford to be the author of it; whereupon, in a post-script to his ode, *Lord Auckland's Triumph*, he denounced Gifford as a

swindler, scoundrel, pimp, fool, and villain. In reply Gifford published his
Epistle to Peter Pindar (1800).

The *Epistle* is prefaced by seventeen pages of vituperative prose on
Wolcot's career and reputation. Gifford rejects any protest against his
severity: "Peter is not a chicken. What would mangle another, only
tickles him . . . he must be 'cut to the bone,' before he will begin to wince."
The same view dictates his violence in the poem and, in his view, makes
"tickling" satire irrelevant. As a result Gifford lacks the savage detachment
Pope displays in the Sporus portrait (see above pp. 65–6); he is intent on
revenge alone; he attempts brutally to bludgeon Wolcot rather than, with
an astringent wit, to reduce him to ridiculous proportions. The *Epistle* is not
"diminishing" satire (as is Dryden's in *Mac Flecknoe*); rather is it of a Skel-
tonic kind which works through weight of abuse.

>While many a NOBLE NAME, to virtue dear,
>Delights the public eye, the public ear,
>And fills thy canker'd breast with such annoy
>As Satan felt* from innocence and joy;
>5 Why, Peter, leave the hated culprit free,
>And vent, poor driveller, all thy spite on me?
>
>While pure Religion's beam, bane to thy sight,
>O'er many a mitre sheds distinguished light,
>And Prelates, in the path their SAVIOUR trod,
>10 In trembling hope, "walk humbly with their God";
>Why, Peter, leave the hated culprits free,
>And vent, poor driveller, all thy spite on me?
>
>While, with a radiance yet to courts unknown,
>Calm, steady dignity surrounds the Throne,
>15 And the tried worth, the virtues, of thy King,
>Deep in thy soul infix the mortal sting;

>*—— aside the Devil turned
>For envy, yet with jealous leer malign
>Ey'd them askance.——
>   MILTON.

4 n. *Paradise Lost*, iv. 502–4.

10 *"walk humbly . . . God":* Micah, vi. 8.

13–16 *While, with . . . sting:* From 1785 onwards Wolcot published a
number of satires against George III and his Court; the *Lousiad* (1785–95)
and *Instructions to a Famous Laureate* (1787) were the best known.

F

Why, Peter, leave the hated culprit free,
And vent, poor driveller, all thy spite on me?

    Alas! scarce enter'd on the rolls of fame,
20 And but to ONE LOVED CIRCLE known by name,
How can I stead thee? Thou mayst toil, and strain,
Ransack for filth thy heart, for lies thy brain,
Rave, storm,—'tis fruitless all. Abuse, be sure,
Abuse of ME, will ne'er "one sprat" procure,
25 Bribe one night-cellar to admit thee in,
Purchase one draught of gun-powder and gin;
Seduce one brothel to display its charms,
Nor hire one hobbling strumpet to thy arms.

    False fugitive! back to thy vomit flee—
30 Troll the lascivious song, the fulsome glee,
Truck praise for lust, hunt infant genius down,
Strip modest merit of its last half-crown,
Blow from thy mildew'd lips, on virtue blow,
And blight the goodness thou can'st never know;
35 'Tis well. But why on ME?—While every tongue
Of thy rank slanders, ranker life, yet rung,
Pronounc'd thy name with mingled hate and dread,
And pour'd its whole abhorrence on thy head;
I spoke not, wrote not: ne'er did aught of thine
40 Profane, thank Heaven! one thought, one word, of mine.
True: when I heard thy deep-detested name,
A shivering horror crept through all my frame,
A damp, cold, chill, as if a snake or toad,
Had started unawares across my road;
45 Yet I kept silence: still thy spleen or pride,
(Thy better demon absent from thy side)

20 *And but . . . name:* The reference is obscure. It may signify the group of writers associated with *The Anti-Jacobin*, or, ironically, the Della Cruscans.

21 *stead:* be of use to.

26 *gun-powder:* some fiery drink (*O.E.D.*).

30 *Troll:* sing with great vigour.

31 *Truck:* barter a precious object for something less worthy.

Urg'd thee to new assaults. THERE is a time,
When slowness to resist, becomes a crime;
'TIS HERE! the hour of sufferance now is o'er,
50 And scorn shall screen thee from my arm no more.

Unhappy dotard, see! thy hairs are grey—
In fitter lists thy waning strength display:
Go, dip thy trembling hands in coward gore,
And hew down Wests and Copleys by the score;
55 But touch not ME, or, to thy peril know,
I give no easy conquest to the foe.
Come then, all filth, all venom as thou art,
Rage in thy eye, and rancour in thy heart,
Come with thy boasted arms, spite, malice, lies,
60 Smut, scandal, execrations, blasphemies;
I brave 'em all. Lo, here I fix my stand,
And dare the utmost of thy tongue and hand,
Prepar'd each threat to baffle, or to spurn,
Each blow with ten-fold vigour to return.—

65   But WHAT is HE, that, with a Mohawk's air,
"Cries havock, and lets slip the dogs of war?"

---

51 *Unhappy dotard . . . grey:* Wolcot was 62.

54 *And hew . . . score:* Wolcot devoted much satirical attention to members of the Royal Academy, including Benjamin West (1738–1820), the historical painter, and John Singleton Copley (1737–1815), the portrait-painter. See, for example, his *Farewell Odes for 1786.*

59-60 *Come with . . . blasphemies.* Together with the use of "venom", these lines are strongly reminiscent of Pope's *Epistle to Dr. Arbuthnot*, ll. 320-2 (see above p. 65). Cf. also l. 129 below.

63-4 *Prepar'd each . . . return.* On 18 August 1800 (after the publication of the *Epistle*) Gifford had to repulse a physical attack by Wolcot.

65 *Mohawk:* a ruffian (frequently referred to as "mohock") of the kind that infested the streets of London at night in the early eighteenth century.

66 *"Cries havock . . . war":* Julius Caesar*, III. i. 273.(Johnson had used these words of Junius in his pamphlet on the Falkland Islands dispute, 1771. See *Works,* ed. A. Murphy, 1792, viii. 129.)

A bloated mass,* a gross, unkneaded clod,
A foe to man, a renegade from God,

67 n. Lengthy footnotes are characteristic of Gifford's *Baviad* and *Maeviad*, as well as of T. J. Mathias's *Pursuits of Literature* (1797). Gifford is here replying to charges made by Wolcot in his postscript to *Lord Auckland's Triumph*. "Sappho" is Wolcot's friend Mrs. Mary ("Perdita") Robinson (1758–1800), the deserted mistress of the Prince of Wales. She was one of the Della Cruscans; she wrote (among many other pieces) a sonnet-series, *Sappho and Phaon*, and signed some of her poems "Sappho"; and she was the object of Coleridge's poems, "A Stranger Minstrel" (1800) and "Alcaeus to Sappho" (1800). Mrs. Robinson suffered latterly from paralysis of her legs. The "friend" whose ruin Gifford was accused of meditating was the Rev. William Peters (1742–1814) a minor painter; they had quarrelled about 1787.

* Now respecting "bloated masses," and illiberal reflections on natural infirmities in general, most admirable are the observations of Peter Pindar. "I *may* have said, that a fellow with the form of the letter Z, who publicly attacks an unfortunate woman for a disorder of which the Divine Being is the sole Author, is little less than a demon or a fool." Peter alludes to a couplet in the Baviad, in which Mrs. Robinson (the *unfortunate woman* here meant) is said to be moving on crutches towards the grave to light and wanton measures. It is probable that neither Peter nor the lady understood a syllable of what they read; otherwise they must have seen, that no reflection was intended on her "disorder," whoever was the cause of it, but on the improper use she made of what the pious Peter is pleased to call a divine visitation.

But a word with you, "Sappho." This is the second time you have wantonly fallen in my way. I humbly beseech you to let it be the last. I have sometimes more plainness than patience, and may be tempted to say what we shall both be sorry for. You rely, it may be, on the prowess of your flash-man—so, I think, they call Peter—you might rely with infinitely more wisdom, on a broken reed: for, to tell you a secret, which I care not how soon you repeat to Peter, I fear him even less than I do you—and *c'est beaucoup dire, ça*.

I did not think to waste another word on myself; but now I am on the subject, I will just observe, that the "friend whose ruin I meditated" has the justest of all possible claims to the patronage and protection of the immaculate Peter.

As I am not quite certain that he has commissioned Peter to fling down the gauntlet for him, I shall say little at present. Many years ago, I drew up an *attested* account of the rise, progress, and termination of this dear "friend's" connection with me. I have kept it concealed from every eye, and did, indeed, intend to destroy it; because I have no longer a wish to disturb the repose of an impotent enemy. It is, however, in Peter's power to compel me to publish it in my own defence,—and as some encouragement for him to recur again to an

From noxious childhood to pernicious age,
70   Sacred to infamy, through every stage.

CORNWALL remembers yet his first employ,
And shuddering tells with what infernal joy,
His little tongue in blasphemies was loos'd,
His little hands in deeds of horror us'd:
75   While mangled insects strew'd his cradle o'er,
And limbs of birds distained his bib with gore.

Anon, on stronger animals he flew
(For with his growth his savage passions grew);
And oft, what time his violence fail'd to kill,
80   He form'd the insidious drug* with wicked skill;
Saw with wild joy, in pangs till then untry'd,
Cats, dogs, expire; and curs'd them as they died!

With riper years a different scene began,
And his hate turn'd from animals to man:
85   Then letters, libels, flew on secret wings,
And wide around infix'd their venom'd stings;
All fear'd, where none could ward, the coming blow,
And each man ey'd his neighbour as his foe;
Till dragg'd to day, the lurking caitiff stood,
90   (Th' accursed cause of many a fatal feud),

71-6 *Cornwall remembers . . . gore:* Wolcot was born in Devon, but went to school in Cornwall, where he later became an apothecary-surgeon. There is no reliable evidence to prove the charge of sadism.

* Let not the reader who shudders at this, therefore disbelieve it. Almost the first accounts I remember to have had of this man, (and they were from one of his own profession, from one who knew him well) related to the execrable use he made of his knowledge as an apothecary's boy, in torturing and destroying animals.

affair of which he is as ignorant as of every thing else, I will assure him—I am about to speak a bold word—that in the narrative I have ready for the press, he will see his protégé depicted, and *most truly* depicted, with a perverseness of head, and a depravity of heart, worthy of all his envy! Meanwhile I congratulate the gentleman on his alliance with Peter Pindar, and the "unfortunate woman" his associate. It does him honour. Peter Pindar, Mrs. R——, and the Rev. Mr. —— do, in fact, form such a constellation of chastity, morality, and piety, as has not often appeared to enlighten and sanctify this lower world!

And begg'd for mercy in so sad a strain,
So wept, so trembled, that the injur'd train
Who, cowring at their feet, a MISCREANT saw,
Too mean for punishment, too poor for law,
95 O'erlook'd ('twas all they could) his numerous crimes,
And shipp'd him off "to ape and monkey climes."

THERE, while the negroes view'd with new disgust,
This prodigy of drunkenness and lust,
Explore the darkest cells, the dirtiest styes,
100 And roll in filth at which *their* gorge would rise;
He play'd one master-trick to crown the whole,
And took, O Heavens! the sacerdotal stole!
How shook the altar when he first drew near,
Hot from debauch, and with a shameless leer,
105 Pour'd stammering forth the yet unhallowed prayers,
Mix'd with convulsive sobs, and noisome airs!—
Then rose the people, passive now no more,
And from his limbs the sacred vestments tore;
Dragg'd him with groans, shouts, hisses, to the main,
110 And sent him to annoy these realms again.

Cornwall, that fondly deem'd herself reliev'd,
Ill-fated land! once more the pest receiv'd;
But, wary and forewarn'd, observ'd his course,
And track'd each slander to its proper source;
115 'Till indignation, wide and wider spread,
Burst in one dreadful tempest on his head.

96 *And shipp'd . . . climes:* In 1768 Wolcot went to Jamaica as physician to the household of the Governor, Sir William Trelawney. The phrase "ape and monkey climes" is from *The Dunciad,* I. 233.

101-10 *He play'd . . . again:* To further his career and increase his income the deist Wolcot was ordained in the Anglican Church, in 1769, but there is no evidence to substantiate Gifford's vivid description of the consequences. The reason for his return to England was the death of his patron, Trelawney.

111-16 *Cornwall, that . . . head:* After his return to Cornwall (1773), his satires frequently caused offence to the citizens of Truro, where he lived. On one occasion, in 1779, he had to give sureties for his good behaviour.

Then flight, pale flight, ensu'd!—'TWERE long to trace
His mazes, as he slunk from place to place;
To count, whene'er unearth'd, what pumps he bore,
120 What horse-ponds, till the country he forswore,
And, chac'd by public vengeance up and down,
(Hopeless of shelter) fled at length to town:
Compell'd in crowds to hide his hated head,
And spung'd on dirty whores for dirty bread.

125 * * * * * * * * * * * * * * *
* * * * * * * * * * * * * * *

LO, HERE THE REPTILE! who, from some dark cell,
Where all his veins with native poison swell,
Crawls forth, a slimy toad, and spits and spues,
130 The crude abortions of his loathsome muse,
On all that Genius, all that Worth holds dear,
Unsullied rank, and piety sincere;
While idiot mirth the base defilement lauds,
And malice, with averted face, applauds!

135 LO, HERE THE BRUTAL SOT! who, drench'd with gin,
Lashes his wither'd nerves to tasteless sin;
Squeals out (with oaths and blasphemies between)
The impious song, the tale, the jest obscene;
And careless views, amidst the barbarous roar,
140 His few grey hairs strew, one by one, the floor!

LO, HERE THE WRINKLED PROFLIGATE! who stands
On nature's verge, and from his leprous hands
Shakes tainted verse; who bids us, with the price
Of rancorous falsehoods, pander to his vice,
145 Give him to live the future as the past,
And in pollution wallow to the last!

122 *fled at . . . town:* With his protégé, the young painter John Opie, Wolcot went to London in 1781.

125 * * *: *The British Critic* (xvi, 194), a journal friendly to Gifford, considered this couplet too indecent to print; he therefore replaced it by asterisks in all editions after the first.

Enough!—Yet, Peter! mark my parting lay—
See! thy last sands are fleeting fast away;
And, what should more thy sluggish soul appal,
150 Thy limbs shrink up—THE WRITING ON THE WALL!—
O! check, a moment check, the obstreperous din
Of guilty joy, and hear the voice within,
The small, still voice of conscience, hear it cry,
An Atheist thou *may'st* live, but can'st not die!

155 Give then, poor tinkling bellman of three-score!
Give thy lewd rhymes, thy lewder converse o'er;
Thy envy, hate—and, while thou yet hast power,
On other thoughts employ the unvalu'd hour;
Lest as from crazy eld's diseaseful bed,
160 Thou lift'st, to SPIT AT HEAVEN, thy palsied head,
The BLOW arrive, and thou, reduc'd by fate,
To change thy phrenzy for despair too late;
Close thy dim eyes a moment in the tomb,
To wake for ever in THE LIFE TO COME,
165 Wake to meet HIM whose "Ord'nance thou hast slav'd★,"
Whose Mercy slighted, and whose Justice brav'd!

FOR ME—Why shouldst thou with abortive toil,
Waste the poor remnant of thy sputtering oil,
In filth and falsehood? Ignorant and absurd!
170 Pause from thy pains, and take my closing word;
Thou canst not think, nor have *I* power to tell,
How much I SCORN and HATE thee—so, farewell.

★ —— the lust-dieted man
That slaves thy ordinance, &c.
KING LEAR.

150 *The Writing on the Wall:* see Daniel, v. 5-29.
155 *bellman:* a town crier or night watchman who called the hours.
159 *eld:* old age.
165 n. *Lear*, IV. i. 70.

George Gordon, Lord Byron

THE VISION OF JUDGMENT
BY QUEVEDO REDIVIVUS

BEFORE Byron (1788–1824) could write his best satires he had to abandon his attempts to follow the main eighteenth century tradition in the heroic couplet. As late as 1817 he was convinced that he and his contemporaries were immeasurably inferior to Pope, "the little Queen Anne's man" (see *Works of Byron: Letters and Journals*, ed. R. E. Prothero, 1922, iv. 169). But in the September of that year he discovered John Hookham Frere's *Whistle-craft* poem. It was a revelation to him; he recognised what possibilities for witty, colloquial, and urbane poetry existed in the *ottava rima* as used by Frere. He chose the form at once for the comic satire of *Beppo* (1818); he adapted it to a variety of uses, serious as well as comic, in *Don Juan* (1819–24); and in his greatest poem, *The Vision of Judgment*, he made it answer the full range of his needs from the expression of aristocratic contempt, through humorous but sometimes savage mockery, to serious indictment. Byron's discovery of the *ottava rima*, then, effected his liberation from the Popeian tradition.

The Vision was provoked not by the death of George III—to which Byron's reaction was surprisingly humane—but by Robert Southey's laureate-poem, *A Vision of Judgment* (published on 11 May 1821). This was a feeble production: its Preface unmistakably linked Byron with "the Satanic school" of poetry; and its arrogant conservatism was the work of an apostate republican. Byron reacted immediately. "It is my intent"— he told Thomas Moore—"to put the said George's Apotheosis in a Whig point of view, not forgetting the Poet Laureate for his preface and other demerits" (*Letters and Journals*, v. 385). He began his poem on 7 May 1821; he broke off; then, after a burst of creative activity, he completed it on 4 October. It eventually appeared (without the Preface) in the first issue of the radical journal, *The Liberal*, on 15 October 1822. Fifteen months later the publisher, John Hunt, was held legally responsible for a poem which calumniated "the late king and wounded the feelings of his present Majesty". He was fined £100.

Byron was undoubtedly conscious of the detail of Southey's poem when writing his own; but *The Vision* remains an independent poem, not a parody. Stanzas 1–15 introduce the scene, the King's death and funeral, in a tone which is now flippant, now bitter, but is certainly "by way of reversing rogue Southey's" (*Byron's Correspondence*, ed. John Murray, 1922, ii. 203). Stanzas 16–84 show Byron most aware of the structure of Southey's poem; he had particularly in mind the sections of that work entitled "The Gate of Heaven" and "The Accusers". Byron's Satan, however, is not the crude ogre created by Southey; he is an aristocratic spokesman for the millions oppressed under George's rule, and voices Byron's own politico-moral indictment of the dead King. As Junius had done, Byron admits George's domestic virtues only to condemn more severely his public crimes against humanity. Wilkes and Junius were George's accusers in Southey's work; so they are in Byron's: but he presents them as responsible spokesmen for the "cloud of witnesses". All dignity is stripped from the Laureate himself, who is the main concern of Byron's last twenty-one stanzas. He is mocked as man, poet, and apostate.

Andrew Rutherford stresses Byron's preoccupation in *The Vision* with satirising Southey's presumption in predicting the damnation of all radical opponents of the king's and his own political conservatism (*Byron*, 1961, pp. 215–37). Rutherford rightly emphasises Byron's tolerance, his self-identification with general, erring humanity, Wilkes's refusal to testify against George in order to secure his damnation, and the poet's bitter exposure of Southey who proclaims his willingness to decide

> who shall enter heaven or fall.
> I settle all these things by intuition,
> Times present, past, to come—Heaven—Hell—and all. (ll. 804–6)

But the theme of moral corruption is equally strong and comprehensive. George, Byron argues, was ultimately responsible for all the repressive, inhuman acts of his reign; Wilkes, though admirable for political courage at one stage, had "turned to half a courtier ere [he] died" (l. 570); Junius, despite his excellent defiance of George, lacked the moral fibre to reveal his identity and accept the consequences—he was "*really—truly*—nobody at all" (l. 640); and Southey, formerly a republican, was now a time-server and an hypocrite. Over against them all stands the poet—ironically choosing Satan as his mouthpiece—proclaiming or implying his values of moral courage, humanity, and above all, freedom.

The text is from *The Works of Byron: Poetry*, ed. E. H. Coleridge (1922 edn.), iv. 481–525.

PREFACE

It hath been wisely said, that "One fool makes many"; and it hath been poetically observed—

> "Fools rush in where angels fear to tread."

1 *One fool makes many:* Scott quotes this proverb in a letter to Byron, 6 November 1813 (see J. G. Lockhart, *Memoirs of the Life of Scott*, 1837–8, iii. 101).

3 *Fools rush . . . tread:* Pope, *Essay on Criticism*, l. 625.

If Mr. Southey had not rushed in where he had no business, and where he never was before, and never will be again, the following poem would not have been written. It is not impossible that it may be as good as his own, seeing that it cannot, by any species of stupidity, natural or acquired, be *worse*. The gross flattery, the dull impudence, the renegado intolerance, and impious cant, of the poem by the author of "Wat Tyler," are something so stupendous as to form the sublime of himself—containing the quintessence of his own attributes.

So much for his poem—a word on his preface. In this preface it has pleased the magnanimous Laureate to draw the picture of a supposed "Satanic School," the which he doth recommend to the notice of the legislature; thereby adding to his other laurels the ambition of those of an informer. If there exists anywhere, except in his imagination, such a School, is he not sufficiently armed against it by his own intense vanity? The truth is that there are certain writers whom Mr. S. imagines, like Scrub, to have "talked of *him*; for they laughed consumedly".

I think I know enough of most of the writers to whom he is supposed to allude, to assert, that they, in their individual capacities, have done more good, in the charities of life, to their fellow-creatures, in any one year, than Mr. Southey has done harm to himself by his absurdities in his whole life; and this is saying a great deal. But I have a few questions to ask.

1stly, Is Mr. Southey the author of *Wat Tyler*?

9 *renegado:* See below, l. 33 and n.

10 *Wat Tyler:* Southey's drama, written in 1794, published in 1817.

15 *Satanic School:* Southey, Preface to *A Vision of Judgment* (1821): "Men of diseased hearts and depraved imaginations, who, forming a system of opinions to suit their own unhappy course of conduct, have rebelled against the holiest ordinances of human society, and hating that revealed religion which, with all their efforts and bravadoes, they are unable entirely to disbelieve, labour to make others as miserable as themselves, by infecting them with a moral virus that eats into the soul! The school which they have set up may properly be called the Satanic school" (*Works* (1838), x. 205-6).

20-1 *like Scrub . . . consumedly:* See Farquhar, *The Beaux' Stratagem* (1707), III, i.

2ndly, Was he not refused a remedy at law by the highest judge
30 of his beloved England, because it was a blasphemous and seditious
publication?

3rdly, Was he not entitled by William Smith, in full parliament,
"a rancorous renegado"?

4thly, Is he not poet laureate, with his own lines on Martin the
35 regicide staring him in the face?

And, 5thly, Putting the four preceding items together, with what
conscience dare *he* call the attention of the laws to the publications
of others, be they what they may?

I say nothing of the cowardice of such a proceeding; its meanness
40 speaks for itself; but I wish to touch upon the *motive*, which is
neither more nor less than that Mr. S. has been laughed at a little
in some recent publications, as he was of yore in the *Anti-jacobin*,
by his present patrons. Hence all this 'skimble scamble stuff'" about
"Satanic," and so forth. However, it is worthy of him—"*qualis*
45 *ab incepto*".

If there is anything obnoxious to the political opinions of a
portion of the public in the following poem, they may thank Mr.
Southey. He might have written hexameters, as he has written
everything else, for aught that the writer cared—had they been
50 upon another subject. But to attempt to canonise a monarch, who,

29-31 *Was he...publication?:* Southey's *Wat Tyler* was published without
his permission and when he had renounced his youthful republicanism. In
1821 he was refused an injunction against the publishers. Lord Chancellor
Eldon stated that "a person cannot recover in damages for a work which is,
in its nature, calculated to do injury to the public".

32-33 *Was he . . . renegado?:* William Smith, M.P. for Norwich, spoke of
"the settled, determined malignity of a renegado" (Hansard, *Parliamentary
Debates*, xxxv (1817), 1090), in the Commons on 14 March 1817. He went
on (col. 1091) to describe *Wat Tyler* as "the most seditious book that was
ever written".

34-5 *Is he . . . face?:* One of Southey's juvenile poems is an "Inscription
for the Apartment in Chepstow Castle, where Henry Martin, the Regicide,
was imprisoned thirty years." (It was parodied by Canning and Frere in the
first issue of *The Anti-Jacobin*.)

41-2 *Mr. S....Anti-jacobin:* See *supra*, pp. 151–3.

48 *hexameters:* In the preface to *A Vision* Southey explains at length why
he wrote his poem "in imitation of the ancient hexameter".

whatever were his household virtues, was neither a successful nor a patriot king,—inasmuch as several years of his reign passed in war with America and Ireland, to say nothing of the aggression upon France—like all other exaggeration, necessarily begets opposition. In whatever manner he may be spoken of in this new 55 *Vision*, his public career will not be more favourably transmitted by history. Of his private virtues (although a little expensive to the nation) there can be no doubt.

With regard to the supernatural personages treated of, I can only say that I know as much about them, and (as an honest man) have 60 a better right to talk of them than Robert Southey. I have also treated them more tolerantly. The way in which that poor insane creature, the Laureate, deals about his judgments in the next world, is like his own judgment in this. If it was not completely ludicrous, it would be something worse. I don't think that there is much more 65 to say at present.

QUEVEDO REDIVIVUS

P.S.—It is possible that some readers may object, in these objectionable times, to the freedom with which saints, angels, and spiritual persons discourse in this *Vision*. But, for precedents upon such 70 points, I must refer him to Fielding's *Journey from this World to the next*, and to the Visions of myself, the said Quevedo, in Spanish or translated. The reader is also requested to observe, that no doctrinal tenets are insisted upon or discussed; that the person of the Deity is carefully with-held from sight, which is more than can 75 be said for the Laureate, who hath thought proper to make him talk, not "like a school-divine", but like the unscholarlike Mr. Southey. The whole action passes on the outside of heaven; and Chaucer's *Wife of Bath*, Pulci's *Morgante Maggiore*, Swift's *Tale of a Tub*, and the other works above referred to, are cases in point of the freedom 80 with which saints, etc., may be permitted to converse in works not intended to be serious.

Q. R.

57–8 *expensive to the nation:* George III had fifteen children by his queen, Charlotte.

72 *Quevedo:* Francisco Gomez de Quevedo published six Sueños or Visions in 1635.

77 *like a school-divine:* Pope, *Imitations of Horace*, Bk. II, ep. 1, l. 102.

Mr. Southey being, as he says, a good Christian and vindictive,
85 threatens, I understand, a reply to this our answer. It is to be hoped
that his visionary faculties will in the meantime have acquired a
little more judgment, properly so called: otherwise he will get himself into new dilemmas. These apostate jacobins furnish rich
rejoinders. Let him take a specimen. Mr. Southey laudeth grievously
90 "one Mr. Landor," who cultivates much private renown in the shape
of Latin verses; and not long ago, the poet laureate dedicated to
him, it appeareth, one of his fugitive lyrics, upon the strength of a
poem called "*Gebir*." Who could suppose, that in the same Gebir
the aforesaid Savage Landor (for such is his grim cognomen)
95 putteth into the infernal regions no less a person than the hero of
his friend Mr. Southey's heaven,—yea, even George the Third!
See also how personal Savage becometh, when he hath a mind. The
following is his portrait of our late gracious sovereign:

(Prince Gebir having descended into the infernal regions, the
100   shades of his royal ancestors are, at his request, called up to
his view; and he exclaims to his ghostly guide)—

" 'Aröar, what wretch that nearest us? what wretch
Is that with eyebrows white and slanting brow?
Listen! him yonder who, bound down supine,
105   Shrinks yelling from that sword there, engine-hung;
He too amongst my ancestors! I hate
The despot, but the dastard I despise.
Was he our countryman?'
                    'Alas, O king!
110   Iberia bore him, but the breed accurst
Inclement winds blew blighting from north-east.'
'He was a warrior then, nor fear'd the gods?'
'Gebir, he feared the Demons, not the gods,
Though them indeed his daily face adored;
115   And was no warrior, yet the thousand lives
Squandered, as stones to exercise a sling,
And the tame cruelty and cold caprice—
Oh madness of mankind! addressed, adored!' "

90-3 *Mr. Landor . . . Gebir:* Walter Savage Landor (1775–1864) published
a volume of Latin verses (*Idyllia Heroica*) in 1820. *Gebir* appeared in 1798.
102-18 *Aröar, what . . . adored:* Gebir iii. 184–99.

I omit noticing some edifying Ithyphallics of Savagius, wishing
to keep the proper veil over them, if his grave but somewhat indis- 120
creet worshipper will suffer it; but certainly these teachers of "great
moral lessons" are apt to be found in strange company.

119 *Ithyphallics:* the metre used in Bacchic hymns. ("Savagius" comes
from the title-page of Landor's volume of Latin verses.)

I

SAINT PETER sat by the celestial gate:
　　His keys were rusty, and the lock was dull,
So little trouble had been given of late;
　　Not that the place by any means was full,
5　But since the Gallic era "eighty-eight"
　　The Devils had ta'en a longer, stronger pull,
And "a pull altogether," as they say
At sea—which drew most souls another way.

II

The Angels all were singing out of tune,
10　And hoarse with having little else to do,
Excepting to wind up the sun and moon,
　　Or curb a runaway young star or two,
Or wild colt of a comet, which too soon
　　Broke out of bounds o'er the ethereal blue,
15　Splitting some planet with its playful tail,
As boats are sometimes by a wanton whale.

III

The Guardian Seraphs had retired on high,
　　Finding their charges past all care below;
Terrestrial business filled nought in the sky
20　Save the Recording Angel's black bureau;
Who found, indeed, the facts to multiply
　　With such rapidity of vice and woe,
That he had stripped off both his wings in quills,
And yet was in arrear of human ills.

5 *Gallic era "eighty-eight":* the French Revolution. This date was either
intended as a comprehensive reference to the revolutionary movement
which preceded the outbreak of the Revolution in 1789, or was required by
the rhyme.

IV

25 His business so augmented of late years,
    That he was forced, against his will, no doubt,
  (Just like those cherubs, earthly ministers,)
    For some resource to turn himself about,
  And claim the help of his celestial peers,
30   To aid him ere he should be quite worn out
  By the increased demand for his remarks:
  Six Angels and twelve Saints were named his clerks.

V

  This was a handsome board—at least for Heaven;
    And yet they had even then enough to do,
35 So many Conquerors' cars were daily driven,
    So many kingdoms fitted up anew;
  Each day, too, slew its thousands six or seven,
    Till at the crowning carnage, Waterloo,
  They threw their pens down in divine disgust—
40 The page was so besmeared with blood and dust.

VI

  This by the way; 'tis not mine to record
    What Angels shrink from: even the very Devil
  On this occasion his own work abhorred,
    So surfeited with the infernal revel:
45 Though he himself had sharpened every sword,
    It almost quenched his innate thirst of evil.
  (Here Satan's sole good work deserves insertion—
  'Tis, that he has both Generals in reversion.)

VII

  Let's skip a few short years of hollow peace,
50   Which peopled earth no better, Hell as wont,
  And Heaven none—they form the tyrant's lease,
    With nothing but new names subscribed upon 't;

48 *in reversion:* i.e. Napoleon and Wellington automatically become Satan's property when they die. (Napoleon died two days before Byron began his *Vision*.)

Twill one day finish: meantime they increase,
  "With seven heads and ten horns", and all in front,
55 Like Saint John's foretold beast; but ours are born
Less formidable in the head than horn.

VIII

In the first year of Freedom's second dawn
  Died George the Third; although no tyrant, one
Who shielded tyrants, till each sense withdrawn
60   Left him nor mental nor external sun:
A better farmer ne'er brushed dew from lawn,
  A worse king never left a realm undone!
He died—but left his subjects still behind,
One half as mad—and t'other no less blind.

IX

65 He died! his death made no great stir on earth:
  His burial made some pomp; there was profusion
Of velvet—gilding—brass—and no great dearth
  Of aught but tears—save those shed by collusion:
For these things may be bought at their true worth;
70   Of elegy there was the due infusion—
Bought also; and the torches, cloaks and banners,
Heralds, and relics of old Gothic manners,

X

Formed a sepulchral melodrame. Of all
  The fools who flocked to swell or see the show,
75 Who cared about the corpse? The funeral
  Made the attraction, and the black the woe,

54-5 *With seven . . . beast:* Revelation, xvii. 3.

57-8 *In the . . . Third:* He died on 29 January 1820. 1820 was notable for the outburst of revolutionary activity in southern Europe, especially in Italy (where Byron was writing). The first "dawn" of Freedom was at the time of the French Revolution, 1789.

59-60 *till each . . . sun:* Cf. Southey, *A Vision*, i:
      "this was the day when the herald
Breaking his wand should proclaim, that George our King was departed.
Thou art released! I cried: thy soul is deliver'd from bondage!
Thou who hast lain so long in mental and visual darkness,
Thou art in yonder heaven! thy place is in light and in glory."

There throbbed not there a thought which pierced the
    pall;
   And when the gorgeous coffin was laid low,
It seemed the mockery of hell to fold
80 The rottenness of eighty years in gold.

XI

So mix his body with the dust! It might
    Return to what it *must* far sooner, were
The natural compound left alone to fight
    Its way back into earth, and fire, and air;
85 But the unnatural balsams merely blight
    What Nature made him at his birth, as bare
As the mere million's base unmummied clay—
Yet all his spices but prolong decay.

XII

He's dead—and upper earth with him has done;
90   He's buried; save the undertaker's bill,
Or lapidary scrawl, the world is gone
    For him, unless he left a German will:
But where's the proctor who will ask his son?
    In whom his qualities are reigning still,
95 Except that household virtue, most uncommon,
Of constancy to a bad, ugly woman.

78-80 *And when . . . gold:* Cf. Southey, *A Vision,* ii:
  "So by the Unseen comforted, raised I my head in obedience,
  And in a vault I found myself placed, arch'd over on all sides.
  Narrow and low was that house of the dead. Around it were coffins,
  Each in its niche, and palls, and urns, and funeral hatchments;
  Velvets of Tyrian dye, retaining their hues unfaded;
  Blazonry vivid still, as if fresh from the touch of the limner;
  Nor was the golden fringe, nor the golden broidery tarnish'd."

92 *German will:* George II pocketed his father's will and never acted on it;
Byron may be suggesting that a similar fate awaited any will left by George
III, whose relations with his heir were notoriously bad.

XIII

"God save the king!" It is a large economy
 In God to save the like; but if he will
Be saving, all the better; for not one am I
100 Of those who think damnation better still:
I hardly know too if not quite alone am I
 In this small hope of bettering future ill
By circumscribing, with some slight restriction,
The eternity of Hell's hot jurisdiction.

XIV

105 I know this is unpopular; I know
  'Tis blasphemous; I know one may be damned
For hoping no one else may e'er be so;
  I know my catechism; I know we're crammed
With the best doctrines till we quite o'erflow;
110 I know that all save England's Church have shammed,
And that the other twice two hundred churches
And synagogues have made a *damned* bad purchase.

XV

God help us all! God help me too! I am,
  God knows, as helpless as the Devil can wish,
115 And not a whit more difficult to damn,
  Than is to bring to land a late-hooked fish,
Or to the butcher to purvey the lamb;
  Not that I'm fit for such a noble dish,
As one day will be that immortal fry
120 Of almost every body born to die.

XVI

Saint Peter sat by the celestial gate,
  And nodded o'er his keys: when, lo! there came
A wondrous noise he had not heard of late—
  A rushing sound of wind, and stream, and flame;
125 In short, a roar of things extremely great,
  Which would have made aught save a Saint exclaim;
But he, with first a start and then a wink,
Said, "There's another star gone out, I think!"

XVII

But ere he could return to his repose,
130   A Cherub flapped his right wing o'er his eyes—
At which Saint Peter yawned, and rubbed his nose:
    "Saint porter," said the angel, "prithee rise!"
Waving a goodly wing, which glowed, as glows
    An earthly peacock's tail, with heavenly dyes:
135 To which the saint replied, "Well, what's the matter?
Is Lucifer come back with all this clatter?"

XVIII

"No," quoth the Cherub: "George the Third is dead."
    "And who *is* George the Third?" replied the apostle:
"*What George? what Third?*" "The King of England,"
        said
140   The angel. "Well! he won't find kings to jostle
Him on his way; but does he wear his head?
    Because the last we saw here had a tustle,
And ne'er would have got into Heaven's good graces,
Had he not flung his head in all our faces.

XIX

145   "He was—if I remember—King of France;
    That head of his, which could not keep a crown
On earth, yet ventured in my face to advance
    A claim to those of martyrs—like my own:
If I had had my sword, as I had once
150   When I cut ears off, I had cut him down;
But having but my *keys*, and not my brand,
I only knocked his head from out his hand.

XX

"And then he set up such a headless howl,
    That all the Saints came out and took him in;

145 *King of France:* Louis XVI, guillotined 21 January 1793.
149-50 *If I . . . off:* Cf. John, xviii. 10.

155 And there he sits by Saint Paul, cheek by jowl;
      That fellow Paul—the parvenù! The skin
Of Saint Bartholomew, which makes his cowl
      In heaven, and upon earth redeemed his sin,
So as to make a martyr, never sped
160 Better than did this weak and wooden head.

XXI

"But had it come up here upon its shoulders,
      There would have been a different tale to tell:
The fellow-feeling in the Saint's beholders
      Seems to have acted on them like a spell;
165 And so this very foolish head Heaven solders
      Back on its trunk: it may be very well,
And seems the custom here to overthrow
Whatever has been wisely done below."

XXII

The Angel answered, "Peter! do not pout:
170   The King who comes has head and all entire,
And never knew much what it was about—
      He did as doth the puppet—by its wire,
And will be judged like all the rest, no doubt:
      My business and your own is not to inquire
175 Into such matters, but to mind our cue—
Which is to act as we are bid to do."

XXIII

While thus they spake, the angelic caravan,
      Arriving like a rush of mighty wind,
Cleaving the fields of space, as doth the swan
180   Some silver stream (say Ganges, Nile, or Inde,

156 *parvenù:* St. Paul, unlike St. Peter, was not associated with Jesus during His earthly Ministry; he is therefore regarded as an upstart by St. Peter.

156-8 *The skin . . . heaven:* According to tradition St. Bartholomew was flayed alive and then crucified.

Or Thames, or Tweed), and midst them an old man
  With an old soul, and both extremely blind,
Halted before the gate, and, in his shroud,
Seated their fellow-traveller on a cloud.

XXIV

185 But bringing up the rear of this bright host
    A Spirit of a different aspect waved
His wings, like thunder-clouds above some coast
    Whose barren beach with frequent wrecks is paved;
His brow was like the deep when tempest-tossed;
190   Fierce and unfathomable thoughts engraved
Eternal wrath on his immortal face,
And *where* he gazed a gloom pervaded space.

XXV

As he drew near, he gazed upon the gate
  Ne'er to be entered more by him or Sin,
195 With such a glance of supernatural hate,
    As made Saint Peter wish himself within;
He pottered with his keys at a great rate,
    And sweated through his Apostolic skin:
Of course his perspiration was but ichor,
200 Or some such other spiritual liquor.

XXVI

The very Cherubs huddled all together,
  Like birds when soars the falcon; and they felt
A tingling to the tip of every feather,
  And formed a circle like Orion's belt

---

184 *Seated their . . . cloud:* Cf. Southey, *A Vision*, iii:
"Then I beheld the King. From a cloud which cover'd the pavement
His reverend form uprose: heavenward his face was directed,
Heavenward his eyes were raised, and heavenward his arms were
    extended."

185-92 *But bringing . . . space:* Miltonic echoes are numerous here. Cf.
Paradise Lost, i. 599-604; vi. 865.

205 Around their poor old charge; who scarce knew whither
    His guards had led him, though they gently dealt
  With royal Manes (for by many stories,
    And true, we learn the Angels all are Tories).

XXVII

  As things were in this posture, the gate flew
210   Asunder, and the flashing of its hinges
  Flung over space an universal hue
    Of many-coloured flame, until its tinges
  Reached even our speck of earth, and made a new
    Aurora borealis spread its fringes
215 O'er the North Pole; the same seen, when ice-bound,
  By Captain Parry's crew, in "Melville's Sound".

XXVIII

  And from the gate thrown open issued beaming
    A beautiful and mighty Thing of Light,
  Radiant with glory, like a banner streaming
220 Victorious from some world-o'erthrowing fight:
  My poor comparisons must needs be teeming
    With earthly likenesses, for here the night
  Of clay obscures our best conceptions, saving
  Johanna Southcote, or Bob Southey raving.

207 *royal Manes:* the spirits or "shades" of dead kings.

216 *By Captain . . . Sound:* Sir William E. Parry, *Journal of a Voyage performed in the years 1819–20* (1821–4), p. 135.

224 *Johanna Southcote:* Joanna Southcott (1750–1814), a religious fanatic. In 1792 she began to write doggerel prophecies and to claim supernatural gifts; she attracted many disciples.

224 *Southey raving:* Cf. *A Vision*, iv.
  "Eminent on a hill, there stood the Celestial City;
  Beaming afar it shone; its towers and cupolas rising
  High in the air serene, with the brightness of gold in the furnace,
  Where on their breadth the splendour lay intense and quiescent:
  Part with a fierier glow, and a short quick tremulous motion,
  Like the burning pyropus; and turrets and pinnacles sparkled
  Playing in jets of light, with a diamond-like glory coruscant.
  . . . Drawing near, I beheld what over the portal was written:
  This is the Gate of Bliss, it said."

XXIX

225 'Twas the Archangel Michael: all men know
    The make of Angels and Archangels, since
There's scarce a scribbler has not one to show,
    From the fiends' leader to the Angels' Prince.
There also are some altar-pieces, though
230   I really can't say that they much evince
One's inner notions of immortal spirits;
But let the connoisseurs explain *their* merits.

XXX

Michael flew forth in glory and in good;
    A goodly work of him from whom all Glory
235 And Good arise; the portal past—he stood;
    Before him the young Cherubs and Saints hoary—
(I say *young*, begging to be understood
    By looks, not years; and should be very sorry
To state, they were not older than St. Peter,
240 But merely that they seemed a little sweeter).

XXXI

The Cherubs and the Saints bowed down before
    That arch-angelic Hierarch, the first
Of Essences angelical who wore
    The aspect of a god; but this ne'er nursed
245 Pride in his heavenly bosom, in whose core
    No thought, save for his Maker's service, durst
Intrude, however glorified and high;
He knew him but the Viceroy of the sky.

XXXII

He and the sombre, silent Spirit met—
250   They knew each other both for good and ill;
Such was their power, that neither could forget
    His former friend and future foe; but still
There was a high, immortal, proud regret
    In either's eye, as if 'twere less their will

255   Than destiny to make the eternal years
       Their date of war, and their "Champ Clos" the spheres.

XXXIII

       But here they were in neutral space: we know
         From Job, that Satan hath the power to pay
       A heavenly visit thrice a-year or so;
260   And that the "Sons of God", like those of clay,
       Must keep him company; and we might show
         From the same book, in how polite a way
       The dialogue is held between the Powers
       Of Good and Evil—but 'twould take up hours.

XXXIV

265   And this is not a theologic tract,
         To prove with Hebrew and with Arabic,
       If Job be allegory or a fact,
         But a true narrative; and thus I pick
       From out the whole but such and such an act
270   As sets aside the slightest thought of trick.
       'Tis every tittle true, beyond suspicion,
       And accurate as any other vision.

XXXV

       The spirits were in neutral space, before
         The gate of Heaven; like eastern thresholds is
275   The place where Death's grand cause is argued o'er,
         And souls despatched to that world or to this;
       And therefore Michael and the other wore
         A civil aspect: though they did not kiss,
       Yet still between his Darkness and his Brightness
280   There passed a mutual glance of great politeness.

256 *Champ Clos:* i.e. lists or tilt-yard.

265-8 *And this . . . narrative:* Byron is alluding to J. M. Good's translation of *Job* from the Hebrew, in 1812. With scholarly citations from Hebrew and Arabic, Good dilates on the biographical and historical character of *Job*.

274-5 *like eastern . . . o'er:* The gateways of eastern cities were used as places for public deliberation, the administration of justice, and the reception of visiting dignitaries.

XXXVI

The Archangel bowed, not like a modern beau,
    But with a graceful oriental bend,
Pressing one radiant arm just where below
    The heart in good men is supposed to tend;
285 He turned as to an equal, not too low,
    But kindly; Satan met his ancient friend
With more hauteur, as might an old Castilian
Poor Noble meet a mushroom rich civilian.

XXXVII

He merely bent his diabolic brow
290   An instant; and then raising it, he stood
In act to assert his right or wrong, and show
    Cause why King George by no means could or should
Make out a case to be exempt from woe
    Eternal, more than other kings, endued
295 With better sense and hearts, whom History mentions,
Who long have "paved Hell with their good intentions".

XXXVIII

Michael began: "What wouldst thou with this man,
    Now dead, and brought before the Lord? What ill
Hath he wrought since his mortal race began,
300   That thou canst claim him? Speak! and do thy will,
If it be just: if in this earthly span
    He hath been greatly failing to fulfil
His duties as a king and mortal, say,
And he is thine; if not—let him have way."

---

296 *paved Hell . . . intentions:* See Boswell, *Life of Johnson*, ed. Hill-Powell, 1934, ii. 360.

297-8 *What wouldst . . . Lord?:* Byron is here closely following the structure of Southey's poem. The fifth section of his poem, entitled "The Accusers", shows George—"Calm in his faith he stood, and his own clear conscience upheld him"—arraigned by his former opponents. They include Wilkes and Junius.

XXXIX

305 "Michael!" replied the Prince of Air, "even here
      Before the gate of Him thou servest, must
     I claim my subject: and will make appear
      That as he was my worshipper in dust,
     So shall he be in spirit, although dear
310   To thee and thine, because nor wine nor lust
     Were of his weaknesses; yet on the throne
     He reigned o'er millions to serve me alone.

XL

     "Look to *our* earth, or rather *mine*; it was,
      Once, more thy master's: but I triumph not
315 In this poor planet's conquest; nor, alas!
      Need he thou servest envy me my lot:
     With all the myriads of bright worlds which pass
      In worship round him, he may have forgot
     Yon weak creation of such paltry things:
320 I think few worth damnation save their kings,

XLI

     "And these but as a kind of quit-rent, to
      Assert my right as Lord: and even had
     I such an inclination, 'twere (as you
      Well know) superfluous; they are grown so **bad**,
325 That Hell has nothing better left to do
      Than leave them to themselves: so much more **mad**
     And evil by their own internal curse,
     Heaven cannot make them better, nor I worse.

XLII

     "Look to the earth, I said, and say again:
330   When this old, blind, mad, helpless, weak, poor
          worm
        Began in youth's first bloom and flush to reign,
          The world and he both wore a different form,

321 *quit-rent:* a nominal rent in place of services formerly rendered to the
lord of the manor.
330 *this old ... worm:* Cf. Shelley, Sonnet: *England in 1819:* "An old, mad,
blind, despised, and dying king."

And much of earth and all the watery plain
    Of Ocean called him king: through many a storm
335 His isles had floated on the abyss of Time;
For the rough virtues chose them for their clime.

XLIII

"He came to his sceptre young; he leaves it old:
    Look to the state in which he found his realm,
And left it; and his annals too behold,
340   How to a minion first he gave the helm;
How grew upon his heart a thirst for gold,
    The beggar's vice, which can but overwhelm
The meanest hearts; and for the rest, but glance
Thine eye along America and France.

XLIV

345 " 'Tis true, he was a tool from first to last
    (I have the workmen safe); but as a tool
So let him be consumed. From out the past
    Of ages, since mankind have known the rule
Of monarchs—from the bloody rolls amassed
350   Of Sin and Slaughter—from the Cæsars' school,
Take the worst pupil; and produce a reign
More drenched with gore, more cumbered with the slain.

XLV

"He ever warred with freedom and the free:
    Nations as men, home subjects, foreign foes,
355 So that they uttered the word 'Liberty!'
    Found George the Third their first opponent. Whose
History was ever stained as his will be
    With national and individual woes?
I grant his household abstinence; I grant
360 His neutral virtues, which most monarchs want;

340 *a minion:* John Stuart, third Earl of Bute (1713–92), became Secretary of State in 1761, and Prime Minister 1762–3.

359–62 *I grant . . . lord:* Cf. Junius: ". . . is it any answer to your people, to say, 'That among your domestics You are good-humoured; That to one lady you are faithful; That to your children you are indulgent?" (*Letters,* 1791 edn., pp. 25-6).

XLVI

"I know he was a constant consort; own
   He was a decent sire, and middling lord.
All this is much, and most upon a throne;
   As temperance, if at Apicius' board,
365 Is more than at an anchorite's supper shown.
   I grant him all the kindest can accord;
And this was well for him, but not for those
Millions who found him what Oppression chose.

XLVII

"The New World shook him off; the Old yet groans
370   Beneath what he and his prepared, if not
Completed: he leaves heirs on many thrones
   To all his vices, without what begot
Compassion for him—his tame virtues; drones
   Who sleep, or despots who have now forgot
375 A lesson which shall be re-taught them, wake
Upon the thrones of earth; but let them quake!

XLVIII

"Five millions of the primitive, who hold
   The faith which makes ye great on earth, implored
A *part* of that vast *all* they held of old,—
380   Freedom to worship—not alone your Lord,
Michael, but you, and you, Saint Peter! Cold
   Must be your souls, if you have not abhorred
The foe to Catholic participation
In all the license of a Christian nation.

364 *Apicius:* the proverbial gourmet.

369 *The New . . . off:* The American colonies declared their independence
in 1783.

383 *The foe . . . participation:* George opposed Catholic Emancipation,
particularly in 1795 and 1807.

XLIX

385   "True! he allowed them to pray God; but as
        A consequence of prayer, refused the law
        Which would have placed them upon the same base
           With those who did not hold the Saints in awe."
        But here Saint Peter started from his place
390   And cried, "You may the prisoner withdraw:
        Ere Heaven shall ope her portals to this Guelph,
        While I am guard, may I be damned myself!

L

        "Sooner will I with Cerberus exchange
           My office (and *his* is no sinecure)
395   Than see this royal Bedlam-bigot range
           The azure fields of Heaven, of that be sure!"
        "Saint!" replied Satan, "you do well to avenge
           The wrongs he made your satellites endure;
        And if to this exchange you should be given,
400   I'll try to coax *our* Cerberus up to Heaven!"

LI

        Here Michael interposed: "Good Saint! and Devil!
           Pray, not so fast; you both outrun discretion.
        Saint Peter! you were wont to be more civil:
           Satan! excuse this warmth of his expression,
405   And condescension to the vulgar's level:
           Even Saints sometimes forget themselves in session.
        Have you got more to say?"—"No."—"If you please,
        I'll trouble you to call your witnesses."

LII

        Then Satan turned and waved his swarthy hand,
410   Which stirred with its electric qualities
        Clouds farther off than we can understand,
           Although we find him sometimes in our skies;
        Infernal thunder shook both sea and land
           In all the planets—and Hell's batteries
415   Let off the artillery, which Milton mentions
        As one of Satan's most sublime inventions.

415-16 *Let off . . . inventions: Paradise Lost*, vi. 482-91.

LIII

This was a signal unto such damned souls
   As have the privilege of their damnation
Extended far beyond the mere controls
420   Of worlds past, present, or to come; no station
Is theirs particularly in the rolls
   Of Hell assigned; but where their inclination
Or business carries them in search of game,
They may range freely—being damned the same.

LIV

425 They are proud of this—as very well they may,
   It being a sort of knighthood, or gilt key
Stuck in their loins; or like to an "entré"
   Up the back stairs, or such free-masonry.
I borrow my comparisons from clay,
430   Being clay myself. Let not those spirits be
Offended with such base low likenesses;
We know their posts are nobler far than these.

LV

When the great signal ran from Heaven to Hell—
   About ten million times the distance reckoned
435 From our sun to its earth, as we can tell
   How much time it takes up, even to a second,
For every ray that travels to dispel
   The fogs of London, through which, dimly beaconed,
The weathercocks are gilt some thrice a year,
440 If that the *summer* is not too severe:

LVI

I say that I can tell—'twas half a minute;
   I know the solar beams take up more time
Ere, packed up for their journey, they begin it;

426 *gilt key:* A gold key was part of the insignia of the Lord Chamberlain.

440 *the summer . . . severe:* possible allusion to Horace Walpole's famous remark: "The summer has set in with its usual *severity*" (*Works of Byron: Poetry*, ed. E. H. Coleridge, iv. 505 n.).

But then their Telegraph is less sublime,
445 And if they ran a race, they would not win it
'Gainst Satan's couriers bound for their own clime.
The sun takes up some years for every ray
To reach its goal—the Devil not half a day.

LVII

Upon the verge of space, about the size
450 Of half-a-crown, a little speck appeared
(I've seen a something like it in the skies
In the Ægean, ere a squall); it neared,
And, growing bigger, took another guise;
Like an aërial ship it tacked, and steered,
455 Or *was* steered (I am doubtful of the grammar
Of the last phrase, which makes the stanza stammer;

LVIII

But take your choice): and then it grew a cloud;
And so it was—a cloud of witnesses.
But such a cloud! No land ere saw a crowd
460 Of locusts numerous as the heavens saw these;
They shadowed with their myriads Space; their loud
And varied cries were like those of wild geese,
(If nations may be likened to a goose),
And realised the phrase of "Hell broke loose".

LIX

465 Here crashed a sturdy oath of stout John Bull,
Who damned away his eyes as heretofore:
There Paddy brogued "By Jasus!"—"What's your wull?"
The temperate Scot exclaimed: the French ghost swore
In certain terms I shan't translate in full,
470 As the first coachman will; and 'midst the war,
The voice of Jonathan was heard to express,
"*Our* President is going to war, I guess."

464 *Hell broke loose:* Milton, *Paradise Lost*, iv. 918.

471 *Jonathan:* a generic name for a United States citizen.

LX

Besides there were the Spaniard, Dutch, and Dane;
    In short, an universal shoal of shades
475 From Otaheite's isle to Salisbury Plain,
    Of all climes and professions, years and trades,
Ready to swear against the good king's reign,
    Bitter as clubs in cards are against spades:
All summoned by this grand "subpœna", to
480 Try if kings mayn't be damned like me or you.

LXI

When Michael saw this host, he first grew pale,
    As angels can; next, like Italian twilight,
He turned all colours—as a peacock's tail,
    Or sunset streaming through a Gothic skylight
485 In some old abbey, or a trout not stale,
    Or distant lightning on the horizon *by* night,
Or a fresh rainbow, or a grand review
Of thirty regiments in red, green, and blue.

LXII

Then he addressed himself to Satan: "Why—
490   My good old friend, for such I deem you, though
Our different parties make us fight so shy,
    I ne'er mistake you for a *personal* foe;
Our difference is *political*, and I
    Trust that, whatever may occur below,
495 You know my great respect for you: and this
Makes me regret whate'er you do amiss—

LXIII

"Why, my dear Lucifer, would you abuse
    My call for witnesses? I did not mean
That you should half of Earth and Hell produce;
500   'Tis even superfluous, since two honest, clean,

475 *Otaheite's isle:* Tahiti.

G

True testimonies are enough: we lose
  Our Time, nay, our Eternity, between
The accusation and defence: if we
Hear both, 'twill stretch our immortality."

LXIV

505 Satan replied, "To me the matter is
      Indifferent, in a personal point of view:
    I can have fifty better souls than this
      With far less trouble than we have gone through
    Already; and I merely argued his
510   Late Majesty of Britain's case with you
    Upon a point of form: you may dispose
    Of him; I've kings enough below, God knows!"

LXV

Thus spoke the Demon (late called "multifaced"
  By multo-scribbling Southey). "Then we'll call
515 One or two persons of the myriads placed
      Around our congress, and dispense with all
    The rest," quoth Michael: "Who may be so graced
      As to speak first? there's choice enough—who shall
    It be?" Then Satan answered, "There are many;
520   But you may choose Jack Wilkes as well as any."

513-14 *late called . . . Southey:* Cf. *A Vision*, v:
    "Many-headed and monstrous the Fiend; with numberless faces—
. . . Caitiffs, are ye dumb? cried the multifaced Demon in anger."

520-1 *Jack Wilkes . . . Sprite:* John Wilkes (1727-97), the notorious political
opponent of arbitrary government. He attacked Bute's administration in
The North Briton and was prosecuted for libel (in 1763) in connection with
the famous issue, "No. 45". Cf. Southey, *A Vision*, v:
      "Beholding the foremost,
  Him by the cast of his eye oblique, I knew as the firebrand
  Whom the unthinking populace held for their idol and hero,
  Lord of Misrule in his day."

For Wilkes's appearance and well-known squint, see Hogarth's caricature
or Zoffany's portrait.

LXVI

A merry, cock-eyed, curious-looking Sprite
    Upon the instant started from the throng,
Dressed in a fashion now forgotten quite;
    For all the fashions of the flesh stick long
525 By people in the next world; where unite
    All the costumes since Adam's, right or wrong,
From Eve's fig-leaf down to the petticoat,
Almost as scanty, of days less remote.

LXVII

The Spirit looked around upon the crowds
530   Assembled, and exclaimed, "My friends of all
The spheres, we shall catch cold amongst these clouds;
    So let's to business: why this general call?
If those are freeholders I see in shrouds,
    And 'tis for an election that they bawl,
535 Behold a candidate with unturned coat!
Saint Peter, may I count upon your vote?"

LXVIII

"Sir," replied Michael, "you mistake; these things
    Are of a former life, and what we do
Above is more august; to judge of kings
540   Is the tribunal met: so now you know."
"Then I presume those gentlemen with wings,"
    Said Wilkes, "are Cherubs; and that soul below
Looks much like George the Third, but to my mind
A good deal older—bless me! is he blind?"

LXIX

545 "He is what you behold him, and his doom
    Depends upon his deeds," the Angel said;
"If you have aught to arraign in him, the tomb
    Gives license to the humblest beggar's head

533-4 *If those . . . bawl:* Wilkes was famous for his persistence in seeking
election to Parliament from the freeholders of Westminster, 1768-9.

To lift itself against the loftiest."—"Some,"
550   Said Wilkes, "don't wait to see them laid in lead,
For such a liberty—and I, for one,
Have told them what I thought beneath the sun."

LXX

"*Above* the sun repeat, then, what thou hast
    To urge against him," said the Archangel. "Why,"
555   Replied the spirit, "since old scores are past,
    Must I turn evidence? In faith, not I.
Besides, I beat him hollow at the last,
    With all his Lords and Commons: in the sky
I don't like ripping up old stories, since
560   His conduct was but natural in a prince.

LXXI

"Foolish, no doubt, and wicked, to oppress
    A poor unlucky devil without a shilling;
But then I blame the man himself much less
    Than Bute and Grafton, and shall be unwilling
565   To see him punished here for their excess,
    Since they were both damned long ago, and still in
Their place below: for me, I have forgiven,
And vote his *habeas corpus* into Heaven."

LXXII

"Wilkes," said the Devil, "I understand all this;
570   You turned to half a courtier ere you died,

557 *I beat . . . last:* After his unopposed re-election in 1774, Wilkes tried repeatedly to get the Commons to rescind the resolution in which he had been described as blasphemous and obscene; he finally succeeded in 1782.

564 *Bute and Grafton:* See above l. 340 and note. Bute was an avowed enemy of Wilkes; Augustus Henry Fitzroy, third Duke of Grafton (1736–1811), was his unreliable friend.

568 *habeas corpus:* Wilkes was denied *habeas corpus* when he was arrested in 1763.

570 *You turned . . . died:* In 1774 Wilkes was Lord Mayor of London, and City Chamberlain 1779–97; in 1790 he voted against the Whigs, and suspicions that he was a turncoat were current.

And seem to think it would not be amiss
    To grow a whole one on the other side
Of Charon's ferry; you forget that *his*
    Reign is concluded; whatsoe'er betide,
575 He won't be sovereign more: you've lost your labour,
For at the best he will but be your neighbour.

LXXIII

"However, I knew what to think of it,
    When I beheld you in your jesting way,
Flitting and whispering round about the spit
580   Where Belial, upon duty for the day,
With Fox's lard was basting William Pitt,
    His pupil; I knew that to think, I say:
That fellow even in Hell breeds farther ills;
I'll have him *gagged*—'twas one of his own Bills.

LXXIV

585 "Call Junius!" From the crowd a shadow stalked,
    And at the name there was a general squeeze,

584 *I'll have . . . Bills:* In November 1795 (as the result of an attack on George) the "Seditious Meetings" and "Treasonable Practices" Acts were passed. They were designed to gag criticism of the constitution at a time of vigorous campaigning by the radical reformers.

585 *Junius:* The identity of this talented, bitter opponent of authoritarian government—in his letters to *The Public Advertiser*, 1769–72—has not been established. His contemporaries attributed the *Letters* to innumerable authors (including Edmund Burke, Horne Tooke, Chatham, and Edward Gibbon); Lord Shelburne or Sir Philip Francis appear the most likely candidates. Cf. Southey, *A Vision*, v:

"Who might the other be, his [Wilkes's] comrade in guilt and in suffering,
Brought to the proof like him, and shrinking like him from the trial?
Nameless the libeller lived, and shot his arrows in darkness;
Undetected he pass'd to the grave, and leaving behind him
Noxious works on earth, and the pest of an evil example,
Went to the world beyond, where no offences are hidden.
Mask'd had he been in his life, and now a visor of iron
Rivetted round his head, had abolish'd his features for ever."

So that the very ghosts no longer walked
   In comfort, at their own aërial ease,
But were all rammed, and jammed (but to be balked,
590   As we shall see), and jostled hands and knees,
Like wind compressed and pent within a bladder,
Or like a human colic, which is sadder.

LXXV

The shadow came—a tall, thin, grey-haired figure,
   That looked as it had been a shade on earth;
595 Quick in its motions, with an air of vigour,
   But nought to mark its breeding or its birth;
Now it waxed little, then again grew bigger,
   With now an air of gloom, or savage mirth;
But as you gazed upon its features, they
600 Changed every instant—to *what*, none could say.

LXXVI

The more intently the ghosts gazed, the less
   Could they distinguish whose the features were;
The Devil himself seemed puzzled even to guess;
   They varied like a dream—now here, now there;
605 And several people swore from out the press,
   They knew him perfectly; and one could swear
He was his father; upon which another
Was sure he was his mother's cousin's brother:

LXXVII

Another, that he was a duke, or knight,
610   An orator, a lawyer, or a priest,
A nabob, a man-midwife; but the wight
   Mysterious changed his countenance at least
As oft as they their minds: though in full sight
   He stood, the puzzle only was increased;
615 The man was a phantasmagoria in
Himself—he was so volatile and thin.

LXXVIII

The moment that you had pronounced him *one*,
　　Presto! his face changed, and he was another;
And when that change was hardly well put on,
620　　It varied, till I don't think his own mother
(If that he had a mother) would her son
　　Have known, he shifted so from one to t'other;
Till guessing from a pleasure grew a task,
At this epistolary "Iron Mask".

LXXIX

625　For sometimes he like Cerberus would seem—
　　"Three gentlemen at once" (as sagely says
Good Mrs. Malaprop); then you might deem
　　That he was not even *one*; now many rays
Were flashing round him; and now a thick steam
630　　Hid him from sight—like fogs on London days:
Now Burke, now Tooke, he grew to people's fancies,
And certes often like Sir Philip Francis.

LXXX

I've an hypothesis—'tis quite my own;
　　I never let it out till now, for fear
635　Of doing people harm about the throne,
　　And injuring some minister or peer,
On whom the stigma might perhaps be blown;
　　It is—my gentle public, lend thine ear!
'Tis, that what Junius we are wont to call,
640　Was *really—truly*—nobody at all.

624 *Iron Mask:* This allusion to the "Man in the Iron Mask" picks up Southey's reference in the last two lines quoted in the preceding note. (The identity of Louis XIV's state-prisoner has never been satisfactorily settled.)

625-7 *like Cerberus . . . Malaprop:* See Sheridan, *The Rivals* (1775), IV. ii.

LXXXI

I don't see wherefore letters should not be
   Written without hands, since we daily view
Them written without heads; and books, we see,
   Are filled as well without the latter too:
645 And really till we fix on somebody
   For certain sure to claim them as his due,
Their author, like the Niger's mouth, will bother
The world to say if *there* be mouth or author.

LXXXII

"And who and what art thou?" the Archangel said.
650   "For *that* you may consult my title-page,"
Replied this mighty shadow of a shade:
   "If I have kept my secret half an age,
I scarce shall tell it now."—"Canst thou upbraid,"
   Continued Michael, "George Rex, or allege
655 Aught further?" Junius answered, "You had better
First ask him for *his* answer to my letter:

LXXXIII

"My charges upon record will outlast
   The brass of both his epitaph and tomb."
"Repent'st thou not," said Michael, "of some past
660   Exaggeration? something which may doom
Thyself if false, as him if true? Thou wast
   Too bitter—is it not so?—in thy gloom
Of passion?"—"Passion!" cried the phantom dim,
"I loved my country, and I hated him.

LXXXIV

665 "What I have written, I have written: let
   The rest be on his head or mine!" So spoke
Old "*Nominis Umbra*"; and while speaking yet,
   Away he melted in celestial smoke.

650 *For that . . . page:* The title-page reads: *The Letters of Junius. Stat Nominis Umbra.*

665 *What I . . . written:* Cf. John, xix. 22.

Then Satan said to Michael, "Don't forget
670   To call George Washington, and John Horne Tooke,
       And Franklin";—but at this time there was heard
       A cry for room, though not a phantom stirred.

LXXXV

At length with jostling, elbowing, and the aid
       Of Cherubim appointed to that post,
675 The devil Asmodeus to the circle made
       His way, and looked as if his journey cost
Some trouble. When his burden down he laid,
       "What's this?" cried Michael; "why, 'tis not a
            ghost?"
       "I know it," quoth the Incubus; "but he
680 Shall be one, if you leave the affair to me.

LXXXVI

"Confound the renegado! I have sprained
       My left wing, he's so heavy; one would think
Some of his works about his neck were chained.
       But to the point; while hovering o'er the brink
685 Of Skiddaw (where as usual it still rained),
       I saw a taper, far below me, wink,
And stooping, caught this fellow at a libel—
No less on History—than the Holy Bible.

LXXXVII

"The former is the Devil's scripture, and
690   The latter yours, good Michael: so the affair

670-1 *To call . . . Franklin:* All could have testified against George III:
George Washington (1732–99), the American general and first President;
John Horne Tooke (1736–1812), the English radical reformer; and Benjamin
Franklin (1706–90), one of the authors of the American Declaration of
Independence. (Southey includes Washington among George's "Absolvers",
and quotes Franklin against Wilkes in the notes to *A Vision*.)

675 *Asmodeus:* A demon who delights in the follies of mankind; he figures
in Le Sage's *Le Diable Boiteux* (1707).

685 *Skiddaw:* Southey's home was in Keswick near the foot of Skiddaw.

Belongs to all of us, you understand.
    I snatched him up just as you see him there,
And brought him off for sentence out of hand:
    I've scarcely been ten minutes in the air—
695   At least a quarter it can hardly be:
    I dare say that his wife is still at tea."

LXXXVIII

Here Satan said, "I know this man of old,
    And have expected him for some time here;
A sillier fellow you will scarce behold,
700   Or more conceited in his petty sphere:
But surely it was not worth while to fold
    Such trash below your wing, Asmodeus dear:
We had the poor wretch safe (without being bored
With carriage) coming of his own accord.

LXXXIX

705 "But since he's here, let's see what he has done."
    "Done!" cried Asmodeus, "he anticipates
The very business you are now upon,
    And scribbles as if head clerk to the Fates.
Who knows to what his ribaldry may run,
710   When such an ass as this, like Balaam's, prates?"
"Let's hear," quoth Michael, "what he has to say:
You know we're bound to that in every way."

XC

Now the bard, glad to get an audience, which
    By no means often was his case below,
715 Began to cough, and hawk, and hem, and pitch
    His voice into that awful note of woe
To all unhappy hearers within reach
    Of poets when the tide of rhyme's in flow;
But stuck fast with his first hexameter,
720 Not one of all whose gouty feet would stir.

719 *hexameter:* See above Preface, l. 48 and note.

XCI

But ere the spavined dactyls could be spurred
   Into recitative, in great dismay
Both Cherubim and Seraphim were heard
   To murmur loudly through their long array;
725   And Michael rose ere he could get a word
      Of all his foundered verses under way,
     And cried, "For God's sake stop, my friend! 'twere best—
     '*Non Di, non homines*'—you know the rest."

XCII

A general bustle spread throughout the throng,
730   Which seemed to hold all verse in detestation;
   The Angels had of course enough of song
    When upon service; and the generation
Of ghosts had heard too much in life, not long
   Before, to profit by a new occasion:
735   The Monarch, mute till then, exclaimed, "What! what!
   Pye come again? No more—no more of that!"

XCIII

The tumult grew; an universal cough
   Convulsed the skies, as during a debate,
When Castlereagh has been up long enough

---

721 *spavined:* i.e. halting, lame.

728 *Non Di, non homines:* Horace, *Ars Poetica*, l. 373. ("Neither gods nor men" allow a poet to be second-rate, according to Horace; if a poem is not excellent it is utterly rejected.)

735-6 *The Monarch . . . that!:* George III's habit of hesitant repetition was ridiculed by Peter Pindar in *Instructions to a Celebrated Laureat,* his conversational incompetence in the *Epistle to Boswell* (see above p. 138).

736 *Pye:* Henry James Pye (1745–1813), the frequently ridiculed poet laureate (from 1790).

739 *Castlereagh:* Robert Stewart, Viscount Castlereagh (1769–1822), Chief Secretary 1799; War and Colonial Secretary 1805; and Foreign Secretary 1812–22.

740   (Before he was first minister of state,
        I mean—the *slaves hear now*); some cried "Off, off!"
            As at a farce; till, grown quite desperate,
        The Bard Saint Peter prayed to interpose
        (Himself an author) only for his prose.

XCIV

745   The varlet was not an ill-favoured knave;
            A good deal like a vulture in the face,
        With a hook nose and a hawk's eye, which gave
            A smart and sharper-looking sort of grace
        To his whole aspect, which, though rather grave,
750   Was by no means so ugly as his case;
        But that, indeed, was hopeless as can be,
        Quite a poetic felony "*de se.*"

XCV

        Then Michael blew his trump, and stilled the noise
            With one still greater, as is yet the mode
755   On earth besides; except some grumbling voice,
            Which now and then will make a slight inroad
        Upon decorous silence, few will twice
            Lift up their lungs when fairly overcrowed;
        And now the Bard could plead his own bad cause,
760   With all the attitudes of self-applause.

XCVI

        He said—(I only give the heads)—he said,
            He meant no harm in scribbling; 'twas his way
        Upon all topics; 'twas, besides, his bread,
            Of which he buttered both sides; 'twould delay
765   Too long the assembly (he was pleased to dread),
            And take up rather more time than a day,
        To name his works—he would but cite a few—
        "Wat Tyler"—"Rhymes on Blenheim"—"Waterloo."

752 *felony 'de se': felo de se*, or suicide.
768 *Wat Tyler . . . Waterloo: Wat Tyler*, published 1817; *Battle of Blenheim*,
1800; and *The Poet's Pilgrimage to Waterloo*, 1816.

XCVII

He had written praises of a Regicide;
770   He had written praises of all kings whatever;
He had written for republics far and wide,
  And then against them bitterer than ever;
For pantisocracy he once had cried
  Aloud, a scheme less moral than 'twas clever;
775 Then grew a hearty anti-jacobin—
Had turned his coat—and would have turned his skin.

XCVIII

He had sung against all battles, and again
  In their high praise and glory; he had called
Reviewing "the ungentle craft," and then
780   Became as base a critic as e'er crawled—
Fed, paid, and pampered by the very men
  By whom his muse and morals had been mauled:
He had written much blank verse, and blanker prose,
And more of both than any body knows.

XCIX

785 He had written Wesley's life:—here turning round
  To Satan, "Sir, I'm ready to write yours,
In two octavo volumes, nicely bound,
  With notes and preface, all that most allures
The pious purchaser; and there's no ground
790   For fear, for I can choose my own reviewers:
So let me have the proper documents,
That I may add you to my other saints."

769 *Regicide:* See Preface, ll. 34–5 and note.

773 *pantisocracy:* a scheme devised by Southey, Coleridge, and Robert Lovell for founding a quasi-communistic society on the banks of the Susquehanna River.

778-9 *he had . . . craft:* in *The Remains of Henry Kirke White* (4th edn., 1810), i. 23.

785 *Wesley's life:* published in 1820.

C

Satan bowed, and was silent. "Well, if you,
    With amiable modesty, decline
795 My offer, what says Michael? There are few
    Whose memoirs could be rendered more divine.
Mine is a pen of all work; not so new
    As it was once, but I would make you shine
Like your own trumpet. By the way, my own
800 Has more of brass in it, and is as well blown.

CI

"But talking about trumpets, here's my 'Vision'!
    Now you shall judge, all people—yes—you shall
Judge with my judgment! and by my decision
    Be guided who shall enter heaven or fall.
805 I settle all these things by intuition,
    Times present, past, to come—Heaven—Hell—and all,
Like King Alfonso. When I thus see double,
I save the Deity some worlds of trouble."

CII

He ceased, and drew forth an MS.; and no
810   Persuasion on the part of Devils, Saints,
Or Angels, now could stop the torrent; so
    He read the first three lines of the contents;
But at the fourth, the whole spiritual show
    Had vanished, with variety of scents,
815 Ambrosial and sulphureous, as they sprang,
Like lightning, off from his "melodious twang".

807 *King Alfonso*: Alfonso X, King of Castile (1221–84), is said to have
remarked that "had he been consulted at the creation of the world, he would
have spared the Maker some absurdities" (Byron).

816 *melodious twang*: Byron may have remembered that Scott, *The
Antiquary* (1816), ch. ix, quotes John Aubrey on "Apparitions" from his
Miscellanies upon Various Subjects: "At Circencester, 5th March, 1670, was
an apparition. Being demanded whether good spirit or bad, made no
answer, but instantly disappeared with a curious perfume, and a melodious
twang."

CIII

Those grand heroics acted as a spell;
   The Angels stopped their ears and plied their pinions;
The Devils ran howling, deafened, down to Hell;
820   The ghosts fled, gibbering, for their own dominions—
(For 'tis not yet decided where they dwell,
   And I leave every man to his opinions);
Michael took refuge in his trump—but lo!
His teeth were set on edge, he could not blow!

CIV

825 Saint Peter, who has hitherto been known
   For an impetuous saint, upraised his keys,
And at the fifth line knocked the poet down;
   Who fell like Phaeton, but more at ease,
Into his lake, for there he did not drown;
830   A different web being by the Destinies
Woven for the Laureate's final wreath, whene'er
Reform shall happen either here or there.

CV

He first sank to the bottom—like his works,
   But soon rose to the surface—like himself;
835 For all corrupted things are buoyed like corks,
   By their own rottenness, light as an elf,
Or wisp that flits o'er a morass: he lurks,
   It may be, still, like dull books on a shelf,
In his own den, to scrawl some "Life" or "Vision",
840 As Welborn says—"the Devil turned precisian."

828 *fell like Phaeton:* Cf. Southey, *A Vision,* xii:
     "as the happy company enter'd
Through the everlasting Gates; I too, press'd forward to enter . . .
But the weight of the body withheld me . . .
And my feet methought sunk, and I fell precipitate."

835 *For all . . . corks:* Byron's note reads—"A drowned body lies at the bottom till rotten; it then floats, as most people know."

840 *As Welborn . . . precisian:* Massinger, *A New Way to Pay Old Debts* (1633), I. i. 8. "Precisian" was, in the seventeenth century, almost synonymous with "Puritan"; it means one who is punctilious in religious observance.

CVI

As for the rest, to come to the conclusion
  Of this true dream, the telescope is gone
Which kept my optics free from all delusion,
  And showed me what I in my turn have shown;
845 All I saw farther, in the last confusion,
    Was, that King George slipped into Heaven for one;
And when the tumult dwindled to a calm,
I left him practising the hundredth psalm.

848 *the hundredth psalm:* A psalm of thanksgiving (well known in the metrical version as the "Old Hundredth"). See especially vv. 4-5: "Enter into his gates with thanksgiving . . . Be thankful unto him. For the Lord is good; his mercy is everlasting." It is perhaps significant that Southey opens three of the last sections of his *Vision* with a near-quotation from Psalm 24:

"Lift up your heads, ye Gates; and ye everlasting Portals,
  Be ye lift up!"

Southey's purpose is seriously emotive; Byron's is ironic.